DEVOLUTION
and
CONSTITUTIONAL
DEVELOPMENT in the
CANADIAN NORTH

DEVOLUTION
and
CONSTITUTIONAL DEVELOPMENT in the CANADIAN NORTH

edited by Gurston Dacks

Carleton University Press
Ottawa, Canada
1990

© Carleton University Press Inc. 1990

ISBN 0-88629-110-0 (paperback)
    0-88629-118-6 (casebound)

Printed and bound in Canada

Carleton Public Policy Series 3

Canadian Cataloguing in Publication Data
    Dacks, Gurston, 1945-
        Devolution and constitutional development in the
        Canadian North

(Carleton public policy series ; PPS 3)
ISBN 0-88629-118-6 (bound).--
    ISBN 0-88629-110-0 (pbk.).

    1.Representative government and representation --
Northwest Territories.   2. Representative government
and representation--Yukon Territory.   3. Northwest
Territories--Politics and government--1951--
4. Yukon Territory--Politics and government--
1953-   . 5. Northwest Territories--Constitutional
history. 6. Yukon Territory--Constitutional
history. I. Title. II. Series.

JL462.D33 1990   320.9719   C90-090266-3

Distributed by: Oxford University Press Canada,
                70 Wynford Drive,
                Don Mills, Ontario,
                Canada. M3C 1J9
                (416) 441-2941

Cover design: Aerographics Ottawa

Acknowledgement

Carleton University Press gratefully acknowledges the support
extended to its publishing programme by the Canada Council
and the Ontario Arts Council.

This book has been published with the help of a grant from the
Social Science Federation of Canada, using funds provided by
the Social Science and Humanities Research Council of Canada.

TABLE OF CONTENTS

Themes and Linkages

Preface

In the summer of 1987, six university researchers decided to join forces to form the Consortium for Devolution Research. This book is one of the fruits of that decision.[1] It results from a process which deserves description, both to introduce the reader to this volume and to assist future researchers.

The heart of this process was the consensus among the members of the Consortium that, to the fullest extent possible, northern research should be structured as a collaboration between researchers and northerners. While university-based researchers are legitimately driven by their own curiosity, we believe that they should attempt to make the research they conduct in the North as relevant as possible to the interests of northerners. Further, we believe that the results of research ought to be effectively communicated to northerners. This belief reflects considerations of both principle and pragmatism. In terms of principle, the North confronts a staggering set of challenges. To the extent that the quality of the response to these challenges depends on the quality of information which is applied to them, it serves the regional and national interest to maximize the flow of information to all northerners and others who have a role in meeting these challenges. A second consideration of principle is that social scientists take up substantial amounts of northerners' time and thought; it is only fair to repay their generosity by sharing research results with them. Pragmatically, social scientists need to be sensitive to the need to encourage northerners to continue to give their time generously. It seems reasonable that respondent diffidence to social science research will be reduced to the extent that subjects feel some ownership of research, in the sense of having contributed to its design, and expect some benefit in the form of receiving the information which studies produce.

The Consortium's research process reflected these considerations in two ways. The first was to involve northerners in the design of the research. The second was to go to unusual lengths to disseminate the results of the research. To accomplish the first goal, the Consortium identified the relevant parties to the devolution process — the territorial and federal governments and the aboriginal groups of the territories. The Consortium advised these bodies of the nature of its intended research and sought, and received, permission to proceed. In June of 1988, the Consortium held a workshop and invited the governments and aboriginal groups to send representatives. The purposes of this workshop were to discuss and refine the assumptions and objectives of the research project; to help the members of the Consortium to revise their plans for their case studies and to discuss how best to disseminate the results of the Consortium's research.

A year later, the Consortium convened a second workshop in Yellowknife at which its members presented drafts of the chapters which comprise this volume. The members of the Consortium hoped that this workshop would serve both of their primary goals for their relationship to northerners. They hoped that the guests would comment on the research and in this way contribute to the process of its revision and refinement. They also hoped that the meeting would serve a dissemination function by returning the results of their research quickly to the people who had assisted them in the research and to northerners in general. To promote wide dissemination, representatives of the northern media were invited, and some funded, to observe the second workshop along with the aboriginal groups and governments which had been invited to the first workshop.

The members of the Consortium felt that this elaborate process represented a very substantial response to the difficult problem of involving northerners effectively in university-based research. The procedure involved significant effort on the part of the Consortium members and could only have been contemplated because of the commitment of the agencies which funded the research, in particular the Donner Canadian Foundation, to the principle of involving northerners in research. The process accomplished many of its goals. The members of the Consortium received invaluable advice from their guests. Undoubtedly, as they made their individual ways to interview respondents, the generous welcome they received owed something to the effort the

Consortium had invested in involving the subjects of their research in its design. The representatives of the media who attended the second workshop came away better informed about devolution and the complex interactions among the processes of constitutional development in the North. The workshops provided an opportunity for some of the participants in the devolution process to share their ideas outside the workshop sessions in an informal setting which was rarely available to them in the course of their work.

At the same time, the process did not fully meet our expectations. The disappointments deserve mention in order to encourage future northern researchers to develop realistic expectations, to anticipate pitfalls and to improve on our process. The first disappointment was the uneven participation of the aboriginal organizations. Several of the organizations made extremely forceful and constructive presentations at the first workshop, offering insights which richly informed the subsequent work of the Consortium. However, none of the five aboriginal groups was represented at both workshops, despite the Consortium's policy of paying the expenses of those who attended. Moreover, the aboriginal representatives at the second workshop were reticent in commenting on the ideas presented. This experience can be attributed to a number of factors. The major explanation, in our opinion, and one which all researchers must face, is that the aboriginal organizations are understaffed and overstressed. Faced with pressing demands to pursue their land claims, challenge threatened land uses ranging from uranium mines to low level bomber flights, manage relations with the federal minister and their own grass roots and secure their funding, the aboriginal organizations find it very difficult to assign staff to read research papers and to attend workshops which improve their understanding of long-term issues, but which do not help them fight the fires which surround them here and now. This is one of the most intractable problems facing the northern researcher who believes in an open and collaborative research process. Conceivably, aboriginal organizations will involve themselves more actively in research which they, themselves, sponsor. However, researchers who seek to secure aboriginal involvement through aboriginal sponsorship or joint-venturing of their research may find incompatibilities between their interests, assumptions and approaches and those of the aboriginal groups; limitations on their ability to disseminate their findings and problems of credibility to the extent that their research touches on issues in which their sponsor has a direct interest. There is no one correct answer to this problem. Each researcher must decide the purpose and intended beneficiaries of his or her research, undertanding clearly that it cannot serve all audiences equally.

A second problem with the Consortium's process was the reticence of the governmental representatives when commenting on the conclusions of the case studies and theme papers. This contrasted markedly with the full presentations concerning their policies which they made at the first workshop and with the candour they displayed in their interviews with individual members of the consortium concerning their case studies. Undoubtedly the presence of the media contributed to the great caution which the governmental representatives exercised. Where the members of the Consortium felt that there were questions of fact and even interpretation which could be addressed in front of the media, the governmental officials saw a risk of being perceived as speaking out of turn, of violating the ground rules of the civil servant-ministerial relationship by commenting incorrectly or imprudently, in the eyes of their ministers, on the policies of their governments. The Consortium decided to include the media at the workshop in order to interest them in devolution, inform them about it and in this way help them to report on it in the future. A press conference on what is an incremental process of administrative change seemed most unlikely to attract much media attendance. The workshop seemed a more newsworthy event, a judgment which was supported by the significant media turnout. This success, however, came at the cost of reduced feedback, at least in the public sessions. It may be that public dissemination and substantial discussion of research among the primary actors being studied are incompatible goals.

However, even with the media absent at the final wrap up session of the workshop, the civil servants relaxed their guards only modestly. They may have found it difficult to put aside the partisan attitude which can mark intergovernmental discussions of devolution. Generally, both levels of government support the principle of devolution, but there are many matters to be negotiated, occasionally with some difficulty. It may have been the case that the civil servants did not want to offer comments in the expansive context of an acadmic workshop which might come back to haunt them when they returned to the negotiating table. Quite possibly they felt less restrained by this concern at the first workshop because it dealt at a general level with questions of methodology and dissemination. In contrast, they may have felt particularly reticent at the second workshop because it addressed particular examples of devolution regarding which they did not wish to compromise their governments' very tangible interests by speaking inappropriately.

Whatever the reasons, the Consortium's experience cautions researchers planning processes for involving northerners in their research that their goals for these processes are likely to involve contradictions. These must be identified and a balance struck among them with a clear understanding of the trade-offs. It might seem preferable to duck the challenges which these contradictions pose. However, the temptation to do so should be resisted for the reasons outlined above. Academic research must protect its independence. At the same time, the legitimate interests that northerners, and others, have in research which is being conducted about them and with which they are asked to assist creates an unavoidable obligation on the part of researchers to consult with their subjects concerning both the design of research and its results.

A project as large as the Consortium's program of research depends on the generosity and co-operation of a great many people. The members of the Consortium owe their greatest debt of gratitude to the politicians, civil servants and leaders and staff of the aboriginal organizations whom they interviewed. All of the governments and aboriginal organizations supported the Consortium's research and almost without exception, requests for interviews were accepted and those interviewed devoted a great deal of time and energy to conveying their understanding of devolution to the researchers. Particularly notable was the hospitality and patience of several individuals who were visited by a succession of researchers from the Consortium, each working on his or her own case study.

The members of the Consortium also acknowledge with thanks the financial support of the Donner Canadian Foundation, the Social Sciences and Humanities Research Council of Canada and the government of Alberta. I personally wish to express my thanks to Gail Sinclair of Donner Canadian, who could not possibly have been more supportive in her role as project officer for the Consortium. Her insights and inquiries on matters both northern and administrative were enormously helpful; indeed so much so that I consider her an honorary seventh member of the group. Thanks also are due to David Knight and Pauline Adams of Carleton University Press for the efficiency and quality of their production of this volume.

Each researcher has his or her own debts to acknowledge. For myself, I am grateful to Audrey Bell-Hiller and Allan Tupper, respectively the administrative officer and chairman of the Department of Political Science of the University of Alberta, for the consideration and energy which they devoted to facilitating the work of the Consortium. Finally, thank you Barb for your generosity and resilience in accommodating the demands which my devolution research placed on you and for the support you always give me.

NOTES

[1]   Others include a two-part series on the CBC radio IDEAS series, entitled *True to the North*, broadcast in April of 1990, and a special issue (#5, Summer 1990) of *The Northern Review*.

Introduction

Gurston Dacks

Great Britain's cession of Rupert's Land to Canada in 1870 began a process of constitutional development which is only now entering its final stages. L.H. Thomas' admirable book, *The Struggle for Responsible Government in the North-West Territories 1870-97*,[1] describes this process by which the territorial government and its relations with Ottawa matured to the point at which provincial status for Alberta and Saskatchewan became inevitable.

The Yukon and the Northwest Territories are today treading a path which leads in the same direction but which takes a more complex and interesting route. The constitutional development of Canada's northern Territories today differs from its historic prairie analogue in that it intimately involves a set of actors who played no direct role in the pursuit of responsible government which Thomas described. These players are the aboriginal peoples of northern Canada. The situation of these peoples contrasts greatly with that of the Indians and Métis of the plains a century ago. For example, northern aboriginal groups comprise large proportions of the populations of the two Territories. Moreover, they have the right to vote, unlike their historic counterparts. Their constitutional efforts draw strength from the legal recognition which the concept of aboriginal rights now enjoys, even if these rights are not well defined. Northern aboriginal leaders are highly sophisticated in dealing with non-aboriginal governments. They and their people have had ample opportunity to observe the experience of the aboriginal communities of southern Canada and to draw from that lesson a determination to build a future for themselves free from the blight of social marginalization, a fate they already endure to varying degrees. Finally, they operate in a different context. While the sympathy that non-aboriginal Canadians have for

1

native people has its limits, they do tend to understand that the social and living conditions native Canadians endure are unacceptable and that Canada has an obligation to its native peoples to improve these conditions and to redress historic wrongs.[2] The impact of this sentiment on governments should not be overstated. However it does compel them to give a higher priority to aboriginal concerns than did their predecessors of a century ago.

With this consciousness and strength, and the passive but significant sympathy of non-aboriginal Canadians — beyond the reach of the aboriginal peoples of the plains a century ago — northern natives have redefined the meaning of constitutional development on Canada's frontier. What was once solely an exercise in the realm of public administration is now equally a struggle about the future of inter-ethnic relations in the North. As the papers in this collection will note, the aboriginal peoples of the North base their political positions on the fundamental conviction that they constitute social collectivities whose continuity through history is the major legacy which their ancestors have bequeathed to them and which they can, and must, pass on to their children and to future generations. They believe that the future vitality of their social collectivities is not only their dominant political interest, but also their basic and inalienable constitutional right. They doubt that this right can be adequately expressed or safeguarded through the medium of the existing territorial governments because, as elsewhere in Canada, these governments operate on the basis of majority rule, a principle which gives no special consideration to the particular needs of minority social collectivities.

In this regard, the Territories represent microcosms of Canadian national politics. Like the aboriginal groups of northern — and for that matter southern — Canada, Quebec is asserting its historic understanding of itself as a cultural collectivity with rights which need to be asserted alongside the rights of individuals and of the Canadian majority. These claims do not fit comfortably with the liberal individualism which dominates Canadian political thinking. However, Canada's most historic minorities — aboriginal and Québécois — fear ever more strongly that this liberalism is exposing them to an assimilationist flood which they will not survive as peoples with their cultures intact. Their shared response is to claim a greater measure of self-determination. It is unlikely that future events in Quebec and the Territories, despite their similar logic, will directly influence one another to a significant degree. However, they are linked by their common logic, that of a minority collectivity asserting rights in the face of an uncomprehending majority. If the majority of Canadians can broaden their approach to politics to accommodate the concept of collective rights, then a philosophical obstacle — although not a variety of practical obstacles — to a redefined Canada in which both aboriginal peoples and Québécois can feel at home may be gained. If not, then the unifying national consensus which Canada has sought for more than a century will continue to elude us.

The papers which follow, then, illuminate at least three processes or features of Canadian constitutional life. The first of these is the issues which arise when different constitutional cultures, one based on individualism, the other on collectivity, confront each other. The second is Thomas's historical theme of the completion of Canada in the constitutional sense of approaching the ultimate status of provincehood, or possibly some form of near or quasi-provincehood, thus bringing a uniformity of governmental institutions to all of the regions of the country. The third is the contrasting circumstances between the present and the century-old process which Thomas described. Much has changed, but the question still remains whether the North can do a better job than southern Canada of fashioning an inter-ethnic relationship which will both provide for good government and honour the self-definitions of the aboriginal peoples of the North so that they will be able to participate successfully in the future life of their homeland.

The Relevance of Devolution

In the latter half of the 1980s, it appeared that the northern devolution process formed a large part of the answer to this question. Devolution is the transfer of authority from a senior

3

government to a junior one. As Peter Clancy's historical paper, Chapter One in this volume, recounts, Ottawa's relations with the territorial governments have featured a long series of such transfers. Indeed, by the time the Progressive Conservatives gained power nationally in 1984, both territories controlled many of the powers which the provinces exercise under the *Constitution Act, 1867*.

The election of the Conservatives accelerated this process, so much so that it appeared to be the dominant process of constitutional development in the North, particularly outstripping progress on claims in the NWT. The relevance of a vigorous unfolding of devolution was the implication that the northern territories would develop constitutionally much as the provinces to the south had almost a century earlier. Provincehood, after all, is basically a combination of jurisdictional authority and constitutional status. As is argued in the chapter "Devolution and Political Development in the Canadian North," when devolution enhances jurisdiction, it also strengthens the argument in favour of enhancing status. Most importantly, it appeared to be doing this through a process which was only modestly structured to take into account the collective interests of the aboriginal peoples of the North, whose agendas government preferred to address through claims negotiations. In both Territories, aboriginal groups signed Memorandums of Understanding (MOUs) to attempt to safeguard their rights in the devolution process. In the Yukon, they succeeded because the territorial government delayed devolution in deference to their claims. In the NWT the aboriginal groups felt that the government's methods of bringing about devolution violated their agreements, and this caused conflict.

At the end of the decade, this conflict abated as the devolution process lost some of its momentum relative to the land claims process. For its part, the Government of the Northwest Territories had taken control of two large programs, forestry and fire suppression in 1987 and health services in the western Arctic in 1988. Because its resources were stretched to implement these transfers, it was limited in its ability to pursue new transfers. The negotiation of a settlement of the Dene/Métis aboriginal claim and of an Agreement-in-Principle for the Inuit claim anticipate that these, and not devolution, will create boards and agencies which will manage the land, water and resources which are so culturally and economically important to the aboriginal people of the Territories.

While no longer the leading constitutional process in either Territory, devolution remains a key element in the strategies of both territorial governments as they approach provincial status. In addition, the individual future transfers of jurisdiction will influence the balance between collectivity and individualism in the constitutional development of the North and, in this way, the fate of the aboriginal political agenda. Because of its impact on these three basic issues, an understanding of devolution is essential for understanding the final stages of the maturing of Canada's constitutional frontier whose beginning Thomas described.

Studying Devolution

Devolution has already been defined as the transfer of jurisdiction from a senior government to a junior government. In the case of devolution from the Government of Canada to the territorial governments, devolution actually covers several different types of transfer. These include the sale of a Crown corporation, the Northern Canada Power Commission; delegation, as in the case of the freshwater fisheries; devolution of administrative responsibilities to be carried out under federal legislation and the actual devolution of legislative as well as administrative authority as is proposed for onshore oil and gas. It seems reasonable to consider all of these to be cases of devolution, in that they all expand the jurisdiction of the territorial governments. It is also fruitful to consider devolution as both a theoretical concept and as an administrative process. Viewed theoretically, devolution can be seen as an instance of decolonization which can be usefully related to the literature on political development in the Third World. Viewed as an administrative process, the study of devolution can contribute to understandings of institutional change in general and, as

Katherine Graham suggests, to particular issues of development administration in the Third World.

In the chapters which follow, this subject should be differentiated from another devolution process which is also currently under way. This process is the transfer to the provinces of the responsibility for delivery of services such as health care, education and social programming to status Indians. These two types of devolution differ very substantially, not least because devolution of Indian programming to the provinces bears no implications for the constitutional status of the provinces, whereas devolution to the North can importantly affect the constitutional future of the two Territories. The research reported within the chapters of this book focusses exclusively on this northward process of devolution.

The use of a single word,"devolution" to identify this subject suggests both a unity and a certainty of process and outcome which obscure the reality of constitutional development in the North. In reality, as the case studies demonstrate and Katherine Graham's chapter on implementation argues, devolution has been a fragmented process. While informed by the overarching goal of empowering territorial governments, devolution has been less a single process than a set of specific instances each of which is shaped by the unique synergy of a number of variables.

The first of these variables is the actors or agencies which negotiate specific examples of devolution. Each territorial government decides its own devolution priorities and preferred timing and, with very few exceptions, negotiates with the federal government independent of the other territory. The lists of powers transferred to each of the Territories differ markedly. This should not be surprising as the Territories differ in the degree to which their government structures are institutionalized, in the politics of the relationship between their respective aboriginal populations and territorial governments and in their natural resources. These differences have encouraged the two Territories to approach devolution differently, the Yukon more gradually, the NWT more aggressively. In addition, the devolu-

6

tion process has been a classic illustration of the heterogeneity of the federal government. The Department of Indian Affairs and Northern Development (DIAND), as the agency of the federal government mandated to oversee northern constitutional development, has attempted to promote devolution. However, it has had to address the concerns of central agencies concerning the fit between specific devolution initiatives and national priorities, such as budgetary implications or the encouragement of northern energy resource development in the national interest. DIAND has also had to interact with individual line departments whose responsibilities have been or may be devolved. These departments have varied greatly in their response to devolution. Some, such as Energy, Mines and Resources, have resisted forcefully. Others, such as Health and Welfare Canada, have been highly supportive.

Some actors, such as DIAND, have figured in all of the instances of devolution. However, because the cast of characters is unique for each case, depending on the function being devolved, the outcomes of the various cases inevitably have differed. The number of actors, federal and territorial, native and non-native, those at the centre of the process and those in the communities, raises an epistemological problem for students of the devolution process — which of the conflicting descriptions and judgments of the devolution process is most credible? Whose reality is real? For example, federal officials maintain that, while some central agencies in Ottawa approached the devolution process as an opportunity for budget cutting, the experience has been that responsibilities have been devolved with the same or greater funding than Ottawa had allocated to the function before the transfer. However, the Yukon government insists that "Another problem in pursuing devolution is federal resistance to pay the full cost for the Yukon to take over new responsibilities."[3] The only viable response to such disagreements is to accept both interpretations as real and to report the diversity of understandings concerning both fact and interpretation. The authors of the chapters in this volume understand the contentious nature of devolution and have attempted to credit the various perspectives they encountered. They have tried to base their interpretations on the objective interests and behaviours of each of the actors, and to acknowledge, where relevant, that their conclusions represent inferences based on these two factors, rather than on judgments which value the perspectives of certain actors above those of others. This is particularly important in case studies such as John O'Neil's where local views diverge greatly from those of the territorial government and have few resources with which to compete with it for legitimacy.

A second variable which has led to contrasts among the various transfers has been the nature of the responsiblity being devolved. For example, some transfers, such as management of smaller airports, have no direct bearing on aboriginal claims. Other transfers, such as management of forests, can have profound implications. Some transfers, such as the freshwater fishery case, only involve the transfer of administrative respon- sibility and are therefore relatively easy to negotiate in a legal sense. Other transfers devolve the power actually to make laws, not merely to administer the federal government's legislation. These legislative devolutions raise complex questions about ensuring that the territorial government receives adequate legislative authority to withstand jurisdictional challenges when it attempts to put its new power into effect. Personnel and financial issues varied across cases. In some instances, the desire was merely to devolve existing programs. In others, such as forest firefighting in the NWT, pressure to change federal government practices seen as unsatisfactory was a major motive for seeking devolution.

The cases reported in this book represent a cross section of the devolution experience. They were selected for several reasons. First, the selection of cases allows for an appreciation of the different views of various groups concerning devolution. Because these perspectives owe a great deal to the specifics of the cases in which these different players were directly involved, care was taken to select cases which involved all of the aboriginal groups of the Territories and a number of federal government line departments. Second, the cases selected for study span the time continuum of devolution. The health care devolution in the

NWT has already been accomplished. Forestry and aspects of wildlife management are in the very last stages preceding their devolution. The northern accords are only beginning to be negotiated. Selecting cases at different stages of development has made it possible to assess the extent to which participants in later devolutions have learned from earlier experiences. It also has made it possible to observe, as Katherine Graham has noted, that the devolution process has very much been an iterative process, rather than one which has followed a clear, uniformly applied blueprint. Third, the cases describe examples of delegation, administrative transfer and devolution of both administrative and legislative authority, in this way identifying the full range of questions which can be raised by the different forms of devolution.

The diversity of the devolution experience and the collegial nature of the Consortium for Devolution Research dictated a particular structure for this book. Each researcher examines a particular case of devolution. The devolution of health care in the NWT is studied by both Geoffrey Weller and John O'Neil, the former focussing a political scientist's vision on the federal-territorial interaction, the latter considering as a medical anthropologist the linkage between the territorial government and one of the regions of the NWT. Five thematic chapters also revisit the cases in order to address questions of context, contrasts, commonalities and consequences in the overall devolution process and to attempt to explain these patterns. The visions of the six members of the Consortium differ on some matters, such as the legitimacy of each of the territorial governments and the degree of ultimate power that will be exercised by management boards established as a result of claims settlements. Beyond the implicit persuasion involved in reading one another's draft chapters, there has been no attempt to homogenize the judgments of the authors, who present their evidence and invite readers to form their own opinions.

To enable the authors to present their cases fully and for the benefit of readers who may be interested in particular case studies rather than the span of the devolution experience, the chapters have been edited in a fashion which allows them to stand alone. Their relative mutual independence comes at the cost of some repetition, particularly concerning the linkage of devolution to other processes of constitutional development. However, there is simply no way to avoid this repetition and do justice to the diversity of interpretation which is unavoidable among six scholars, each of whom has focussed on a particular element of a complex process.

Prospects for Future Research On Devolution

The research reported in this volume covers only one stage of the devolution process. It clearly demonstrates that, even within the brief span of time observed, the process has ebbed and flowed, changing as federal and territorial ministers, other constitutional processes and the powers to be devolved have varied. Devolution remains very much in process. Researchers in the future will find valuable insights into the overall pattern of constitutional and political growth in the North in the processes which lead to the transfer of the remaining provincial-type powers that remain in Ottawa's hands. Moreover, even after powers have been transferred, the implementation of the transfers presents challenges and uncertainties which politicans and administrators will have to overcome and scholars document. Prominent among these will be the relative power of the aboriginal groups and the territorial governments over the management of lands, water and the other resources of the North. As "The Quest for Northern Oil and Gas Accords" in this volume explains, how this power is shared will decide the values which will guide the future economic development of the North, in particular the Northwest Territories. The public government institutions for managing these resources will be created through the claims settlements, but the adequacy of the support they receive and the administration of their policies will be determined by the territorial governments, empowered through the devolution process. To the extent that economic opportunity very strongly influences life choices and validates the self-definition of the various ethnic groups of the North, the balance between these forces will prove utterly fundamental in shaping the future societies of the North.

It also remains to be seen how fully the benefits of devolution will be enjoyed at the regional and community levels. As Peter Clancy and Frances Abele demonstrate, devolution has brought improved delivery of services to the residents of the small communities of the North. At the same time, it has not increased their control over these aspects of their lives as fully as they had anticipated before powers such as health care in the NWT were devolved. A consensus on the roles of the territorial government, the regions and the local communities remains to be forged, most significantly in the NWT before it will be possible to judge the full impact of devolution.

The interaction between devolution and other constitutional questions also requires future research. In the near future, aboriginal self-government in both Territories and division of the Northwest Territories will become increasingly prominent questions, whose resolutions will be influenced by the way in which the devolution process is played out.

All of these prospects guarantee the continuing relevance of research into the devolution process, research which will draw on our understanding of the devolution process as it has already unfolded, as described in the chapters which follow.

NOTES

1   (Second edition, Toronto: University of Toronto Press, 1978).

2   J. Rick Ponting, "Political Obstacles and Opportunities in Public Opinion Pertaining to Aboriginal Constitutional Reform: Highlights of the University of Calgary National Survey," David C. Hawkes and Evelyn J. Peters, eds., *Issues in Entrenching Aboriginal Self-Government*, (Kingston: Institute of Intergovernmental Relations, Queen's University, 1987), pp. 36-38.

3   Executive Council Office, Government of Yukon, Green Paper on Constitutional Development, (Whitehorse: Government of Yukon, 1990), p. 10.

1 Politics by Remote Control: Historical Perspectives on Devolution in Canada's North

Peter Clancy

Since 1985, the issue of devolution has assumed a leading role on the political agendas of Canada's northern Territories. It has accelerated the prospect of territorial autonomy, even if full provincial standing under the constitution remains elusive. The advent of devolution has also complicated the process of settling aboriginal claims, in no small part because Ottawa appears to be simultaneously negotiating the same issues at two separate "tables". Equally, the federal government's willingness to accelerate the transfer of jurisdictions and administrative programs to the territories, after at least two decades of prevarication, raises serious questions about Ottawa's long-range commitment and intentions in the North.

Without questioning the centrality of devolution to the contemporary political scene, this paper seeks to explore the historical antecedents of today's initiatives. In one sense, a process of devolution has been underway in the territorial north for more than a century. By taking a reading of the earlier episodes, we may achieve a more measured appreciation of today's events. At the same time, it will become clear that "devolution" has encompassed a richer and more diverse set of political relations than the contemporary focus admits. This reveals not only the process of issue definition in the North, but also the distinct and potentially rivalrous projects which have been advanced under the rubric of devolution. In developing this argument, I will suggest that a continuing analytical thread runs through the history of devolution politics. It links the nineteenth century Commissioner and Council model which was pioneered in the Yukon, the centrally directed and heavily bureaucratized administrative model which dominated the NWT until relatively recently, the plethora of decentralizing experiments undertaken at the field administration level, the unique structures being created by aboriginal claims settlements, and the provincialist expansion of existing territorial authorities. Each is a response to a colonial state system straining to reconcile the imperatives of national and northern resident control. In this, devolution constitutes a vast and varied field of manoeuvre, a contested terrain where the sponsors and beneficiaries of many political projects collide.

The paper will proceed as follows. An initial section will consider the concept of devolution and review the prime sites and mechanisms of devolution initiative in the North over the years. This will be followed by an analysis of devolution as a political strategy. It will highlight some of the leading strategies from the birth of the Yukon to the present round of federal-territorial transfer negotiations. I will suggest that the emergence of each devolution option is a function of the wider configuration of state institutions, but that the prospects for fulfilling such strategies depend on the political coalitions which underlie them. Taken together, the history of these devolution projects helps illustrate some fundamental patterns of political conflict in the North.

Devolution as a Concept

Part of its conceptual ambiguity stems from the simplicity of the impulse which underlays devolution. Harold Wilson, no stranger to devolution politics, described it as "a boring word, a boring and soporific subject so far as legislation is concerned, but potentially one of the most powerful means of achieving one of the highest aims of democracy, bringing the process of decision-making as close as possible to the people affected by it."[1] Yet in the realm of popular politics, devolution has been anything but soporific. It has served as a rallying cry for generations of peripheral movements seeking more direct control of their affairs. The fact that devolution combines a spatial with an institutional dimension emphasizes that it is pre-eminently a program for northern resident interests, straining against absentee or remote political control.

As it has figured in Canada's north, the concept is both precise and diffuse. Perhaps the classical connotation is the transfer of power or authority from a central government to a regional or local one. In everyday political discourse, it is commonly understood as a matter of transferring "provincial-style" government programs from Ottawa to the territorial authorities. At the same time, the term is used less rigorously to describe *any* action which furthers responsible government or local political participation, as well as territorial autonomy. In this sense a former NWT government leader has referred to the "devolution" of departmental accountability to ministers, while the same government released a discussion paper on local government reform entitled "Design for Devolution." Only a decade ago, NWT Commissioner Hodgson promoted a government-wide "devolution" exercise aimed at expanding community-level involvement in the delivery of the core territorial programs. More recently, Ottawa's northern reference manual discussed the prospects for "devolution of *de facto* responsible government." Despite these inconsistencies, and the terminological confusion which undoubtedly follows, all of these formulations are compatible with bringing decision making closer to the people.

When the question of devolution is approached in a historical light, the rather simple impulse immediately becomes a complex, multi-faceted phenomenon. Two variables help illustrate the range of variation and complication. Accepting that devolution involves a transfer of decision-making capacity toward those most immediately affected, it is important to ask *of what* and *to whom* the transfer pertains?

The singularity of the federal crown presence in the North must be emphasized. Since the Territories lack their own "crowns," they are encompassed within the Crown of Canada, with the result that their governments are an extension of the Crown of Canada. As a further consequence, the classically federal notion of jurisdictional transfer could not apply. This was clear as far back as 1870, in the "old" Northwest Territories from which both modern territorial governments descend. By the terms of transfer from Great Britain, Ottawa's hold on Rupert's Land and the Northwestern Territory was exhaustive. Yet despite its dominant position, Ottawa fashioned a synthesis of imperial and federal principles to offer the Northwest hinterland a modicum of home rule. By the terms of the *Temporary Government Act, 1869* and successive versions of the *Northwest Territories Act,* Parliament vested a limited executive authority in the Lieutenant-Governor of the NWT, to be exercised on instruction from the Governor-in-Council.[2] An appointed Territorial Council was devised to support the Lieutenant-Governor in his executive capacity. Parliament also conferred a set of legislative powers (a truncated version of the s.92 headings of the *Constitution Act, 1867)* on the Lieutenant-Governor-in-Council of the NWT. The consent of this legislative authority was required to raise revenues or spend territorial funds. Any Territorial Ordinance was subject to disallowance by the Governor-in-Council for two years following assent (thus paralleling the crown prerogative in Canada, and in the provinces). It is noteworthy that the creation of distinct executive and legislative authorities neither implied nor required a distinct territorial administrative agency. Initially the federal apparatus assumed this role. A policing and judicial system was established, with the North West Mounted Police as the constabulary and appointed stipendiary magistrates as the justices. After 1873, the Department of the Interior brought together all of the remaining agencies of consequence in the Northwest: Indian Affairs, the Geological Survey, the Dominion Lands Administration, and a general administrative component. This all-purpose bureaucracy, which Thomas has called "a veritable colonial office in its dealings with western and northern Canada,"[3] retained its general structure for the next 50 years.

During its first 30 years, the constitutional politics of the old Northwest was driven by two major imperatives. One pushed toward responsible government, similar in terms to that established in the Province of Canada in 1848. Here the Crown relied on an executive council which was itself drawn from and responsible to the membership of an elected chamber. This culminated in 1897 with the appropriate amendments to the *NWT Act* and instructions to the Lieutenant-Governor. It is important to note that this arrangement effectively applied only to the "organized" part of the NWT, that is, the prairie section (the four provisional districts) which alone enjoyed electoral representation. The other imperative was toward territorial autonomy, whose ultimate expression would be the constitutional status of provincehood. In the Northwest, this cause gathered added strength after 1897. For Saskatchewan and Alberta significant results were attained in 1905, though it was not until 1930 that the Natural Resources Agreements completed the transfer process. As we have seen, the jurisdictional issue remains a prime thread of the devolution process in the North today. At the same time, the twin imperatives bear equally on devolution writ large, and as a result both have become intimately bound up with twentieth century politics in the "residual" Northwest and Yukon Territories.

Thus far it has been suggested that devolution may affect the allocation of executive, legislative or administrative functions, and that the devolution of any one function need not be accompanied by either of the others. Indeed it is precisely the absence of responsible government which permits such disconnected relations of authority. It remains to discuss a second question, concerning the prospective addressees of any potential transfers. In light of their politically subordinate and sub-constitutional status, it is natural to look first at the federal-territorial axis. Within the federal domain, delegations may be made without the limitations which the courts have stipulated for delegations in the federal-provincial realm. The Parliament of Canada can delegate to the Commissioner-in-Council the power to legislate on designated subjects. Likewise the federal Governor-in-Council can delegate executive authority to the Commissioner. Part of this may involve the establishment of separate territorial administrative agencies. Over the past 120 years, the enabling statutes (principally the *Northwest Territories Act* and the *Yukon Act*) have been revised periodically to reflect the changing terms of this quasi-colonial relationship. While Ottawa's desire to support and respect the territorial governments makes such an action unlikely, it is also important to note that Parliamentary supremacy makes equally efficient the reverse process of taking back powers from the territorial regimes.

Legally, of course, this intergovernmental relationship is little different from that which arises between provincial authorities and the municipal units which are established by provincial statute. One point of contrast, which lends a proto-constitutional quality to the northern power grid, is the tradition that federal territories have advanced over time toward provincehood.

While federal-territorial relations carry the most prominent constitutional overtones, these statutory delegations form only one plane of devolution. Quite distinct from this are flows to the sub-territorial level. This embraces both regional and local recipients which have emerged over the past 30 years. While a legislative dimension is not ruled out, the most relevant focus here is administrative. It has sprung from organizational problems of matching hierarchies of authority to the forbidding problems of distance, and to the tremendous variation in conditions on the ground. The tensions between headquarters and field organizations exert a profound effect on the design, and delivery of and responsibility for policy measures. Rather than delegating legal authority, the key mechanism here is the decentralization of organizational capacity. At the sub-territorial level, this can lodge at a number of points. The regional or area service centre, and the local community are leading examples, whose roles have been subject to virtually continual adjustment since their inauguration in the 1950s.

Most recently an additional field of action has been opened up by the political arrangements being concluded as part of aboriginal claims settlements in the Territories. Although this process is ongoing, the terms of powerful new authorities can be discerned in the Inuvialuit, Yukon Indian, Dene-Métis and Nunavut settlement areas. Particularly important are a variety of joint decision-making ("co-management") bodies. Established under public authority, they guarantee the claimant organizations parity of representation on the designated boards and committees. Not only do these settlement provisions enjoy a powerful constitutional position in law. They have become particularly important in the areas of land, water and resource management, and environmental regulation. Significantly, these are areas where Ottawa's jurisdictional defence has been most intractable. These arrangements also reflect a tactical shift in the native approach to settling claims. Considerable attention is now directed toward formalizing a generalized interest in territorial lands for purposes of resource management, in addition to fee simple title to large tracts of land (which was the original focus of many aboriginal groups).

Such a brief survey can only begin to illustrate the variations which are concealed within the rubric of devolution. Table 1 presents one approach to apprehending and comparing possible outcomes. It classifies devolution relationships by two variables: the type of function subject to transfer (devolution *of what*); and the type of authority involved in the transaction (devolution *to whom*). Within each category, an attempt is made also to identify the policy mechanisms on which the devolution occurs.

TABLE 1

	Executive	Legislative	Administrative
Federal-Territorial	"Chief Executive Officer"	"Commissioner in Council"	Pre-1950 delegations: NWT
	NWT Act	*NWT Act*	
	Yukon Commissioner - Controller of the Yukon	Section 13 Headings Amendments: "Game" 1949 see p. 74	NWT Council-Northern Admin. Branch, Post 1950 NAB-GNWT Transfer 1967
Territorial-Sub-Territorial a) regional b) local	1977 Devolution, GNWT Regional School Boards Regional Health Boards		1977 Decentralization GNWT Hunter and Trapper Association administration of Community Hunter and Trapper Assistance Programs
Federal/Territorial-Native Claimants	Inuvialuit Final Agreement, 1984. - Joint Management Committees Dene/Métis and Nunavut Claims provisions	Prospective future arrangements in Aboriginal Self-Government	Inuvialuit Final Agreement, 1984. Sub-allocation of harvesting quotas by Inuvialuit Game Council and Hunter and Trapper Committees

Devolution as a Political Strategy

Thus far we have canvassed the potential sites and relationships by which devolution may arise, along with the means of putting it into effect. The present section will examine the broad patterns of devolution initiative which have arisen historically in the North. The specific transactions discussed above might be viewed as the building blocks from which broader strategies are constituted. To speak of "strategy" in this sense is to introduce a new set of analytical factors: interests, coalitions, contradictions, conscious goals and unintended consequences. Here devolution might constitute a political strategy in its own right, or it may represent a subordinate thrust in a broader program of action. It is important to bear this distinction in mind. Yet in any case, devolution becomes pre-eminently "political." Where in the previous section devolution options could be presented in essentially functional terms, the options can no longer be viewed as disembodied conduits for allocative decisions.

To explain the variety of forms of devolution initiative, we will advance the hypothesis that both the substance and the priority attached to devolution will be directly related to the broader institutional configuration, identified by time and place. To the extent that territorial autonomy can be advanced along executive, legislative or administrative fronts, devolution will be so defined. Five distinct political strategies are discussed below, each carrying direct implications for the status of devolution. The dates associated with each strategy are indicative rather than exclusive, since periods of significant overlap characterize the transitions between strategies.

Yukon, 1898-1965: Settler Colonialism

The institutional development of the Yukon represents the first, and the most complete example of modern territorial government. By the time news of the Klondike gold rush began to spread, Ottawa had already designated the Yukon a Provisional District within the NWT. But it was really with the passage of the 1898 *Yukon Act* that the terms of territorial government took form. In effect, the Yukon assumed a status modelled after the

Northwest Territories. The federal Governor-in-Council was given the power to appoint a "Commissioner" as head of the executive, to administer the government under instructions from Ottawa.[4] By a similar arrangement, the Commissioner-in-Council was given power to legislate over a set of subjects set by the Act, with the federal government holding the power to disallow ordinances. Ottawa also directed the Commissioner to establish the seat of government in Dawson. The massive immigration of prospectors over the next decade saw the Yukon population swell by tens of thousands. In the years which followed, amendments were made to the *Yukon Act*, transforming the Council from a purely appointed body, to one which combined appointed and elected members, and ultimately to a purely elected chamber. During this time the size of the Council grew from four appointees to 10 elected members. In addition to his role as the territorial chief executive, the Commissioner also directed the federal administration by virtue of an additional appointment as Controller of the Yukon. This enabled the work of the two fledgling administrations to be co-ordinated.[5]

Just as the gold rush had made necessary some form of territorial institutions, its eventual decline exposed them to review and retreat. *Yukon Act* amendments empowered Ottawa to abolish the Commissioner's position and the Council if necessary. Political resistance by the resident population led Ottawa to reverse a 1918 plan to restore an appointed Council, though it could not prevent the reduction in the number of elected members from ten to three. Postwar retrenchment also saw the office of Commissioner abandoned (with his duties passing to the Gold Commissioner), along with a drastic scaling down of administrative commitment. This inaugurated a period aptly described as "thirty years of eclipse."[6] While the national significance of the territory had waned, its institutional form remained relatively intact. It had evolved through two quite distinct constitutional regimes. The first, created in 1898, represented "a reversion to the pre-1875 territorial constitution — the most primitive form which had ever existed in the NWT."[7] The second, a product of the 1908 amendments, "strongly resembled a provincial constitution."[8] The key political force which drove the transition between them was the settler element. While this was coloured secondarily by the American prospector presence (which raised issues of sovereignty) and the anarchic tendency of the frontier (raising concern for law and order), the Yukon was transformed by immigration into a largely Euro-Canadian society. This generated pressures and obligations to extend the political conventions of settled southern Canada. In effect, the Yukon was a "white settler society," whose political trajectory, and stake in political devolution, would remain anchored to that fact.

Despite its curtailed capacity to govern, the Yukon "model" of territorial government was, by the 1930s, confirmed. It had secured a germinal provincial-type authority. When socio-political conditions again allowed, the distinct system of resident Commissioner and elected Council, together with the dual (federal and territorial) administrations, could advance anew. The Yukon's second historical boom occurred during and after the Second World War. Again it was a massive population influx, this time consisting of thousands of military personnel, whose defence-related works projects were of sufficient magnitude to trigger a renewed cycle of territorial growth. The territorial population doubled between the censuses of 1941 and 1951.

The Yukon was nicely positioned to advance here. Critical to its take-up capacity was the existence of a territorial civil service. With the restoration of the office of Commissioner in 1948, the Yukon Territorial Government (YTG) once again enjoyed a full-time administrative head. In this context devolution assumed the form of administrative transfers from Ottawa to Whitehorse. While it was far from an urgent and comprehensive plan of transfers, a number of programs made the shift over the post-1948 period.[9] Their variety underlined the increasingly complex character of territorial government in the era of the welfare state. Some involved the administrative transfer of functions still provided by federal departments but under the legislative authority of the Yukon Council. These included the corrections service (1962) and the maintenance of the Alaska Highway (1964). Others involved the YTG exercising its legislative responsibility by contracting the provision of services to federal agencies. This had arisen in the health field (with the Northern Health Service in the Department of National Health and Welfare, 1954) and later applied to police services (with the RCMP, 1962). In still other cases, Ottawa transferred new legislative powers to the Yukon (administration of justice, excepting the Attorney General function, 1969). An unusual case arose with the freshwater fishery, in which the equivalent of provincial status called for Ottawa to *delegate* regulatory powers under the federal *Fisheries Act*. Despite the Yukon Council's ambitions, the eventual delegation covered only the narrow function of sports fish licensing in 1972. While the pace of such transfers never approached a torrent, the process slowed to a trickle after 1968. DIAND was forced to reconsolidate in light of two pivotal events: the repudiation by native groups of the 1969 White Paper; and the frontier resource boom ushered in by the Prudhoe Bay oil strike in Alaska.

The Northwest Territories, 1905-1965: Administrative Fusion

Despite a similar location on the northern frontier, the governmental model for the residual Northwest Territories stands in striking contrast to the Yukon. For its first half century, the "new" NWT was distinguished by the predominance of federal administrative institutions, which, regardless of the formal terms of the *NWT Act*, penetrated all aspects of the state. Not only did this enable the Ottawa authorities to minimize the expense of the territorial government. By pre-empting the development of separate resident institutions, including channels of northern resident representation, it launched the Territory on a unique constitutional trajectory. One consequence was to radically limit the relevance of devolution at executive or legislative levels. At the same time, it brought the administrative dimension of devolution to the forefront.

By statutory design, the NWT shared most of the leading terms of the 1898 *Yukon Act*: a Commissioner with executive and legislative responsibilities, an appointed Council, a provision for the federal disallowance of Ordinances, and a circumscribed list of provincial-style powers. (Yet it would take the NWT

70 years to traverse the distance which the Yukon had covered between 1898-1908.) It was in the application of these provisions that the major departures arose. Rather than a full-time Commissioner, the Governor-in-Council designated a federal civil servant to the role. The RCMP Comptroller held the position until 1919, when it shifted to the Deputy Minister of the Interior. Furthermore, not only was the seat of government designated as Ottawa, but no Council members were appointed for more than 15 years. Zaslow suggests that in terms of political evolution, this arrangement pushed the NWT back into the pre-1870 era.[10] Administrative support for the NWT government was provided by the federal bureaucracy.

In at least one respect, this arrangement failed to meet constitutional muster. In 1920, the Commissioner-in-Council had passed an *Entry Ordinance,* with the aim of controlling the social turbulence associated with white immigration to the Mackenzie region. This measure was overturned by the courts on the grounds that the Commissioner had no Council from which to seek advice. Ottawa made remedy by appointing a Council of six senior public servants whose departments figured prominently in the North. By contrast to the resident and representative character of the Yukon model, the NWT system was embedded in the federal bureaucracy. Zaslow has described the NWT Council aptly as:

> an interdepartmental advisory committee, co-ordinating the activities of several federal departments within the Territories, and its decisions, whether administrative or legislative, relied for implementation upon the funds and personnel of those Departments - notably Indian Affairs, Mines, Public Works, and National Defence as well as its immediate connection with the NWT and Yukon Branch of the Department of the Interior.[11]

In effect, the Government of the NWT disappeared into the federal state system for the North. In fact, the Council was only one of several such co-ordinating bodies, operating alongside committees handling wildlife conservation, sovereignty, and financial cost-sharing. The Council became necessary only when enabling legislation was needed to authorize departmental policy.

With these alternative institutions, the NWT government was as functional in its setting as was the Yukon in its. Lacking a white settler influx (in fact fearing just such an eventuality), the NWT government was joined to the federal cause of protecting the indigenous native population which was its special responsibility by law. Though not entirely insignificant, the settler population lacked the proportions to mount a Yukon-style campaign for home rule. When occasional petitions were received from white residents, the government responded with specific concessions in the form of local authorities or school boards.

While the NWT could not match the Yukon's preoccupation with representative government, it did face major challenges at the administrative level. In fact it was in this fashion that devolution first surfaced in the NWT. Two types of problem proved especially intractable, and gave rise to continual experimentation. One involved the selection of a prime agency to *deliver* territorial programs. The other concerned co-ordination in the field, where it was often common for several agencies to finance or deliver similar programs for distinct clienteles (Indian, Eskimo and white).

The interpenetration of administrations can be in part explained by the need, more pronounced in the NWT than in the Yukon, to reconcile two of Ottawa's distinct statutory mandates: one for Indians and one for federal crown territories. The first began in the North with the conclusion of Treaties 8 (1898) and 11 (1921) with the Indians of the Mackenzie District (though not the Yukon). The relevance of section 91(24) to the North grew with the Supreme Court judgment *Re Eskimos* (1930), which brought them under federal jurisdiction though not under the *Indian Act*. Alongside this stood Ottawa's general jurisdiction over the North, from which the police, geological survey, lands administration, and Council stemmed. In the first generation of northern administration, responsibilities were frequently transferred between federal agencies by Cabinet decision. In this way the Department of the Interior was designated the general administrator for the NWT government (1920), Eskimo affairs were added to its mandate (1926), and Indian and Eskimo health was transferred to National Health and Welfare (1945).

With the postwar expansion of the federal state in the fields of health, education and welfare, the scale of commitment grew dramatically in the North as well.[12] The prime seat of this administration for the NWT was a new Northern Administration Branch (NAB) within the Department of Northern Affairs. Between 1954 and 1960 the budget of the Branch increased eight fold. Particularly complicated was the task of co-ordinating the three separate agencies responsible for providing public services: the Indian Affairs Branch (status Indians), the Northern Affairs Branch (Inuit) and the Council (other residents). This could be met by interdepartmental delegation. The arrangement was formalized in 1952, when the NWT entered a federal-territorial financial agreement covering tax rentals and operating subsidies. This in turn gave rise to a new working group, the Federal-Territorial Committee on Finance, with membership from the Department of Finance, the Bank of Canada, and Department of Northern Affairs and National Resources (DNANR). By virtue of its control over the Agreement, the Committee could also determine the scale of expansion for the NAB, as well as the timing of administrative transfers to the Yukon government.[13]

As it sought to emulate a provincial structure, the NAB spawned discrete "divisions" providing resource, education, welfare, engineering and industrial programs, as well as a liaison unit to the territorial governments.[14] With an initial focus on the design of new programs, the administrative growth was quite heavy at the centre, in Ottawa. By the latter part of the decade the Branch shifted its emphasis to program delivery, which triggered a systematic decentralization of resources to the field. Out of this emerged a multi-tier field structure, with local, regional, and district level offices operating within the NWT.[15] Given that many of the new regions were equivalent in area to the Yukon, the shift of departmental resources to the field was a necessary stage in the growth of an effective territorial administration.

At the same time, the existence of a fully operational bureaucracy in federal hands opened an alternative route to devolution, not by discrete jurisdictional transfers as in the Yukon, but by a single stroke of policy. The 1962 report of the (Glassco) Royal Commission on Government Organization sought to hasten this day. Glassco identified a host of anomalous services, vested in federal hands within and beyond DNANR. Besides recommending the immediate transfer to Commissioner's authority (in both Territories) of programs in the legal, educational and health fields, his broader advice was that "early steps should be taken to establish the framework of a territorial civil service for the Mackenzie Territory." This would permit "progressively greater devolution of authority to territorial centres and progressively greater employment of northern residents in a territorial civil service".[16] Three years later, the report of the (Carrothers) Advisory Commission on the Future of Government in the Northwest Territories set this in motion. The transfer took place, in separate phases for the western and eastern regions, between 1967 and 1970. The GNWT, which as late as 1966 employed only 56 personnel, had grown to 1285 by 1970.

Federal Perspectives on Devolution: The DNANR/DIAND Period

Once the breakdown of the unified bureaucratic apparatus became imminent, it was necessary for the federal government to review its own continuing strategy in the Territories. Much would hinge on where the boundary of provincial style programs was set. In fact Ottawa followed the precedent of the old Northwest, retaining the resource jurisdiction as its own. While this only became clear in the late 1960s, this choice had been determined as much as a decade earlier, in the DNANR between 1954-56. Here the Department's overarching policy mandate was forged in a most turbulent social context which included the cyclical decline of the fur trade, fears of a caribou population crisis, and reports of extreme distress and even starvation among isolated native groups. This prompted Northern Affairs

27

to fashion a program of economic transformation to meet what were regarded as structural problems. The first systematic expression of this strategy appeared in the Deputy Minister's submission in 1955 (as Commissioner of the NWT) to the Gordon Royal Commission.[17] It argued for a co-ordinated federal program of infrastructure investment and tax incentives, to accelerate industrial resource exploitation (chiefly minerals and petroleum) in order to generate wage employment for northern natives whose traditional economic activities faced terminal decline. Over the next 10 years, the Department worked persistently to implement this plan.[18]

Only in the second half of the 1960s did the fruits of this program begin to show. Consequently, at the same time as the NAB's provincial-style programs were being prepared for transfer to the GNWT, Ottawa's resource management authority was actually consolidated. All relevant functions for the management of federal crown lands and sub-surface resources were gathered together, first in the Resource and Economic Development Group of DIAND, and later in an enhanced Northern Economic Development Program headed by its own assistant deputy minister. It was this group within DIAND which provided sustained bureaucratic support for the Mackenzie Valley Gas Pipeline and associated projects.[19]

Consequently, there were really two dimensions to Ottawa's position on devolution. Provincial-type programs of the social and local variety, together with the necessary supporting services, were spun off to the GNWT in a single stroke of administrative devolution. Meanwhile the essential levers for the Department's core economic mandate were not only preserved but expanded in the wake of the NAB's demise. The Department's determination to exercise its residual jurisdiction over crown resources was intensified.

It is interesting to note that during this same period, DIAND was involved in an even greater devolution exercise in its Indian Affairs program. As early as 1964 Ottawa had approached the provinces with proposals to devolve the administration of such programs while retaining the financial responsibility. Provincial disinterest left this proposal stillborn.[20] The question was revived in a more radical form with the White Paper of 1969, and its proposal that Ottawa terminate its special constitutional relationship for Indian peoples. The outcome is well known. Nonetheless if the administrative delegation of the NAB is considered against the devolution goals of the Indian program, it seems evident that Ottawa was able to accomplish in the Territories what it failed ultimately to do in the provinces: shift the delivery of all major programs for Indians to a single, sub-national authority. In aim if not always in deed, DIAND was truly Ottawa's ministry of devolution during the 1960s.

The Northwest Territories, 1960-1979: Provincialism Ascendent

In tracing the history of devolution politics, the early years of the 1960s represent a watershed. Here the previous focus on administrative matters gave way to a wider concern with statutory powers in the executive and legislative realms. This strategy was advanced from two directions. The initial impetus came from the NWT Council, which articulated an increasingly powerful and sophisticated case for the early advance towards provincehood. The leading social elements here were the elected members from the Mackenzie District, speaking primarily on behalf of a town-centred, non-native constituency. Increasingly it was this element which seized control of the "political" issues at Council, while the non-resident appointed members tended to defer on such basic constitutional matters. By the early 1970s, with the territorial civil service firmly grounded in the North, its senior executive officers also took up the issue. This second initiative originated less in a programmatic commitment to provincehood, which was hardly for the Commissioner (as a federal appointee) to decide. Rather it grew out of the need to advance the institutions of territorial authority to their limits, both to demonstrate the government's technical competence, and to shore up its political legitimacy at a time of fundamental controversy. This period concluded in 1979, with the election of the 9th Council, and the retirement of Commissioner Stuart

Hodgson. Together these events signalled the end of a classic provincialist strategy, characterized by the overriding pursuit, although not necessarily attainment, of jurisdictional devolution from Ottawa and local-regional devolution to the communities.

This period opened during the 4th Council (1960-63), when the question of territorial division appeared on the agenda. Knut Lang, an elected member from the Mackenzie Delta, proposed a motion to partition the NWT into separate Mackenzie and Eastern Arctic territories. This was intended to accelerate the advance of a Mackenzie Territory, along parallel lines with the Yukon, while consigning the Keewatin and Franklin Districts to an extended wardship under Ottawa's authority. After a positive response from Ottawa, the initial Council consensus appeared to break down.[21] Eventually the issue was referred to the Carrothers Commission, which in 1966 advised against division. Ottawa then extended elected representation to the central and eastern Arctic areas, and implemented Carrother's proposals for a resident northern government.

Much as it would again in the 1980s, the extended controversy over division sharpened the focus on broader constitutional questions. Indeed, once the GNWT was fully operational in Yellowknife, the elected segments of the 7th and 8th Councils (1970-1979) made the expeditious advance toward provincehood one of their policy preoccupations. A series of resolutions, reports and motions offer evidence to this. On the devolution question, it was committees of Council that provided the principal working forum. The Committee on Provincial-Type Responsibilities produced an Interim Report [1973], which dealt with jurisdictional transfers, and executive and financial responsibility. It not only identified programs eligible for transfer (with estimated costs), but also set out a timetable which would have brought many of them into the GNWT by 1975.[22] In a related move, the Council began to study the comparative financial standing of the NWT as a territory and as a province, yielding the conclusion that "the Northwest Territories as a province in 1974/75 would still be in a position of requiring major deficit financing."[23] The implications of resource mega-projects on territorial fiscal capacity were also closely observed. In a 1975 report, the Standing Committee on Development and Ecology concluded that "through utilizing revenues generated from the proposed Mackenzie Valley pipeline development, the GNWT, if we enjoyed [sic] full provincial status, could exist fiscally independent of the Government of Canada, within Confederation."[24]

While it would be wrong to conclude that the Council was ever of a single mind on such issues, the hegemonic segment during these years was evidently the one promoting provincial expansionism. This became more clear after 1975, in the performance of the first fully elected NWT Council. With the Berger Hearings providing the key forum on pipeline and environmental issues, and DIAND's Office of Native Claims handling the responsibility for aboriginal claims negotiations, the Council found itself little more than a spectator. Correctly recognizing that Ottawa had reclaimed the political initiative in the North to match its economic policy clout, the Council continued to advance the joint cause of responsible government and autonomy. Responding to the arguments advanced by native political groups, it released a statement titled *You've Heard From the Radical Few; Now Hear From the Moderate Many.* In 1977 the Council called for a new public inquiry, under GNWT auspices, to examine political and constitutional issues. When the Commissioner declined to introduce the necessary legislation in January 1977, the Council chose to adjourn without enacting any bills, including the estimates for the upcoming fiscal year. DIAND Minister Allmand subsequently offered the Council the opportunity to collaborate on a new federal policy statement, an invitation which it accepted (along with the expenditure estimates). Its formal submission to Allmand called for the immediate transfer of the jurisdictions identified earlier, as well as the subsequent transfer of "resource management presently under the northern operations branch of IAND (highways and ferry system, forestry, surface rights to land and inland waters, sub-surface rights)."[25]

Although the relations between the Council and the Commissioner were seldom completely harmonious, there emerged a conjunction of interests on many of the broader political issues of the 1970s. In practice, the Commissioner occupied a position somewhere between government mandarin and territorial political leader. As a federal appointee, he was seldom in a position to publicly lobby on issues for which he also advised the DIAND Minister. However his role as chief executive of the most immediate and responsive level of government drew him constantly into domestic politics. By the early 1970s, with the administrative problems of program transfer and organization at least provisionally solved, Commissioner Hodgson began to articulate a broader political vision.[26] Through his addresses to the Council and his interventions in its proceedings, his annual tours to the settlements and his role as general spokesman for the GNWT, he devoted considerable effort to promoting the regime's standing. Particularly as it was directed toward the world outside, it could be construed as a vigorous but familiar exercise in boosterism.[27] Within the North, however, the Commissioner's program amounted to a multi-faceted legitimation campaign. He argued forcefully for a northern pluralism in which cultural variety could be celebrated at the same time as a pan-territorial political identity took root.[28] Assertions such as "We are all northerners together" and an insistence that the northern system involved "one government for all" were characteristic of this approach. Not surprisingly, Hodgson took exception to the broader political objectives of the native organizations, particularly insofar as they undermined the achievements and prospects of his government:

> The basic source of conflict between native organizations and the Territorial Council is, therefore, over the system by which the legitimate interests of native people can be best expressed. The leadership of the Indian Brotherhood and similar organizations advocate that the interests of the native people are different from those of the majority within the Northwest Territories, and can be met only by their own organizations... The Territorial Government, on the other hand, feels equally strongly that because native people constitute the majority within the Territories, their interests can be best served

through representation on the Territorial Council, and through settlement and hamlet councils at the local level.[29]

By the mid-1970s the GNWT was engaged in a struggle for its continuing legitimacy. The native groups tended to dismiss the political relevance of the Commissioner and Council system, instead defining their political futures through land claims and native self-government. The Council's provincialist agenda was obviously out of phase with Ottawa's agenda. In the aftermath of the Berger Report, the federal government implicitly recognized that a crisis of major proportions had arisen on the political and constitutional front. It moved to regain control through the appointment of Bud Drury as Special Constitutional Representative for the NWT (thus relieving DIAND of its failed responsibility) while the Privy Council Office was charged with fashioning a new compromise. (This in turn unleashed the complicated constitutional politics of the 1980s in the North, to be discussed below.)

The direct initiative of the GNWT in this contest was the "devolution and decentralization" policy which Hodgson proposed to the Council early in 1976. Despite its apparently technical aim of adjusting the central-local balance of responsibility and authority, this initiative was pre-eminently political. It represented what the GNWT could do on its own account to enhance local involvement in policy delivery. It began with a critique of past approaches ("adapted from southern models with which the non-native people are at ease but which at times may grate on the sensibilities and values of people raised in another culture").[30] To remedy this, the GNWT would devolve control of its major programs by enabling local authorities to control their terms and allocation: "A decisive step has to be taken when community groups move from a consultative to a controlling to a management role." At the same time, the government would decentralize within its own administrative structure by shifting functions as far as practicable from Yellowknife to the regional and local level. As a political strategy, this was aimed at cultivating new or more positive ties between the GNWT and community-based bodies. Here the insight was to recognize that the process of delivering public programs could so easily break down at the local level, nullifying any chances of success. By delegating the fine decisions on delivery to local groups, the social distance between the GNWT and the community could be better bridged, while depriving rival organizations of a foothold. Particularistic practices could replace universalistic ones. Most tellingly, "Devolution strengthens the political base and in so doing strengthens our possibilities of constructing a fair and ordered northern society with a common sense of purpose."

By the manner of its unfolding, this initiative left unresolved the proportions of devolution and decentralization which would be pursued, and the balance between them. Commissioner Hodgson's general proposal to Council contemplated the transfer to local authorities of territorial program elements in such fields as social work, wildlife, economic development, and recreation. It also held out the prospect of local school boards and community development corporations, which implied even more direct community control. The Commissioner left no doubt as to the scale of this initiative, describing it as an unprecedented "wide-sweeping [sic] transfer of authority and responsibility to a lower level of government".[31] To this end, a Committee on Devolution was struck within the GNWT, with the task of consulting the local communities, reporting the results, and implementing the necessary measures to facilitate transfers. This group consisted of eight senior administrators from the regions and the Executive. Its work would be driven by demand in the communities. It professed no prior agenda, and dismissed the need for universal standards, for "not all communities will react in the same way: the devolution process may have to allow for variations in program development and control between regions and between communities."[32] During 1977, the Committee met with 24 community governments.

This premise of variability acknowledged that the priorities and capacities of communities differed enormously. To have any chance of success, the program would have to harness these differences. At the same time, it was clear that the local government offered not only the prime consultative channel, but

34

the natural recipient, for devolved activities. The Committee was intended as the first phase in a process which would take years to develop. As a parallel and more immediate goal, departments could consider the decentralization question. Both initiatives unfolded over the following five-year period. One of the most notable products of this devolution was the emergence of the regional council system. This began in the Baffin Region, where the Director encouraged meetings of municipal delegates from all settlements to exchange views and develop common positions. It proved to be an effective lever for the Regional Office, as well as the communities, to deal with the vertically organized program departments. One of Hodgson's last major acts as Commissioner was to see the *Regional and Tribal Councils Ordinance* passed in 1979, thus enabling the generalized growth of this new level of decision making.

Structures of Joint Management: Devolution in the 1980s

While significant differences persist between the institutions of government in the two territories, they had converged at least partly, by the late 1970s, along one common plane. Increasingly they faced similar political problems: the need to establish leverage over the mega-projects, to contain Ottawa's new constitutional initiatives, and to reconcile aboriginal claims and the conventions of public government. Given such parallels, it is interesting that many of the creative solutions were pioneered this time in the NWT. The year 1979 inaugurated a period of complicated politics, which gave rise to a tentative synthesis between the native claims agenda and the "greater Territories" agenda. The 9th Council played a critical role in this, acting in striking contrast to its predecessor. For the first time it became possible to speak of the organic representation of native groups in territorial politics, particularly those from the Mackenzie District. This Council was already on its way to reconciling support for comprehensive claims and a devolving, even subordinate territorial government, when Ottawa's constitutional and energy politics began to unfold in the fall of 1980. Faced with examples of federal assertiveness, in the form of the *Canada Oil*

35

and Gas Act and the constitutional patriation package, the issue of a territorial interest versus Ottawa was focussed anew (for both the GNWT and aboriginal claimants at the land claims table). Out of this catharctic encounter there emerged a sustained effort to forge a synthesis of competing political agendas. This possibility was signalled by such statements as the Dene/Métis proposal of 1981, which contended that:

> the Government of Denendeh be a public government rather than a government designed only to protect our rights. We see no reason why a public government cannot be designed by all northerners in a way that makes it truly possible to govern in the interests of all northerners while, at the same time, having special features required to protect and enhance the rights of native people.[33]

At the claims negotiations table, this opened the way for such structures as the joint management board, with policy-making powers over designated aspects of lands, resources or environmental matters. The exact nature of the delegation of ministerial powers remains subject to negotiation and debate. Yet should they be coupled with channels of accountability to native claims beneficiaries, as well as the public at large, these structures point toward a new avenue of devolving executive powers.

The forging of an indigenous constitutional consensus cleared room for creative developments not only on the claims front but for traditional devolution as well. In 1984, the 10th Legislative Assembly approved a priorities statement which included "giving priority to the transfer of the remaining provincial-type powers retained by the federal government."[34] Consultation with the new DIAND Minister, David Crombie, led to a procedural framework for the identification of eligible fields, a negotiating process and the terms for ultimate Cabinet/Ministerial approval.[35] In 1985 the GNWT established a Devolution Office within its Executive Council Secretariat, to co-ordinate that government's initiatives, while DIAND was similarly designated a co-ordinator in Ottawa. The native groups with claims under active negotiation remained acutely sensitive to possible prejudice to their own settlements. To meet this concern, and with Crombie's encouragement, the GNWT signed a Memorandum of Understanding (MOU) in April 1985, which offered the native organizations a formal role in the GNWT side of the transfer process. Furthermore, the MOU classified potential transfer topics according to their salience for claims settlements, and undertook to conclude no agreement in the designated areas of salience without native consent, or the prior conclusion of those claims. Despite continuing questions about the status of the MOU (for example, the Dene and Métis signed it but the Inuit did not), it did open the way for the active discussion of transfers in such major areas as health (1985), forestry (1986) freshwater fisheries (1986) and energy (1988). A separate path of talks applied to subjects which by the terms of the MOU did not directly affect land claims matters.

Perhaps as interesting as the renewed territorial initiative was the reaction in Ottawa. A number of factors certainly helps account for the new federal outlook, including the personal impact of the new minister, his staff, and senior departmental personnel.[36] There was also at least a short-term carry over from the work of the Nielson Task Force on Program Review, which devoted considerable attention to northern resource management programs. Focussing as much on the regulatory tangle as the expenditure implications, the report proposed a "transition toward shared responsibility" with the Territories. This included the possibility of territorial departments of mines, with delegated responsibilities for granting mineral rights, collecting revenues and handling health and safety matters. The report went on to describe DIAND's Lands, Forests and Water program as central to the territorial governments' "aspirations for autonomy". Once a thorough going regulatory reform was complete, the next step would be "a timetable for the delegation of specific 'lands, forest and water management' activities to the territorial governments."[37] In retrospect, Nielsen's overall impact on the post-1985 transfers was more on the principle than on the process. Despite the stress laid on the importance of the land and resource package, all governments have been slow to engage this subject.

Conclusion

It is obviously important to distinguish devolution initiatives from the other constitutional processes unfolding in the North, even while recognizing the implications which the latter may have for the former. In ranging across a century of devolution, dozens of incidents and policy transactions can be identified. Rather than attempt a descriptive rendering of each case, we have focussed here on the broader sweep of northern politics, as a means of highlighting and interpreting the different shapes which devolution has assumed. The space available for the pursuit of devolution, along with its substantive content, can be related to the particular contours of state institutions. It is in this way that devolution can be inserted into or excluded from the policy agenda.

At the same time, devolution lends itself not just to one, but to many strategies, whose political significance must be linked to the underlying social interests which champion or oppose them. In this regard, the constitutional alignments in the North are extraordinarily fluid. A strategy roundly condemned as colonial in the 1970s, can assume the cloak of progressivism little more than a decade later.

There are a great many axes along which to compare devolution initiatives. It is apparent that the driving forces in the two Territories have differed. There are occasional convergences, as when the GNWT sought to catch up to the Yukon in the drive toward provincehood, or more recently with the convergence around aboriginal claims. It is also possible to compare the executive, legislative and administrative dimensions of devolution. Administrative devolution would appear now to be almost complete. It is interesting to note, incidentally, the way in which administrative decentralization has twice coincided with the close of periods of rapid program expansion (1959-62, 1975-79). It is also intriguing that the most thoroughly bureaucratized northern governments (the NAB from 1950-67, and the GNWT from 1967-79) demonstrate such persistent reliance on commissions of inquiry as devices to adjust or recast

their institutional structure, not to mention the profound legitimizing purposes so served. For its part, executive devolution
continues with each advance toward responsible government.
Legislative devolution awaits the final jurisdictional adjustment
involving crown land and resources.

Another salient contrast lies between devolution to the
territorial and to the regional or local levels. Only over the past
decade has this relationship been cultivated at other than the
administrative plane. Both the regional councils and the aboriginal claims machinery point toward very interesting experiments in executive decision making. This must remain tentative, however, since the present stance of the GNWT is to
eliminate the regional bodies in the rationalizing sweep of the
Prime Public Authority concept. Similarly the joint management
phenomenon faces major challenges as it moves from the
agreement-in-principle stage to the final agreement stage of the
claims settlement process. A full understanding of the present
federal-territorial transfer process will certainly need to acknowledge them both. In the meantime, the historical perspective may serve to more clearly illuminate the multiple domains
of devolution in the North.

NOTES

1   Harold Wilson, *Final Term*, London: Weidenfeld and Nicolson, 1979, p. 46.

2   For a detailed study of the development of government in the early Northwest, see L.H. Thomas, *The Struggle for Responsible Government in the Northwest Territories, 1870-1897*, (2nd Ed.) Toronto: University of Toronto Press, 1978.

3   L.H. Thomas, "Introduction" to Chester Martin, *'Dominion Land' Policy*, Toronto: McClelland and Stewart, 1973, p. xiv.

4   Robertson suggests that the title "Commissioner" owes its origin to the fact that when the office was first established in 1895, the most appropriate title was still held by the Lieutenant-Governor of the Northwest Territories, of which the Yukon District was still part. After 1898 the designation of Commissioner was retained. R.G. Robertson, "The Evolution of Territorial Government in Canada", in J.H. Aitchison (Ed.) *The Political Process in Canada*, Toronto: University of Toronto Press, 1963, p. 140.

5   For a detailed discussion of the Yukon during its first, formative decade, see David R. Morrison, *The Politics of the Yukon Territory, 1898-1909*, Toronto: University of Toronto Press, 1968.

6   Janet Moodie Michael, *From Sissons to Meyer: The Administrative Development of the Yukon Government, 1948-1979*, Whitehorse: Yukon Archives, 1987.

7   L.H. Thomas, *The Struggle for Responsible Government in the North-West Territories, 1870-1897*, Toronto: University of Toronto Press, p. 267.

8   Ibid., p. 273.

9   A very informative treatment of these transfers can be found in Janet Moodie Michael, *From Sissons to Meyer: The Administrative Development of the Yukon Government, 1948-79*, Whitehorse: Yukon Archives, 1987.

10 Morris Zaslow, "A Prelude to Self-Government: The Northwest Territories, 1905-1939" in Frank H. Underhill (Ed.). *The Canadian Northwest: Its Potentialities*, Toronto: University of Toronto Press, 1958.

11 Ibid., p. 92. Gordon Robertson has observed that "It is doubtful if any country has provided a more bureaucratic regime than the one that then [1921-1946] governed the Northwest Territo-

ries." R.G. Robertson, "The Evolution of Territorial Government", p. 143.

12   For a revealing account of the task at hand, as seen through the eyes of Ottawa officials, see J. Lesage, "Enter the European: V. Among the Eskimos," *The Beaver*, (Spring 1955).

13   For a description of the work of the Committee, see Fingland, "Administrative and Constitutional Changes", pp. 145-152.

14   A thorough account of these program activities can be found in the Department of Northern Affairs and National Resources, *Annual Report, 1958-59*, Ottawa: Queen's Printer.

15   For a discussion of this phase of NAB development, see F.A.G. Carter and R.A.J. Phillips, "Organizing for Northern Administration: A Practical Problem of Decentralization", *Canadian Public Administration*, 5, Spring 1962.

16   Royal Commission on Government Organization, "Northern Affairs" in Vol.4, *Special Areas of Administration*, Ottawa, Queen's Printer, 1963, p. 163, 166.

17   R.G. Robertson, *The Northwest Territories: Its Economic Prospects*, Ottawa, 1955.

18   One central element in the program was the building of the Great Slave Lake Railway. See Peter Clancy, "Working on the Railway: A Case Study in Capital-State Relations", *Canadian Public Administration*, 30(3) Fall 1987.

19   E.J. Dosman, *The National Interest*, Toronto: McClelland and Stewart, 1975. The extent to which this objective was embraced at the ministerial as well as bureaucratic levels of DIAND can be seen in Arthur Laing, "Northern Resources and Canada's Future" *Arctic*, 20(1) March 1967.

20   See J.R. Ponting and R. Gibbins, *Out of Irrelevance*, Toronto: Butterworths, 1980.

21   For more detail on the division issue of the early 1960s, see Frank Fingland, "Administrative and Constitutional Changes in Arctic Territories: Canada" in R. St. John MacDonald (Ed.), *The Arctic Frontier*, Toronto: University of Toronto Press, 1966, pp. 152-58; and *The Northwest Territories Today*, Ottawa 1963.

22   Northwest Territories Council, 49th Session, "Interim Report of the Provincial-Style Responsibilities Committee", June 1973.

23   Northwest Territories Council, "Comparative Review of the Territorial Government's Financial Position as a Territory and as a Province", Information Item 44-53, 14 June 1974, p. 7.

24   Northwest Territories Council, Standing Committee on Development and Ecology, *Final Report*, 21 January 1975, p. 22.

25   Council of the Northwest Territories, *Priorities for the North*, Yellowknife, 1977, p. 41.

26   An official version of the activities during the first decade of GNWT administration is *Decade of Progress*, Yellowknife, n.d.

27   See, for example, Stuart M. Hodgson, "Development Along the Polar Seas" in *The Empire Club Addresses 1974-75*, Empire Club Foundation, 1976.

28   Hodgson once remarked that "My job was to hold the Territories together, and make it work until the northern people developed an awareness and could speak for themselves." Lois Neely, "Stu Hodgson: Umingmak of the North", *Readers' Digest*, May 1977.

29   Hodgson to J. Chretien, 8 October 1971.

30   Ray Creery, "Devolution in the Northwest Territories," in *Towards Decentralized Government*, Annual Report of the Government of the Northwest Territories, 1977.

31   NWT Council, *Debates*, 58th Session, 8th Council, 26 January 1976, p. 11.

32   Sessional Paper 1-61, *Devolution - A Discussion Paper*, 1st Session, 1977, p. 6.

33   Dene Nation and Métis Association of the N.W.T., *Public Government for the People of the North*, Yellowknife, 1981, p. 3.

34   Government of the Northwest Territories, *Annual Report*, 1985.

35   For a description of these procedures, see GNWT Devolution Office, *Planning For Devolution: Principles, Process and Guidelines*, Yellowknife, 1987.

36   See Frances Abele, "Conservative Northern Development Policy: A New Broom in an Old Bottleneck?", in M.J. Prince (Ed.) *How Ottawa Spends, 1986-87*, Toronto: Methuen, 1986.

37   Task Force on Program Review, Study Team Report, *Natural Resources Program: From Crisis to Opportunity*, Ottawa: Supply and Services, 1986, p. 296.

2 Who Benefits? Devolution of Forest Fire Control and Forest Management to the Northwest Territories and Yukon

Frances Abele

Responsibility for forest fire control and forest management passed from the federal to the Northwest Territories (NWT) government on April 1, 1987. The Yukon is currently engaged in devolution negotiations, with the actual transfer projected for spring 1991.[1] Included in both transfers are the personnel, funding and physical assets (such as buildings and equipment) associated with fire control and forest management. Each territorial government gains the power to set forestry and fire control policy, but ownership of the forests and the land upon which the trees grow is retained by the Crown.

Northerners, particularly those in the NWT, sought the transfer of fire control responsibility as a result of long-term dissatisfaction with federal fire policy. In neither Territory, though, has there been much public interest in overall forest management, despite the forests' obvious importance as wildlife habitat, source of fuel and — potentially — commercial lumber and pulp. When the transfers are complete, all of the difficult decisions about the use of the forests will be in northern hands; the territorial governments will have a chance to do it better.

This chapter reviews the transfer process to arrive at a preliminary assessment of the prospects for this outcome. First, the important northern forest policy issues are highlighted and the concatenation of interests that led to devolution negotiations is considered, for both Territories. Although there are significant and interesting differences, both cases show how the issues of quality of service, administrative arrangements, policy authority, comprehensive land claims and constitutional development are intertwined. The paper concludes with a discussion of the fault lines of power revealed by the devolution process, and some cautionary words about opportunities taken and opportunities missed.

Political Development and Institutional Interests

Devolution is a process of government-building. In any transfer, there are choices to be made about when a new responsibility will be accepted, where it will be lodged, and how it will be organized. Such choices are constrained by financial and physical resources, and considerations of equity to the personnel who are affected. They are constrained as well by the overall political and economic goals of both the "donor" and the "recipient" levels of government.

Because the forests are important as wildlife habitat and generally in the maintenance of the health of the renewable resources sector, they have obvious relevance to comprehensive land claims and any new resource management regimes that might be established by the claims settlements. Although the forests are most relevant to the Council for Yukon Indians and the Dene-Métis claims (since most of the trees are in these geographical areas), devolution of responsibility for forest and fire management is relevant to the Inuit and Inuvialuit as well, for two reasons. First, the general well-being of the ecosystem is important to all northern residents; it is conceivable that future use of the forests could affect air and water quality in other parts of the North. Second, and more immediately, there is the matter of precedent. During the recent round of devolution initiatives (of which the forestry and fire transfer is just one instance), it has been clear that all native organizations are attentive to the possibility that the precedent set for one devolution process could set the direction for future transfers, while precedents established with respect to one or two comprehensive claims could be carried over to the other negotiating tables.

The three governments involved in forest and fire transfer negotiations brought their own distinctive agendas of issues to devolution negotiations. Only some of those goals are relevant to the "quality of service" matters that have long been of particular concern to northern citizens. A major federal motivation (and also a constraint in negotiations) has been the potential for devolution to reduce the size of the federal bureaucracy, and ultimately and indirectly, federal expenditures. Devolution in itself reduces federal "person-years" — that is, the number of people employed in the federal bureaucracy — by transferring the employees to the territorial bureaucracies. This does not produce an immediate reduction in costs to the federal government (since salaries and other resources are transferred with the employees). In the long term, however, federal costs may decline. Once the territorial governments are responsible for delivery of a particular service, they bear the costs of public dissatisfaction. Federal interest in containing northern firefighting expenditures was particularly evident after the devastating — and expensive — fires of 1979-80.[2] Arguably, federal interest in devolution during the 1980s was sustained by the overall Liberal and then Progressive Conservative commitment to reducing the size of the federal deficit by reducing expenditures.[3] Certainly, an important aspect of the federal interest in transferring fire control responsibilities must have been the knowledge that formula funding would insulate federal funders from public pressure and displeasure. Territorial officials and politicians would have to meet fire control needs from within the overall territorial budget.

Also bearing on the federal government, rather more weakly, is the general constitutional and political expectation that Canada's two remaining Territories will continue to make steady progress towards provincehood. In this sense, the recent wave of devolution initiatives is only the continuation of the long-term federal project to strengthen government structures in the Yukon and Northwest Territories by transferring responsibilities, personnel and funding from Ottawa.[4]

If the federal government has thus an interest in reduction of northern service delivery responsibilities, each territorial government has a complementary interest in expanding its reach. The politicians and officials in each territorial government quite naturally seek the full, "provincial" complement of functions, to respond to the demands of the northern electorate and as a consequence of the general tendency of bureaucracies to expand.[5] On the other hand, each government is constrained by other political processes that may affect the shape of territorial institutions. These include outstanding constitutional development questions in the Northwest Territories (formerly addressed most explicity through the now-defunct Constitutional Alliance)[6] and in both Territories, land claims negotiations. Though the territorial governments are not full participants in claims negotiations, the outcome of the claims process has important implications for the future shape of government in both jurisdictions. For each as well, there are serious political consequences for aggravating their sometimes strained relations with territorial native organizations.

Each territorial government faced the same strategic question. In the light of the considerations just enumerated, is it better to negotiate for the transfer of the service "as is," and then, after some experience has been gained, to consider reorganization; or is it better to have an alternative plan in place, so that negotiations concern levels of funding and other arrangements adequate to the alternative (rather than to past practice)? The two governments arrived at contrasting positions with respect to this question, arising from the differing situations of the native organizations in each territory. The Yukon government (YTG) chose to give priority to resolution of outstanding Council for Yukon Indians (CYI) claims issues, and delayed negotiations on devolution. The Government of the Northwest Territories took the first available opportunity to begin negotiating the forestry and fire transfer, contending that the transfer was an administrative matter of improving service delivery, and not an issue that could jeopardize the native cause in claims negotiations. The sources and consequences of the differing choices of the two governments are discussed later in this paper.

Fire Control and Forest Policy Issues

Firefighting is an area in which many northerners have both vital interests and considerable expertise, developed through long experience. Until the transfers now completed in the NWT and in progress in the Yukon, policy authority for firefighting lay with the Ottawa staff of the Department of Indian Affairs and Northern Development (DIAND). DIAND regional staff, based at a Regional Fire Centre in each territory and subordinate district and area offices, carried administrative responsibility. Fires were actually fought by seasonal indeterminate (permanent but not full-time) DIAND employees drawn from many northern communities. These employees (250-300 in the NWT; somewhat fewer in the Yukon) worked during the fire season only. Firefighting was (and is) skilled and difficult work that provided an important and seasonally reliable source of cash income for a significant number of native households.

Probably the most important fire suppression issue for northerners is the federal practice, begun in 1972, of using a system of previously defined priority and observation zones to determine whether or not a particular fire would be fought. Under this policy, only fires in priority zones are automatically attacked. Many northerners have complained that the "lines on a map" that delineate the areas in which fires will be fought were drawn without sufficient attention to local use of the land, particularly the areas of value to hunters and trappers. Some argue as well that other considerations besides simple location should be applied when decisions are made about when and where to attack a fire.

Another concern has been the role of the federal Treasury Board in policing the annual expenditures on firefighting. Under the federal system, after a certain minimum budget had been spent, DIAND regional staff required Treasury Board approval for funds to fight all subsequent fires, including those in the priority zones. Because fires burn faster than bureaucracies make decisions, Treasury Board approval for "extra" expenditures by northern staff was regularly sought after the fact. Although Treasury Board thus never actually prevented a priority zone fire from being fought, neither DIAND regional fire control staff nor the communities they were trying to serve ever worked with a clearly defined, finite budget. This added unnecessary uncertainty and administrative complications.

Finally, northerners have raised concerns about certain departmental decisions with respect to firefighting methods. For various reasons, DIAND grew to rely upon capital-intensive "high tech" firefighting techniques. The use of CL-215 Air Tankers under long-term operations and maintenance contracts to southern-based firms has been particularly controversial.[7] It is argued that these contracts, signed "for national purposes," draw resources that might be better spent using other, less costly equipment: for example, northern-owned fixed-wing planes could be used in some cases where helicopters and imported pilots are now used, a substitution that, they argue, would support local businesses while improving the northern transportation system.

Taken together, the priority zone system, the role of Treasury Board as the distant *eminence grise* of northern fire policy, and DIAND's contractual relations with helicopter companies left a relatively scant role for community advice, despite the efforts of some northern-based federal fire management personnel to consult with the people vitally affected by federal policy. It is not surprising that public pressure for devolution of fire suppression responsibility mounted, especially in the NWT and particularly in years when there was widespread fire devastation. In comparison, there has been relatively little public pressure for the transfer of forest management, probably because there has been little commercial exploitation of the forests so far.

Public interest in territorial administration of the forests has been strongest in the Yukon, where there is probably somewhat more commercial potential and where the forests have been studied as an aspect of the territory's overall plan for economic development.[8] In neither Territory, however, has forest management been a particularly "hot" public issue. Territorial forest management, like fire suppression, has been a responsibility of DIAND under its overall mandate for administration, management and control of northern lands.[9] Compared to some provincial jurisdictions, at least, forest management (as distinct from fire control) was not an elaborately developed federal capacity. Inadequacies in the federal forest management program were highlighted in an evaluation report published by DIAND in 1982.[10] Key problems included the absence of an integrated forest management program, insufficient legislative authority, serious underfunding and poor forest inventory data.

The forests are, of course, of major importance to northerners. Besides their aesthetic and spiritual value, the forests are wildlife habitat. They play an important role in natural water control and they are a primary source of fuel and building materials for many northerners. In both Territories there has been small-scale commercial logging and milling by locally owned enterprises, and in the Yukon some craft-scale manufacturing. Forests are seen increasingly as possible contributors to sustainable economic development; particularly in the Yukon, northern-based forestry enterprises seek a more stable regulatory regime. For all of these reasons, forest management is likely to become a more important public issue in both Territories.

The Transfer of Fire and Forestry Responsibilities to the NWT

It was suggested earlier that the institutional interests had a direct impact on constitutional growth and policy development in the NWT and the Yukon. There is an even larger, still open and looming question, concerning province-like jurisdiction over crown land: in neither Territory is this issue likely to arrive on the public agenda until final land claims agreements have been reached. Besides these large political questions, devolution also raises issues of funding, personnel transfer, legislation and office space. These kinds of questions are neither trivial nor easily resolved under any circumstances; because the forest and fire management transfer negotiations were the first of the revived devolution initiatives, they presented significant challenges for the officials who were involved. Administration, however, is in practice rarely separable from matters of policy — or, ultimately, from political issues. The institutions through which policy is developed have a major impact on actual decisions, since the structure of the institutions determines who has decision-making power and who does not. The administrative structures through which decisions are implemented, similarly, shape the programs authorized by policy decisions, and thus have an enormous effect on the delivery of service. The case of the forest and fire management transfer illustrates this point clearly.

The transfer of fire and forestry responsibilities to the NWT government is a kind of transitional case, because it began before the renewed federal commitment to devolution that came with the election of a Progressive Conservative government to the federal Parliament in 1984. The terrible fires of 1971, which destroyed forests and caribou rangeland, led to a reorganization of the federal fire service and the establishment of the priority zone system. The unprecedented devastation from fire in 1979 (a product of severe drought, reductions in federal budgets, and concentration on fires in the priority zones only) led to public actions by Hunters and Trappers Associations, which in turn led to the federal appointment of an independent Fire Review Panel, a task force report, and significantly increased fire control expenditures. The Government of the Northwest Territories responded to these same concerns by seeking devolution of fire control services during 1980-82. The federal response to this request was initially positive, but for a variety of reasons the process was slowed and finally derailed.[11] After this false start, the issue was revived two years later, after discussion in the NWT Legislative Assembly and a May 1984 letter from the GNWT Minister of Renewable Resources to the Minister of Indian Affairs and Northern Development that formally requested the commencement of negotiations towards devolution of forest and fire management.

In July 1985, the Dene Nation, Métis Association and the Government of the Northwest Territories initialled an Interim Agreement on Key Elements of Lands and Resources. The substance of this agreement is repeated in a Memorandum of Understanding (MOU) on devolution signed by the same three parties in April 1986.[12] The interim agreement and subsequently the MOU committed the parties to "pursue at the Dene-Métis claims table and elsewhere the following: (9.1) an integrated land and water management regime to be co-ordinated with land

and water use planning and impact assessment review; (9.2) the meaningful and influential involvement of Dene and Métis in land and water management and planning [in their] claims area; and (9.3) devolution of responsibility for the management of northern lands and waters." Other sections of the MOU guarantee consultation and "the involvement" of the Dene-Métis in all devolution negotiations, defer devolution of any powers related to claims negotiations or aboriginal rights until the claims agreement has been signed, and provide for cases in which there is not agreement about whether aboriginal rights are affected. In this last case, devolution is again deferred until the claims agreement is signed.

Territorial officials appear to have believed, at first, that the MOU on devolution (and perhaps also the initialled interim agreement) were not meant to apply to the devolution of forest and fire management. This impression was strengthened by yet another MOU signed by the Deputy Minister of Renewable Resources and the Associate Deputy Minister of the Department of Indian Affairs and Northern Development in September 1985. The second MOU was drafted "[w]ith the understanding that both governments are actively considering the progressive devolution of resource management programs and authorities," but it establishes a schedule for forest and fire management programs transfer only. The two deputies also agree to a set of "Guiding Principles" that include some references to the role of "native groups." Examined from the perspective of the native organizations, these guiding principles provide somewhat weaker protection than does the MOU on devolution signed six months later, in April 1986.[13]

Of course, as direction for civil servants, the MOU on devolution (signed by ministers) supersedes any sort of agreement signed by deputies, but there was a period of six months between the signing of the deputies' MOU and the signing of the MOU on devolution. During this period, officials from both levels of government (DIAND regional staff and territorial civil servants from Renewable Resources and Justice) began discussion of such matters as legislative mechanisms, funding, service continuity, buildings, contracts and personnel. During the same

period, information about the forest and fire transfer negotiations and invitations to attend officials' meetings were sent
regularly by the Deputy Minister of Renewable Resources to
leaders of the Dene Nation and Métis Association. The Dene-
Métis, engaged in negotiations for the MOU on devolution, did
not attend these meetings of officials. Their response to the
deputies' MOU is contained in a letter sent to the Minister of
Renewable Resources on October 10, 1985. The Presidents of
the Dene Nation and the Métis Association indicated support for
the devolution of fire control, but not forests, and stated with
respect to fire control that they were concerned with matters of
policy, rather than with the administrative details of the transfer.[14] They identified the forests as integral to overall land and
water management, in which there is an aboriginal interest and
for which an integrated management regime should be negotiated. Although neither document mentions forests, specifically,
this position is consistent with provisions concerning lands and
water management in both the Interim Agreement initialled in
July 1985 and the MOU on devolution signed in April 1986.

In early 1986, just before the MOU on devolution was
signed, the two native organizations agreed to participate in an
"advisory committee" on forest policy (later the Forestry Working
Group). This body was established to advise the Minister of
Renewable Resources, and a consultant was hired to produce a
report for the committee's consideration. At the same time,
federal officials reported a change in their department's stance
on the question of transferring a proprietary interest in the
forests. While they had earlier appeared to accept the territorial
government position that "ownership of the trees" was integral
to effective management, after April 1986 the federal position
was that the proprietary interest could not be transferred until
the Dene-Métis claim was settled. Territorial negotiators disa-
greed with the federal rationale for this change of course, but
were unable to win their point.

The positions of the three parties at this point were as
follows. The Dene-Métis opposed transfer of a proprietary
interest in the forests to the territorial government on the
grounds that the transfer would prejudice ongoing claims

negotiations. The GNWT argued that it was not reasonable to separate fire control from forest management, and further, that effective forest management required that the territorial government acquire a proprietary interest in the trees (though not immediately the land on which the trees were growing); aboriginal interests in the trees could be protected by a caveat in the transfer agreement, which would provide for adjustments in ownership after the settlement of the Dene-Métis claim. The federal position after April 1986 stressed two points: transfer of proprietary interest in the trees might "complicat[e] or prejudic[e] land claims," and it would interfere with the federal Minister's responsibility for territorial land management under the *DIAND Act*.

It appears that the convergence of federal and aboriginal interests accounts for the failure of the territorial government to gain a proprietary interest in the forests along with responsibility for fire control and forest management. The federal position was almost certainly authorized at the political level, by the Minister. It may reflect concern that the controversy over the ownership of the trees could obstruct or prolong claims negotiations needlessly, as well as the recognition that federal purposes (in reducing the size of the department) would be adequately served by the fire transfer alone.[15] In any case, by virtue of this federal position, what was ultimately transferred to the GNWT was legislative authority over most NWT forests and all federal fiscal and physical resources associated with forest management programs.[16] The resources transferred included an annual budget of $25 million, 122.5 person-years with corresponding salaries and benefits, as well as facilities, buildings and assets. The federal government retained proprietary interest in the trees.

On the strength of the MOU on devolution, native leaders wrote to territorial ministers. They requested funding to enable them to conduct independent research and community consultations, a negotiated participation agreement (under the terms of the MOU) and a delay in the deadline for completion of negotiations (by this point identified as October 1986) to allow time for preparation of their positions. Funding for the purposes they identified was not forthcoming (although the Government of the Northwest Territories agreed to pay a per diem and expenses to the native organizations' representative on the forestry advisory committee); nor was a participation agreement completed in time to govern the negotiations.[17] They did achieve a delay to the negotiating process, however. Territorial officials report that the bulk of the government-to-government negotiations on administrative matters related to the transfer occurred from June through December 1986, with the transfer effective April 1, 1987.

The federal and territorial officials charged with negotiating the transfer were affected by the struggles on political matters only episodically; in between times, they faced a number of substantive issues that had to be resolved step by step.[18] One of the most difficult concerned personnel. It will be discussed here as an illustration of the kinds of issues the officials confronted, and because personnel matters appear to be assuming major importance in the Yukon transfer as well. The prospect and then the process of the transfer of forest and fire management to the GNWT brought some months of anxiety for federal staff who had reason to expect that they might be affected by the transfer. There was, first, the federal Work-force Adjustment Policy (WAP), designed for all departmental employees who might be affected by the general federal policy to reduce the size of the civil service. The WAP as it was initially drafted proved inadequate, and was revised midway through the forest and fire transfer. Its general purpose was to make orderly provision for federal employees whose jobs would disappear from the federal staff complement as a result of "down-sizing."[19] Besides concerns over the effectiveness and application of the WAP, there were difficulties in matching the job classification systems of the federal and territorial bureaucracies. Although none experienced a drop in pay, many federal employees who were transferred found that they were classified at a lower level in the territorial system. Anticipation of this effect, coupled with uncertainties arising from the WAP and the delay in the process introduced by the political process, created a good deal of anxiety. In the event, however, 91 percent of affected federal employees ultimately chose to move to the territorial government when the opportunity became available.

Further complications for another category of worker were introduced by the interest of the GNWT in having vacant positions transferred, in order to leave as much room as possible for the application of territorial hiring policies, such as the affirmative action policy. The GNWT position and federal concern over the capacity of WAP to absorb "surplus" staff led to a decision by "senior management of the federal government"[20] to fill vacant positions for the 1986 fire season with term appointments. These positions would normally have been filled as "seasonal indeterminate," meaning that employees who had work in 1986 could expect to have work in subsequent years. As term employees, however, the new firefighters hired in 1986 became unemployed with the end of the fire season. Though most of the affected employees were native (and thus in principle in a good position to be rehired in light of the GNWT's affirmative action policy) very few were in fact rehired in 1987. In part, this can be seen as an effect of the system of "contracting out" firefighting crews to community-held corporations, whose managers made most of the relevant hiring decisions. For the people hired on term positions in 1986, however, the situation was made worse because the limitations of their term appointment, and its variation from normal practice, were apparently not clearly explained at the outset.

There are other personnel issues which do not appear to have surfaced in the transfer at all. One of the potential benefits of devolution is the opportunity it creates for improving the representation of native people in management positions of the territorial civil service. Although the GNWT expressed an interest in having vacant positions transferred to maximize the effectiveness of territorial employment equity policies, consideration was not given, apparently, to developing a system that would make the new positions available to native people. Care would have to have been taken to protect the interests of existing federal employees, and probably training programs for certain positions would have to have been initiated before the transfer itself. As this transfer unfolded, there was apparently not time for such measures.[21]

Another opportunity created by devolution, and one that was most emphatically demanded by northerners, was improvement to firefighting policies. Some promising steps were taken during the transfer to begin the process of developing new policy guidelines. Other, less successful initiatives were taken after the transfer date. Development of a new fire control policy was at first the shared responsibility of staff in the territorial Department of Renewable Resources and the Forestry Working Group (FWG), a body that evolved out of the advisory committee formed to involve native organizations in advising the Minister of Renewable Resources on his new responsibilities. The FWG was attached to another new advisory body, the Denendeh Conservation Board (DCB), itself a product of the claims process.[22]

In late 1989, the DCB accepted the recommendation of the Forestry Working Group to approve a public discussion paper that was expected to form the basis of a draft fire management policy. The plan was to subject the discussion paper to public examination, and then to have fire control specialists in the territorial Department of Renewable Resources prepare a draft policy, based on public commentary. Unfortunately, public response to the fire control discussion paper was very slight.[23] Nevertheless, in early summer of 1990 Renewable Resources staff were drafting a fire control policy for Executive Council consideration in the fall. The FWG was not consulted during the drafting of the policy, but it seems likely that the need for some regular means for public consultation will result in the revival of this body. If not, officials in the Department of Renewable Resources will have to devise another effective means of public consultation, or risk developing a policy that is not seen to be legitimate by the interested public.

After the fire policy is established, of course, it will remain to develop a general policy on forest management. To this end, officials in the Department of Renewable Resources have prepared background discussion papers, but so far these have not been released. A public consultation process broadly similar to the fire policy procedures is envisioned for forest management.

Both policies will be developed within the fiscal framework set in advance by the transfer agreement, which includes some flexibility,[24] and the policies will be implemented using the personnel and physical resources in federal hands at the time of transfer. It is appropriate to pause, at this point, to consider to what extent northerners' original concerns about the adequacy of the federal fire service were addressed in the transfer, and to look also at the upshot of the political struggles that took place "over the heads" of the officials who were negotiating the transfer.

On the adequacy of service, it must be said that the jury is still out. The GNWT is certainly in a better position now to address northerners' concerns about firefighting, but has yet to deliver a new policy. There are both positive and negative signs about the capacity or the willingness of the relevant department's political leadership to ensure that concerned citizens are effectively involved at the appropriate level. Early policy development work apparently went very well, and then a plan for public consultation was ineffective. Because there are still several steps remaining in the process, all judgments must be tentative. With respect to forest management, it must be remembered that here there was no great public pressure for territorial control. The GNWT has acquired legislative authority and new resources; in the absence of public pressure for immediate action, this government has gained an opportunity to develop a new approach. The most immediate task would appear to be the development of a workable regulatory system that takes into account the likelihood that the Denendeh Conservation Board and perhaps other management boards to be established will have somehow to be worked into a territorial government policy process that increasingly emphasizes ministerial responsibility. How this will be done is at the moment far from clear. A second task involves research and analysis — in fact, the development of the capacity in the territorial civil service to support forest policy development, since no such capacity was transferred with the responsibility for management. The development of such expertise in the North appears to be under way.

With respect to the implications of the fire and forestry transfer for the general government-building project in the NWT, at least two observations are possible. In the forest and fire transfer, it is apparent that more than just a general interest in improving a service shaped the process. Distinct departmental interests (and perhaps they were ministerial interests as well) had some effect on the department's actions, particularly the insistence that forest management be included with fire control responsibilities. The sequence of events which prevented the Department of Renewable Resources from gaining a proprietary interest in the forests may reveal a similar imperative governing the behaviour of the federal department as well. In neither case is this evidence of unusual megalomania; it is rather an indication that the politicians who are ultimately responsible for such matters must reckon with the natural tendency of bureaucracies to expand, as well as with pressure from the public, in meeting more general political goals.

Second, the importance of such formal agreements as the Memoradum of Understanding on devolution is evident. The process to negotiate the MOU, and the MOU itself, mitigated the effect of the devolution negotiations on other processes of government building then under way in the NWT — land claim negotiations and public discussion of new constitutions for a divided territory. Concretely, the MOU probably accounts for the political decision of the federal government not to transfer a proprietary interest in trees to the GNWT at the same time as fire control responsibilities and legislative authority were transferred. Although this has created a complex and potentially tricky interim arrangement, it has also left the space for the development of better policy through a respectably public process, provided that the political intention to do this exists.

Prospects for Transfer of Fire and Forest Responsibilities to the Yukon Government

The 1985 decision of the Yukon government to give priority to the settlement of the Council for Yukon Indians land claim effectively delayed most devolution negotiations until the CYI agreement-in-principle was secure. Negotiation of the transfer of the inland fishery and A & B airports has been completed since then, and negotiations on the forestry and fire transfer as well as health are in progress. The original tentative target date for transfer of fire suppression and forest management responsibilities was fall 1990; it now appears likely that the transfer will not occur before spring 1991. This further delay is not the result, so much, of a principled decision taken by Cabinet, nor a reflection of difficulties encountered in negotiations. Rather, the land claims process is absorbing personnel and political resources in both the Council for Yukon Indians and the Yukon government, so that there has been less time and energy for dealing with devolution negotiations. The Yukon government remains committed to proceeding with devolution, now that the claims issue is largely resolved.

Yukon government officials identify two general objectives in seeking the fire control and forest management transfer. First, forestry is viewed as an important sector for economic growth in the Yukon economy. The Yukon 2000 planning exercise highlighted a number of possibilities here, including import substitution (of fuel, milled lumber and building logs), as well as export opportunities to Alaska and Asia. Because regeneration of Yukon forests may require as long as 100 to 150 years, there has been considerable interest in Swedish forestry practices, including the use of replanted forests and the development of small-scale manufacturing enterprises to maximize the economic benefits from the use of the resource. Second, YTG officials see forest management as an integral part of any comprehensive land, water and resource management regime. The current management regime is a complicated patchwork of federal and territorial measures, supported by relatively scant research into such matters as sustainable harvest levels and linkages to other renewable resource sectors such as wildlife harvesting and trapping. Territorial control of forest management is seen as necessary to ensure that commercial uses of the forests can be managed without jeopardy to the ecosystem.[25]

The connection between "ownership of the trees" and land claims is recognized, and in contrast to the Northwest Territories, the Yukon government has excluded the ownership issue from devolution negotiations.

As in the Northwest Territories, fire control is a related issue that seems to have a life of its own. Although there has not been an extraordinarily bad fire season in the Yukon in recent years, there is similar dissatisfaction with the priority zone system. Particularly in the Old Crow region, it is held that federal priorities do not give enough weight to areas important for wildlife harvesting, habitat or traplines. Methods of fire suppression, which rely heavily on "high tech" solutions, are also questioned. The extent to which the Yukon government will actually implement proposed reforms is of course not known, but consideration is being given to a serious reorganization of the fire service. This would involve establishment of local resource management committees with the responsibility to set local priorities in the expenditure of regionally decentralized fire suppression budgets.

A Memorandum of Understanding on Devolution was negotiated by the Council for Yukon Indians and the territorial government in 1985. A joint YTG-CYI Constitutional Development and Program Devolution Working Group has been established. To date, this Working Group appears to have been a less than effective forum for discussion. The CYI has insisted upon being considered a party to devolution negotiations, rather than merely an "interest" to be consulted. It appears that the latter rather than the former involvement has been the case. Still, on the whole, relations between the Yukon government and the native organization have been co-operative. Each requires a healthy working relationship with the other to meet core political goals.

Unresolved personnel issues in the health transfer negotiations have had the effect of slowing progress in the forestry
and fire transfers. In the health transfer, two unions, the Public
Service Alliance of Canada (PSAC) and the Professional Institute
of the Public Service of Canada (PIPS), have pressed vigorously
for a "bridging package" to protect their members who will be
transferred from federal employment to employment with local
health boards. One of these unions, PSAC, represents the
employees who would be affected by the forestry and fire
transfer, and it is expected that the union will press for arrangements for forestry and fire employees commensurate with
those gained for health workers. To date, the Yukon cabinet has
resisted this step, arguing that the health and forestry transfers
are cases of a different kind: the former involves employees
moving from government employment to employment with a
health board; the latter is a "government-to-government" transfer.
At this stage in the negotiations, it is not clear whether this
territorial government position will change.

Conclusions

The current northern political configuration presents many
opportunities. In principle, the processes of comprehensive
claims negotiations, constitutional development and devolution
could all contribute in complementary fashion, to the evolution
of more democratic and responsive public government in the
NWT and the Yukon. Comprehensive claims agreements are
fundamentally an affirmation of aboriginal rights and a form of
compensation to native peoples who now share their homeland
with non-natives. They can also be seen, however, as significant
gestures towards a more equitable future, in which native
peoples in the North will have a better relationship with the
government and their co-residents than has been possible in
other Canadian jurisdictions. In this last respect, the agree-
ments-in-principle and eventual claims agreements have had
and will have some effect on the institutions of government, for
both policy development and administrative practices.

In both territories — though most notably in the NWT —
these very institutions are the rapidly evolving object of public

attention and debate. Northerners have invented a form of public government building that they label "constitutional development," and it is most directly through this process that they express their aspirations for more responsible and responsive government.

As we have seen, devolution of responsibilities from the federal to the territorial governments was seen by many — though not all — in the North as a procedure with major implications for both land claims negotiations and formal constitutional development. On this point, the two territorial governments took initially different strategic positions. The Yukon government chose to delay commencement of negotiations on transfer of forest and fire management responsibilities for a couple of years; this left time for negotiation of a framework Memorandum of Understanding with the CYI and the development of territorial plans for reorganization of the forestry and fire services. The GNWT, on the other hand, for good local reasons, sought an early transfer before extensive plans for the territorial management of these functions were made.

The different choices of the two governments reveal something about how the political institutions of each are now operating. In the Yukon, where constitutional matters are more settled and where the existence of a governing party supports the development of a consistent governmental stance on key policy issues, the territorial cabinet chose to avoid conflict with the claims negotiation process by deferring devolution until claims were settled. As it turned out, devolution was deferred until it was evident that the CYI claim was not going to follow the model of other comprehensive claims, with a single, watershed "ratification" date. Yukon government leaders could delay devolution in favour of claims partly because their constitutional auspices were already settled at a satisfactory level: with responsible government and party politics introduced in the 1970s, the 1980s could safely be seen as a time of consolidation. Furthermore, with the discipline of party politics in place to reinforce Cabinet authority (and the authority of individual ministers), this government was in a position to contain any bureaucratic eagerness for expanded responsibilities.

The Northwest Territories government, on the other hand, chose to pursue devolution and thus also chose to add devolution to the general process of constitutional development that is currently under way. Two factors seem to have contributed to this decision. First, more so than in the Yukon, territorial citizens were extremely dissatisfied with federal management of the fire service. There was considerable pressure for immediate improvement. Second, again more so than in the Yukon, the Government of the Northwest Territories is still "under construction," with all structures much more fluid. The NWT has begun to move towards "province-like" control of the bureaucracy by elected ministers, but the absence of party discipline in the Legislative Assembly and the relative difficulty of maintaining "Cabinet" solidarity, reduce the ministers' power, including their power over the administrative branch.

Perhaps paradoxically, both Territories are now in approximately the same position, in that neither is able yet to assume full responsibility for the forests. Each confronts similar substantive forest policy issues: most generally expressed, it is a matter of finding a way to balance competing goals of conservation, commercial development and local use, and in these circumstances to support the differing economies of both the wage economy centres and the predominantly native communities. Each also faces a similar task of institutional development, as ways and means have to be found for decisions about policy (on fire and on forests generally) that permit co-operation between government and the new native organizations that will exist after the relevant claims are settled.

The challenge in the Northwest Territories was to find a way to link the future-oriented processes of constitutional development and the claims negotiations to the day-to-day shaping of institutions that is integral to devolution, but also necessary ultimately, to the completion of the other two processes. Considering just the devolution of forest and fire responsibilities, it appears that in this sense the transfer was successful. After considerable conflict — costly conflict, particularly for employees affected by these events — the terms of the transfer produced a sensibly open-ended situation. In the Yukon, the task must be seen somewhat differently: there, it will be a matter of negotiating and effecting devolution in such a way that the long, complex process of band-by-band self-government negotiations is not unnecessarily disrupted. In both Territories, there is an ever-present risk of stalemate, and fruitless competition among actors involved in some processes but not others.

These processes are intimately involved in assessing the extent to which services to northerners will be improved by devolution. No answer is possible for the Yukon, since the transfer has not yet occurred. The prospect is favourable, since plans have been made that appear to meet the most important northern concerns, but it remains to be seen whether territorial preparedness will be rewarded with adequate funding from the federal government. Not much of an answer is possible for the NWT, either, for similar reasons. There has not been time for the processes established during the transfer for the development of new policies to actually produce alternative approaches and mechanisms. Here funding is also an issue, particularly as it will affect firefighting after 1990, but even more important will be the extent to which the responsible Minister and advisory boards are able to involve those who are affected by the policy in its development, implementation and evaluation. So far, both positive and negative steps in this direction have been taken, as is revealed in the process developed for involving the Forestry Working Group and the Denendeh Conservation Board in the formulation of a new fire suppression policy, and contrariwise, in the failure of the first round of the public consultation process.

In the end, each territory will be left with a finite budget and the need for consistent public involvement in policy making and more ground-level decisions. These two circumstances will shape each government's ability to respond to northerners' needs after all the issues arising in the course of devolution negotiations have been settled.

Acknowledgments

Revised versions of this paper were read to a public workshop on devolution held in Yellowknife in April 1989, and submitted to *The Northern Review*. The comments of workshop participants were extremely helpful, particularly those of Gurston Dacks. It is a pleasure to acknowledge also the assistance of representatives of the Council for Yukon Indians, the Dene Nation, the Métis Association and the Dene-Métis Negotiating Secretariat, as well as federal and territorial officials. As graduate students, John Crump and Jon Pierce conducted some of the research and preliminary analysis for the earlier version, while Marina Devine commented most helpfully on an earlier draft. Territorial government specialists and Clayton Burke of the Forestry Working Group in the NWT were particularly helpful in educating me about many technical aspects of forest and fire management. Of course none of the above are responsible for the resulting analysis.

NOTES

1   In this paper, the terms "devolution" and "transfer" are used interchangeably to refer to all cases where federal responsibilities, resources, jurisdiction and mandate are passed to a secondary level of government. Some might wish to distinguish between "devolution"(of governing authority) and "transfer" (of administrative responsibility), but such a neat analytical distinction does not serve my analytical purposes.

2   In 1971, 8,290 square kilometres of forest burned, compared to an average of 63 square kilometres in the preceeding decade. The record was set in the 1979-80 fire season, when the area burned increased by 15,675 square kilometres over the previous ten-year average. *Indian and Northern Affairs Canada, Transfer of Fire and Forest Management from Indian and Northern Affairs to the Government of the Northwest Territories: A Summary and Evaluation*, Ottawa, 1988, p. 5.

3   Federal interest in shifting the blame for capped expenditures on forest fires to the North was almost certainly part of the political calculus in Ottawa's decision to proceed with devolution in this area. Though there can have been little optimism in Ottawa about a short term reduction in actual federal expenditures on fire control, devolution did produce a real reduction in person years, raising the potential that in the long run costs could be contained. For one interpretation of the shifting northern policy sands in Ottawa, see Frances Abele, "A New Broom in an Old Bottleneck?" Conservative Northern Development Policy" in Michael J. Prince, ed. *How Ottawa Spends 1985-6: Tracking the Tories*, Toronto: Methuen, 1985 and Frances Abele and Katherine Graham, "Plus Que Ca Change...Northern and Native Policy" in Katherine Graham, ed. *How Ottawa Spends 1987-88: Heading into the Stretch*. Ottawa: Carleton University Press, 1987.

4   See Kenneth Coates, *Canada's Colonies: A History of the Yukon and Northwest Territories*, Toronto: James Lorimer and Company, 1985; Gurston Dacks, *A Choice of Futures: Politics in the Canadian North*, Toronto: Methuen, 1981; David R. Morrison, *The Politics of the Yukon Territory, 1889-1909*, Toronto: University of Toronto Press, 1968; Kenneth Rea, *The Political Economy of the Canadian North*, Toronto: University of Toronto Press, 1968; Morris Zaslow, *The Northward Expansion of Canada, 1914-1967*, Toronto: McClelland and Stewart, 1988.

5   Territorial departments, like government departments every-
     where, have a natural interest in expanding their ambit. From
     within a department, there are usually good strategic and
     practical reasons for doing this, since the civil servants in these
     positions know that there are always more needs to meet, and
     more work to be done, than they have the financial and internal-
     influence resources to accomplish. To some extent, for senior
     officials at least, a larger department enhances both personal
     power and security.

6   The Alliance was composed of the Western and Nunavut Con-
     stitutional Forums, each in turn composed of territorial native
     organization leaders and a representative of the Government of
     the Northwest Territories. The Forums were charged with de-
     veloping new constitutions for a divided Northwest Territories.

7   DIAND regional staff were similarly frustrated by the requirement
     that they work with decisions taken in Ottawa for other than local
     reasons. As is noted in Indian and Northern Affairs Canada,
     Transfer of Fire and Forest Management (p. 21): "[The CL-
     215s]...replaced a DC-6 tanker group.... The federal government's
     entry into this agreement was based on national policy objectives
     and not economic considerations. These aircraft are very expensive
     to operate and matters were complicated by a delay in authori-
     zation of the contract and the resultant training of pilots and high
     insurance increases. There was also a need to provide additional
     aircraft pending late delivery of the CL-215s."

8   Yukon, *Yukon Development Strategy: Forestry*, Yukon 2000
     Sectoral Report. Whitehorse: October 23, 1986; Colin Heartwell,
     The Forest Industry in the Economy of the Yukon. Prepared for the
     Yukon Government, Indian Affairs and Northern Development
     Canada, Canadian Forestry Service, Yukon Forest Industry
     Association. Whitehorse: February 1988.

9   DIAND's authority arises from the *Department of Indian Affairs
     and Northern Development Act. The Territorial Lands Act* provided
     the legislative basis for the management of forests, under the
     Territorial Timber Regulations and (in the NWT) the Forest
     Protection Ordinance.

10   John S. McTavish, *An Evaluation of the Northern Affairs Forest
     Management Program*, Ottawa: Department of Indian Affairs and
     Northern Development, 1982.

11   The most important factors were apparently the absence of an
     agreement between the GNWT and the Dene Nation, and disa-

greement between the territorial and federal governments about funding.

12   Reprinted in Indian and Northern Affairs Canada, *Transfer of Fire and Forest Management.*

13   The protections are weaker for at least two reasons. The first has to do with the status of the signatories, who, as civil servants, cannot make binding political commitments. The second has to do with quite ambiguous references to "affected native groups," a phrase that might refer to community organizations or even to unorganized groups of people, rather than to native organizations (such as the Métis Association and the Dene Nation). Native organizations are never mentioned in the deputy ministers' MOU. Three of the "guiding principles" are relevant: "Transfers will be made through a process of agreement between the federal and territorial governments, with the support and participation of affected native groups." "Transfers will not prejudice further political evolution in the Northwest Territories." "Transfers will not prejudice unsettled native claims."

14   Letter from Steve Kakfwi (President of the Dene Nation) and Larry Tourangeau (President of the Métis Association) to Minister of Renewable Resources Nellie Cournoyea dated October 10, 1985. The author does not have a copy of this letter.

15   The transfer that was negotiated reduced the size of the Northern Affairs program by 14 percent, a reduction that made a respectable contribution to the overall departmental target of 6 percent.

16   The legal details are quite complicated. They are spelled out in Northwest Territories Forest Resources Transfer Agreement, signed by the Minister of Indian Affairs and Northern Development for Canada and the Minister of Renewable Resources and the Commissioner of the Northwest Territories on March 31, 1987. They are summarized clearly in Indian and Northern Affairs Canada, *Transfer of Fire and Forest Management:* "[The GNWT gains] authority to pass Ordinances with respect to fire and forest management on territorial lands under the administration, management and control of the Minister of DIAND. These apply on reserved or withdrawn lands except where the Minister indicates otherwise. Certain deletions respecting timber have been made to the Territorial Lands Act and although the Minister retains administration, management and control of trees, GNWT has responsibility for the legislation."

17   A participation agreement was eventually signed by the parties, too late to bear on these negotiations, but in the spirit of preserving the principle for future negotiations.

18   There is no space here to treat other challenging issues faced by the negotiators, which include staff housing and the general condition of the transferred physical resources, as well as taxation.

19   Work-force Adjustment Policies were developed for all federal departments affected by the Cabinet decision to reduce the size of the federal civil service. In effect, a WAP places "surplus" employees in a privileged position for jobs elsewhere in the civil service, but does not guarantee them employment.

20   Indian and Northern Affairs Canada, *Transfer of Forest and Fire Management*, p. 20.

21   There was very little provision made for training of any staff at all during this transfer. The federal Fire Management Program did expose some GNWT Renewable Resources employees to firefighting procedures during 1986, while some were also included in a fire suppression course during 1987. Territorial training of formerly federal staff did not begin until after the transfer was completed.

22   The DCB was established after the signing of the Dene-Métis claims agreement-in-principle, prefiguring the joint management boards that will be established with the final settlement of the Dene-Métis land claim.

23   This is probably because sufficient or appropriate measures were not taken to solicit responses. Renewable Resources officials report that copies of the discussion paper were mailed to the relevant non-governmental organizations, with a request for commentary, and newspaper advertisements were placed inviting citizens' participation. Considering the other demands upon key commentators' time during this period, and the difficulty of inter-community communications, probably some more elaborate or personal system for soliciting responses would have worked better.

24   An interim funding arrangement was developed for fire suppression, to be replaced by a new regime appropriate to the new territorial policy, then expected by 1990. Under the interim system, the GNWT has access to an $8 million fire suppression account, with the provision that annual shortfall or surplus (less the first $1 million) can be carried over to the next year. There is

also a provision for an additional federal contribution should there be a need for more expenditures during this period. During the three years this funding system is in place, the GNWT is committed to follow the existing priority zone system for firefighting.

25   Yukon forest industry representatives have expressed a strong interest in simplification of the regulatory process, and some concerns about the fairness of decisions taken under the present system. See Colin Heartwell, *The Forest Industry in the Economy of the Yukon*, prepared for the Yukon Government, Indian Affairs and Northern Development Canada, Canadian Forestry Service and the Yukon Forest Industry Association, Whitehorse, 1988.

3 Political Devolution and Wildlife Management

Peter Clancy

To discuss questions of wildlife is to tap a wellspring of northern politics. It is by any measure a "valence" issue, which sharply defines some of the most basic issues of power in the North. Wildlife has been one of the most durable objects of public policy, dating back to the nineteenth century. When the state has intervened, whether in the name of conservation, of protecting native peoples, or of shaping economic growth, its wildlife policies have had a profound impact on northern life. This remains as true today as yesterday. The most basic co-ordinates of wildlife policy are politically contestable: in the Legislative Assembly, at the land claims table, in the community, and in the courtroom. No discussion of devolution politics could ignore its many ramifications in this field.

Yet there are several respects in which the wildlife case differs from some other policy fields affected by devolution. First it is evident that with wildlife, a significant degree of devolution has already occurred. In the case of terrestrial mammals, both the Yukon Territorial Government (YTG) and the Government of the Northwest Territories (GNWT) have held jurisdiction for more than a generation. By studying the record of the territorial game management agencies, we can assess a record of provincial-style control, while also comparing an already devolved wildlife sector to those which remain with Ottawa. This should not suggest that further transfers are not possible. Indeed, territorial involvement in inland fisheries is presently an element of the devolution agenda. Nevertheless the experience of the territorial game services to date remains most pertinent to understanding the impact of jurisdictional devolution on wild-life management.

The wildlife case is equally important to devolution in a second respect. It has been the object of sustained political challenges *within* the Territories. This second consideration is not so much for the constitutional aggrandizement of territorial authorities, as it is to bring control over wildlife programs closer to the people. From this perspective, a jurisdictional transfer simply replaces an absentee legislature and management agency with resident structures. The more radical devolution impulse seeks community control over wildlife policy. This has inspired a variety of institutional proposals and political initiatives over the past two decades. One instance was the GNWT's *internal* "devolution" initiative of the 1970s, an effort to decentralize the delivery of programs wherever possible and involve northern residents in local decision making. Community-based Hunters and Trappers Associations (HTAs) were central to this endeavour.

A more substantial impulse toward devolution in this second sense involves "co-operative" or "joint" management regimes for wildlife. Several versions of these structures have appeared, ranging from the germinal to the mature. Their overriding thrust is to bring together scientific, administrative, and harvester interests, in a common cause. The general principle of co-operative management has won wide acceptance in a very short period of time. Today the principle is being invoked in a wide variety of settings, including the management of wildlife on public lands and the wildlife regimes established by aboriginal claims settlements. It finds additional support in fields where federal agencies retain statutory authority for such species as migratory birds, and fish and marine mammals.

The aboriginal claims arena provides yet another opportunity for addressing the process of local empowerment. At every claims table, negotiations over wildlife have assumed central importance. Whether by defining harvesting rights or guaranteed claimant participation in public decision-making bodies, the settlement packages transform the basis of wildlife management in profound ways.

In sum, an analysis of the wildlife field throws the devolution phenomenon into sharp relief. It allows the comparison of wildlife management programs which are already devolved (in the jurisdictional sense) with those programs which are not. In the case of devolved activities, it highlights not only the strengths but also the limitations of territorial power.

To this end, our discussion will proceed as follows. The first section will introduce wildlife as a policy area. The next section will examine the GNWT's record in terrestrial wildlife management. Since jurisdictional devolution implies a further build-up of this authority, its record to date is of considerable relevance. The discussion will then turn to the aboriginal claims question where it surveys the central developments affecting wildlife in the contemporary settlements. From here the discussion will return to jurisdictional devolution, with an analysis of the recent freshwater fishery delegation in the Yukon. The final section will explore the overall findings and offer some conclusions on the questions posed above.

Wildlife as a Policy Area

> The term wildlife naturally includes all the members of our native Canadian fauna...Strictly speaking, it would include the game, non-game, and fur-bearing mammals, the game and non-game birds, the fishes and other members of our fauna.[1]

The impressive scope of this definition is accepted in principle by virtually all who study or harvest wild species. Yet the self-evident unity of the subject has almost never been sustained, conceptually or practically, in Canadian public policy. Even in the volume cited above, Hewitt went on to limit his discussion, for purposes of the book, to large game mammals and birds. He thereby excluded fur-bearers, fish, and marine mammals. Half a century of subsequent wildlife policy has if anything accentuated this tendency, to the point where today, a unified system of wildlife management seems a rather remote prospect for most parts of Canada.

The segmentation which prevails in science and administration contrasts with the unity of perspective associated with the hunter-trapper-fisherman. For such harvesters, the widest possible range of species knowledge is required. To be sure, harvesters may possess differential levels of expertise across the wildlife spectrum, as some social groups rely more on fish, others on big game, and still others on marine mammals. But the necessity of utilizing multiple species to sustain both the commercial and the domestic sides of the hunting-trapping enterprise places a premium on global expertise regarding wildlife.

While space does not permit a full elaboration here, it might be argued that the contradiction between the specialized/ segmented tradition of management, and the holistic/inte-grated tradition of harvesting, underlies much of the political conflict over wildlife policy. However before we examine concrete instances of this encounter, it is necessary to document the constitutional and administrative field on which it operates. This jurisdictional grid will provide us with a backdrop for the analysis of devolution politics.

1) Game: The *British North America Act, 1867* effectively conferred jurisdiction over land-based wildlife to the provinces, under section 92(16), covering "matters of a merely local or private nature in a province."[2] Statutes commonly applied the term "game" in order to emphasize land-based animals and birds. In contrast to the provinces, land title in the North has continued to rest with the Crown in right of Canada. In Yukon, the Council acquired jurisdiction over game in 1900. This was a statutory delegation from Ottawa to the Territory under the *Yukon Act*. Despite the curtailment of the Yukon Council's jurisdiction following the collapse of the Klondike Gold Rush, it retained control over game.[3] Not until 1948 did the NWT acquire the same status. At that time Ottawa amended the *Northwest Territories Act* to add game to the section 13 powers delegated to the NWT Council. The Council passed a *Game Ordinance* in 1949, consolidating most of the provisions of the former federal *Northwest Game Act.*[4]

2) Fisheries: The fisheries situation offers a significant contrast to game. Here the *British North America Act* assigns the constitutional jurisdiction for "sea coast and inland fisheries" to the federal government. On this basis Ottawa assumed regulatory authority over both the harvesting and habitat aspects of fisheries. The *Fisheries Act* constitutes the main legal instrument, covering fish, marine mammals and crustaceans.[5] Through the courts, the provinces have established a constitutional position in the fisheries field. This began with a provincial crown proprietary right over riverbeds. It conveyed the same power to regulate capture as prevailed on crown land, although it extended to freshwater only. Subsequently, the federal government acceded to provincial requests for enhanced *administrative* control of the inland fisheries. While Ottawa retained the authority to issue the statutory regulations under the *Fisheries Act,* it did so on a province-by-province basis, on the advice of provincial authorities. Meanwhile a series of federal-provincial fisheries agreements spelled out the provincial managerial role.[6]

Significantly, none of these provisions applied to fisheries in the territorial north. Since the territorial governments lacked the constitutional basis for a proprietary claim, Ottawa's jurisdiction remained complete. The Northwest Territories was first mentioned in the 1886 *Fisheries Act,* primarily by way of recognizing special rights of Indians to fish for their own use, without restriction by season or method. Since 1929 regulations have been issued for arctic marine mammals, largely in response to the mounting pressure from commercial harvesting.[7] Following the Second World War, the Department of Fisheries' interest centred on the inland freshwater sector, particularly the Great Slave Lake commercial fishery in the NWT and the salmon sport fishery in the Yukon. Facing considerable pressure from their harvesting constituencies, both Territorial Councils began calling, as early as the 1960s, for the transfer of inland fisheries management.

3) Migratory Birds: As with other wildlife sectors, the jurisdictional basis of bird programs derives from the federal division of powers. The migratory bird category consists of migratory varieties of game birds (mainly waterfowl), non-game birds (auks, loons, murres and the like) and insectivorous (perching) birds. All of these fall under federal jurisdiction, while non-migratory birds fall under provincial law. As a consequence, the hunting of ducks, geese, and swans is regulated by Ottawa, while the hunting of game birds, such as pheasant, grouse, and partridge, is handled by the provinces and territories.[8]

The key legal development for migratory birds occurred early in this century. Alarm was being raised over the devastating impact of market hunting, combined with extensive habitat loss through land reclamation.[9] Given that several nations and multiple jurisdictions were involved, an international treaty offered a powerful means to co-ordinate legislative authority across the entire migratory range. In 1916, the *Migratory Birds Convention* was initialled by Canada, the United States and Mexico. Following its ratification, Parliament enacted the *Migratory Birds Convention Act* in 1918.[10] Today migratory birds remain the leading management responsibility of the Canadian Wildlife Service, in the federal Department of the Environment.

Both the Convention and the Act ignored a central concern of northern hunting. Open seasons for migratory birds could run from September to mid-March, when the birds were in prime condition along the flyway and available to hunters in the southern plains regions.[11] However this posed serious difficulties in the far north, where the birds are only accessible to hunters in the late spring. Though native peoples rely on the spring hunt to provide fresh food during a transitional season, they do so illegally. For their part, management agencies must decide whether to enforce regulations of questionable legitimacy or turn a blind eye to a wholesale violation of the law. In the late 1970s, Canada and the United States initialled a protocol to amend the Convention, by recognizing the importance of aboriginal spring harvests. Despite executive support in both countries, the draft protocol failed to gain ratification in the American Congress, where a coalition of sport hunter lobbies successfully portrayed the northern native harvests as a threat to conservation.

This brief portrait shows that the wildlife policy field is highly fragmented, with legal authority divided between national and territorial levels, and management authority vested in a number of distinct bureaus and agencies. While terrestrial game was devolved to territorial governments decades ago, Ottawa continues to hold responsibilities for fish, sea mammals and migratory birds. It is from these fields that any further jurisdictional transfers will come. However it is one thing to claim a jurisdiction and quite another to exercise it. Does a devolved wildlife program differ significantly from its non-devolved counterpart? To answer this question, the following section examines the performance of the terrestrial game programs under territorial administration.

Devolution in Theory and Practice

Given the constitutional and legal constraints reviewed above, it is improbable that the wildlife field will ever pass wholesale to territorial authorities in the North. Indeed it seems appropriate to ask what features of such devolution make it a desirable option. This can be approached through a review of recent initiatives by the NWT Wildlife Service. Based on two decades of experience, the Wildlife Service offers an invaluable case study of a jurisdictionally devolved administration. It also offers a base line reference against which non-devolved wildlife programs (such as ocean fisheries, sea mammals and migratory birds) can be compared. Equally, it provides a standard of comparison for assessing the alternative styles of political devolution which are part of northern politics today.

Although the *Game Ordinance* was passed by the Northwest Territories Council in 1949, the administrative and enforcement staff remained federal until 1967. At that time the staff function was transferred to the GNWT, becoming the Game Management Service (GMS) of the newly formed Department of Industry and Development. The match was more than a little incongruous. The Department's overriding mandate was the

77

support of small commercial business enterprise, encompassing arts and crafts, forest and fishery projects, tourism and assorted small ventures.[12] The Wildlife Service fit this thrust, to the extent that it supported commercial production, through its embryonic programs for trapper loans, fish camp and bush camp ventures, and fur marketing. However this commercial appreciation of game did not go unchallenged. Arrayed against it were the long-standing principles of wildlife conservation (as embodied in the *Northwest Game Act*), which included the need to *regulate* commercial harvesting. On this rested the historical basis of northern game protection, going back to the early measures covering musk ox, caribou, and migratory birds. While some tension between commerce and conservation was inevitable, game policy has always accorded primacy to the latter. Though it may not have been evident in 1967, a potent contradiction was embedded in the wildlife program.

The term "game management" was probably a misnomer during these years. The *Game Ordinance* was a restrictive statute, and, given the fact that its major provisions were 20 years old, due for a major revision. The field staff, on which depended enforcement, covered the Mackenzie District only, while the balance of the Arctic fell to the RCMP. The research function in wildlife lay not with Yellowknife, but with the Canadian Wildlife Service, which, despite sizable contributions to northern biology, was constrained by the additional claims of its national mandate. Thus there was neither an integrated capacity to take informed decisions nor one to enforce them. All of these matters would draw extended attention in the years to follow.

Without question, 1974 stands out as a watershed year in the development of the GMS. The most dramatic and revealing incident arose in September, with a controversy which struck at the very heart of the program. It began with public allegations of irregularities in big game licensing and sports hunt financing.[13] At issue were charges that the Superintendent of Game had taken game himself in violation of the law, misappropriated public funds, and exercised powers contrary to the *Ordinance*. Not only did this draw sensational attention to the practices of the Service and endanger its political legitimacy in the process, it also precipitated an extensive review of the game programs.

After an internal investigation, the Assistant Commissioner reported no illegal acts, but found the Superintendent to have displayed "a marked lack of judgement."[14] Looking beyond the specific incidents, the report contended that "the present game management policies and practices have failed to keep in pace with current thinking." The proposed remedies included an executive review of the philosophy, structure and organization of the GMS, and the creation of a Game Council to advise the Commissioner on policy matters. The Council members were drawn from politically interested organizations representing native peoples, tourist operators, and big-game hunters.

This controversy clearly anticipated many of the basic political conflicts which would animate wildlife policy for the next decade: conservation against commercial harvesting; staff biologists against the field service; senior executives against policy professionals. However, one fundamental debate remained latent for the time being. This concerned the distribution of wildlife rights and products *among* resident interests in the North: native and non-native, General Hunting Licence and Sports Licence holders, subsistence and recreational harvesters. In such a complex political context, the GMS could not afford to drift. Early in 1975, a GNWT review proposed that the agency be transferred to a new Department of Natural and Cultural Affairs (NCA).[15] There remained, however, the larger challenge of re-establishing the internal administrative coherence and political legitimacy of the wildlife program.

Organizing the Constituency

In the years to follow, the Service laid particular stress on cultivating a relationship with its hunter-trapper clientele. This involved a positive program to organize the harvesters qua harvesters. For this, no existing organization would suffice. The basic approach had already been set in the early 1970s. Within each community the GMS encouraged the local organization of a Hunters and Trappers Association (HTA). These were intended to be non-governmental organizations, whose field of interest and expertise would focus on wildlife drawn broadly. Essentially, the HTAs were allowed to define their own membership by local agreement. Incorporated under the *Societies Ordinance*, each association would select its own leadership, which would hopefully include the most respected and active hunter-trappers. The GMS provided token financial support, initially set at $500 per year per association.

The pattern of growth for HTAs was of necessity uneven. By 1973 the Service reported 28 functioning associations, which ranged in health "from very excellent to marginal."[16] By 1979, the total had increased to 53, of which 10 were Dene Band Councils recognized as HTA equivalents. The existence of hunter forums at the local level, tied directly into the GMS, offered several advantages. To begin with, the HTAs were the only local groups (of the many supported by the GNWT) whose prime field of interest lay beyond the settlements. For the Service this meant that "we have it much easier dealing with a group of people who are genuinely interested in the management of natural resources."[17] The potential uniqueness of the associations went beyond wildlife matters, to include the wider issues of land use and environmental protection. Thus to the extent that their objectives coincided, the HTAs offered the GMS an invaluable network of field intelligence, along with a specialized channel of political advice. This advisory function was readily acknowledged: "The GNWT recognizes these groups as official community spokesmen on all matters concerning the renewable resources of their area."[18] A critical factor in consolidating local support for the HTAs was their capacity to provide discrete benefits to their members. From an early date, the GMS planned to delegate to them the delivery role for harvester assistance programs. By 1977 an initial package, consisting of trapper assistance loans and funds for community hunts and outpost camps, was well along. This dovetailed with a government-wide initiative announced by the Commissioner in 1976, to devolve and decentralize as many programs as practicable to the local level. The HTA network was being transformed, at least in part, from an advisory to an administrative apparatus. The eventual logic was "to increase administrative operating grants to these associations to allow them to ultimately hire secretary/managers to handle their business."[19] It is arguable whether this has yet occurred.

The HTAs have also assumed roles in certain public decision-making processes. Following the revision of the *Wildlife Ordinance* in 1979, it was possible for the Commissioner to delegate to any consenting local association a wide range of powers under the Ordinance. The federal Department of Fisheries also took advantage of the HTA network to consult on the setting of marine mammal regulations in the Arctic. In yet another venue, the HTAs acquired a role in the northern land use planning system, when they were given the opportunity to comment on land use applications within their areas of operation.

The role of an organized clientele was not confined to the local level. In the early 1970s, the GMS began supporting regular regional conferences to which all HTAs were entitled to send delegates. Eventually, annual conferences were adopted in all five regions, with funding for delegate travel budgeted in the basic HTA grants. In 1979 the Fish and Wildlife Service took this logic one step further, by supporting the formation of a NWT Hunters and Trappers Federation. This was intended to serve as an umbrella group for the HTAs in dealing with governments north and south of 60°. While the federation failed to take hold as a permanent association, it has been revived periodically to engage the anti-fur lobby.

The question of who could or should speak on behalf of wildlife harvesters never had a clear answer. The GNWT strongly endorsed the HTA structure because it encompassed, in principle, virtually all active harvesters regardless of race or intensity of effort. However the HTA program came under challenge from another direction, as the native political organizations contemplated the role of wildlife in their claims settlements. There was a potential rivalry for representative status between the HTAs at various organized levels, and the Dene, Métis and Inuit organizations. The Dene Band Councils in the Mackenzie District enjoyed a strong basis in law. In the first instance, this led many elected Band Councils to challenge the municipal government programs of the GNWT. This was most forceful in the Dene communities along the Mackenzie Valley. Faced with the prospect of separate community bodies staking control over wildlife and land issues, most Band Councils preferred to claim this role for themselves. By 1981 the FWS recognized 10 Band Councils in this capacity, although they did not qualify immediately for administrative funding.

For the FWS, the cultivation of an organized clientele served important strategic objectives. It provided a network for the delivery of field programs, and for the potential delegation of local regulatory matters. It also provided a precedent which was adopted by the aboriginal claimant organizations in negotiating the wildlife institutions in their settlements. If it did not automatically bolster the agency's political legitimacy, it certainly helped lay the groundwork for future gains. The revision of the *Game Ordinance* offers a timely case in point.

Modernizing the Ordinance

Between 1975 and 1979, one of the most urgent matters to come before the NWT Council was the proposed revision of the *Game Ordinance*. This statute formed the central legal instrument of wildlife policy. As such, any amendments took on a symbolic as well as a substantive importance. The prospect of its wholesale revision, for the first time since 1960, heightened the stakes considerably. Furthermore, the process revealed much about the competing agendas of the many interests which made up the policy community for northern wildlife. Political organizations such as the Dene Nation, COPE, and the Inuit Tapirisat, which viewed the wildlife field as integral to their land claims settlements, understandably resisted any legal changes aimed at upgrading or modernizing the regulatory role of the state. As the central forum for legislative changes, the NWT Council also revealed its contradictory representative character. Anxious to assert its prerogatives, yet sensitive to the social impact of management policy, the Council tended to be reactive rather than directive. Nevertheless the existence of public forums and their accessibility to resident interests had an unmistakable impact. Particularly when compared to these same groups' experience with federal fish and bird policy, this case demonstrates the effect of legislative and administrative devolution of a socially significant sector.

This issue became one of the first political trials of the Wildlife Service, as it struggled to repair its badly damaged prestige. A decision to review the Ordinance was made as early as 1972. Given that its core provisions dated from 1949, a thorough revision was overdue. For example, terms of the statute were unusually elaborate, necessitating a formal legislative amendment for each proposed change, no matter how minor. A more flexible set of statutory regulations was planned to cover, among other matters, the details of seasons, bags and zoning. In other respects the Ordinance had to confront entirely new problems, such as the environmental impact of industrial mega-projects. To this end, provisions were needed to manage special impact zones, and to control hunting by non-resident project personnel.

When the new Council met in May 1975, the policy atmosphere surrounding wildlife was already tense. Rather than move directly to legislation, the GMS engaged Mr. Frank Bailey, a former wildlife official, to conduct a systematic round of consultations. His task was to solicit community views on the existing statute and any prospective revisions, reporting back on the main themes and variations which arose in the course of the meetings. In both its scope and its informed status, Bailey's consultation provided an indispensible input for the revision.[20]

Yet far from exhausting the consultative process, Bailey's initiative was merely the first phase of three. The Game Advisory Council received Bailey's final report, and went on to consider draft versions of the new ordinance and regulations as they emerged in 1977. A third phase followed from the Government's decision to circulate the drafts for *public* discussion before they received formal legislative consideration.[21] During the summer, the local game officers met with HTAs to explain the proposals. Not surprisingly, this multi-track procedure began to sow confusion, as different drafts and translations found their way into circulation.

The terms of the proposed statute indicated some new directions in management thinking which were taking hold in the FWS. Substantively, there were new provisions dealing with eligibility, permissable hunting practices, commercial ventures based on wildlife, and the use of zoning as a conservation measure. According to the FWS, they shared a common logic. The entire Ordinance "was based on the premise that the native people of the Northwest Territories have the first claim on the use of fish and wildlife resources."[22]

Another striking feature was the scope for local input to the regulatory process. The HTAs were encouraged to get involved across a broad front. For example, in the issuance of General Hunting Licenses, they screened and recommended the acceptance of any new applicants for this most important of harvesting rights in the NWT. At the same time, the waiting period in qualifying for a resident hunting licence was lengthened to two years. In this sense the Ordinance was described aptly as positive discrimination in support of native hunters.[23] HTAs could also secure group trapping licences, and allocate the territories amongst their members. The entire zoning system, used for setting open seasons and harvest quotas, was redesigned in a more flexible fashion, which enabled the HTAs to advise on the detailed terms for their local areas. As far as commercial ventures were concerned, not only did the Ordinance liberalize the terms for marketing country products. It also offered new opportunities for HTAs and other GHL holders to engage in outfitting ventures. Finally, the Ordinance created the new position of "wildlife guardian," by which knowledgeable local persons could act as advisors to the field staff, without getting involved in the enforcement side of patrolling. All points considered, it was no doubt correct that "under this new Ordinance there is more power wielded by the HTAs and Band Councils, quite a lot more power, than in the current Ordinance."[24] After minor amendments, the new *Wildlife Ordinance* was approved in October of 1978, and was enacted early the following year.

Ultimately, this protracted process of legislative revision yielded impressive results for the FWS. As an experiment in public education, its was an unprecedented success. Not only were the communities offered repeated opportunities for input, but the overall level of awareness of the Ordinance, old version and new, increased greatly. Substantively, the *Wildlife Ordinance* gave legal sanction to a more flexible, community sensitive regulatory regime. This, it turned out, was only one co-ordinate of the new management strategy, which became further evident when the GNWT launched its own internal "devolution" initiative after 1976.

Devolution and Decentralization

Periodically over the past decade, the GNWT has announced initiatives aimed at internal decentralization and devolution of program control. This addressed the question of increasing local and regional input to *existing* territorial programs. Several distinct options were bound together here. Decentralization entailed the shift of administrative control from Yellowknife to regional or even local community offices of the GNWT. Decisions formerly made at headquarters or the regions could be made closer to the point of delivery. This implied a significant re-allocation of personnel, job tasks, and authority levels, but was confined to the civil service. By contrast, devolution suggested that control over the actual formulation and design of policies could move closer to the ground. This went beyond the bureaucracy, and raised the prospect of expanded power at the community level. It constituted the GNWT's leading political initiative to win legitimacy for itself in the turbulent climate of the late 1970s.

One common denominator, which would be compatible with any and all such initiatives, was program decentralization. As was seen above, its key policy initiatives left the Wildlife Service well positioned for this phase. Since the devolution initiative stressed institutional experimentation, and acknowledged the uniqueness of program needs, it found in the FWS one of its most willing participants.[25] Of the new considerations being thrust to the fore, staffing and personnel practices posed special challenges. In this area more than most, the field staff constitute a critical link in program delivery. Between 1968 and 1987, the total field establishment grew from 22 to 79 positions.[26] In building this infrastructure the GMS took several steps to attract native people to the field service. A modest in-house game officer training program of the early 1970s has given way to a formal Natural Resource Training program at Arctic College. The GMS also designed a new position of Assistant Officer, to be filled by local people, most often native, who could serve as liaison between the Game Officer and the community.[27]

Embedded in the devolution debate of the early 1980s was a fundamental ambiguity, which turned on the precise degree of decision-making power to be retained by the Department of Renewable Resources (DRR), and the period of time appropriate to its retention. Arguments could be made for a standstill for the duration of the claims negotiating process, for a management devolution to the HTAs as a provisional step compatible with future claims settlements, or for a formal demarcation of residual government responsibilities irrespective of devolution or claims. Within the FWS, there was significant support for the latter. A 1981 review expressed this succinctly:

In general, people programs can go completely or in limited manner to the HTAs/Band Councils, as they are concerned with resource utilization. However wildlife research, wildlife management processes, wildlife administration and enforcement functions must largely remain within the Service. Some parts of each function can be devolved, but without firm control, the Service would lose control of wildlife management in the NWT.[28]

This position effectively put the GMS in the forefront of the GNWT's "devolution and decentralization" initiative. Moreover it completely eclipsed the performance of other wildlife agencies in the North. However it is a measure of the political complexity of the wildlife field that even as these arrangements were unfolding, entirely new initiatives were on the horizon. Perhaps it was inevitable, given the plethora of consultative channels detailed above, that the interested public would look beyond "advice" to claim a direct role in policy making. In fact, this crystallized around the issue of "joint management" or "co-management" of wildlife.

Joint Management Regimes for Wildlife

One of the most innovative policy initiatives of the late 1970s involved the joint decision-making body. Versions of this concept were advanced from many directions: the Berger Report, the aboriginal claims table, the National Parks Service, and the FWS. On the one hand joint management addressed the question of power sharing in claims settlements. On the other, it offered a means to extend popular involvement in the wildlife regime beyond its previous limits. During the 1980s, joint management arrangements won wide acceptance as institutional mechanisms for bringing wildlife users together with scientists and managers in common cause. Many different arrangements fall into this category, ranging from the purely advisory to the delegated decision-making body. In the North today it is reflected in two caribou management boards, the Wildlife Management Advisory Council and the Joint Fisheries Management Committee in the Western Arctic Settlement, the Nunavut Wildlife Board, the Denendeh Conservation Board, the Great Bear Lake Fisheries Committee, and joint wildlife bodies operating in two northern National Parks.[29] The present section will focus on the origins and the issues raised by this arrangement. The claims-related joint bodies will be discussed in greater detail later in the paper.

In the increasingly politicized climate of northern wildlife management, the concept of joint decision making had an obvious relevance. It looked beyond the conflicting bids for exclusive control by government agencies and native claimants, proposing instead a collaborative form of control. Thomas Berger advised in his final report that "the government should ensure meaningful involvement of native organizations in all aspects of wildlife management in the region."[30] The battle to define "meaningful," not to mention "all aspects," was soon joined. The concept of a joint wildlife body had already appeared in the CYI and ITC claims proposals. It was also reflected in the COPE claim, which proposed a variety of "joint management regimes" for wildlife, parks, and land management.

One of the first *federal* agencies to formally embrace the principle of joint management was Parks Canada. Its 1979 policy statement declared that "an agreement will be negotiated between Parks Canada and representatives of local native communities prior to formal establishment of a national park, creating a joint management regime for the planning and management of the national park."[31] By bringing the entire park management plan under joint management, this went well beyond the question of wildlife alone. Thereafter, Parks Canada spent the next several years trimming this formal statement toward a more restrictive focus on wildlife, on northern parks, and on subsistence users.[32]

In fact, questions of institutional design and power sharing were basic to the politics of joint management. On the one side, some wildlife managers seemed to view joint management as a stepped-up form of consultation with local HTAs. This could be done by further decentralizing the local advisory roles already authorized by the new *Wildlife Ordinance*. On the other side, native claimant groups were advancing proposals for decision-making bodies (Boards), to which ministers of the Crown would delegate *de facto* control. This triggered major bureaucratic resistance, at precisely the point where guaranteed rights to be consulted and to advise gave way to guaranteed rights of final decision.

Such tensions might have deadlocked any progress for the duration of aboriginal claims negotiations, had it not been for the "new" caribou crisis.[33] This forced the issue into tangible terms, and gave rise to the Beverley and Kaminuriak Caribou Management Board (BKCMB). The controversy was triggered by the results of GMS population surveys of the massive barren-ground caribou herds. Beginning in 1976 and 1977, the data suggested that far from reproducing their numbers, the herds were in serious net decline. Given their continuing importance in meeting the domestic needs of native peoples across such a wide section of the northern Canadian mainland, any decline which jeopardized the viability of the herds would be calamitous. The experience in Alaska, where the western arctic herd fell precipitously in only a few years, underlined the need for immediate remedies.

The terms of the ensuing debate illustrated the magnitude of the political legitimacy crisis which the FWS faced. The biologists attributed the population declines to the excess of mortality (natural and hunter kill) over recruitment. By contrast, the Keewatin Inuit cited the disruption which mineral exploration activities visited on the caribou herds, particularly through losses on the calving grounds and disruptions to migration routes. According to this alternative perspective, industrial exploration and development posed the prime threat to population growth and herd movement. When the caribou census was released, aboriginal reactions ranged from cautious scepticism to cynical dismissal, particularly where the data failed to square with local experience in encountering caribou on the land. Even to the extent that the numbers were accepted, they could as easily be attributed to exploration crews as hunters. The analytical gulf between hunters and biologists was wide indeed. While the scientists saw the merits of protecting calving grounds, there was still "the main problem with caribou — their decline for reasons unrelated to the activities of the mineral industry."[34]

In any case, the dimensions of the crisis pointed out how far the existing management controls were failing, while the need for political reconciliation opened the way for an innovative response. By 1981 the concept of joint management was already under active consideration both in Yellowknife and Ottawa.[35] In an attempt to bring harvesters and managers together, the governments proposed a joint board concept to native groups. The formal agreement was signed in June of 1982. Of the 13 members appointed to the Board, five represented the co-operating government agencies, while eight represented the harvesting communities contiguous with the range. High among the Board's concerns was the design of a management plan, an information program, and an educational program.[36] It could "recommend" policy changes to ministers, who were obliged to respond, and to offer reasons where advice was not accepted.

It is fair to say that the Beverly and Kaminuriak Caribou Management Board had an effect both as precedent and advertisement. Springing to life under crisis conditions, it demonstrated the value of joint approaches for future management problems. Yet concealed within the structure of the BKCMB were some key questions of institutional design. Answers would be worked out over the next decade of wildlife programming. For example, who appoints delegates to such authorities, and to whom do the delegates answer? To whom do the authorities convey decisions, and what is then done with them? Where is the authority positioned relative to the wildlife management agency? Each new joint initiative was obliged to confront such issues. But in so doing, they confirmed that the joint body had become a fixture in the new wildlife era. Nowhere was this more clearly illustrated than at the land claims table.

Aboriginal Claims and Devolution

No discussion of wildlife policy and devolution can overlook the landmark developments over the past 15 years of negotiating aboriginal claims. Certainly this is formally separate from jurisdictional devolution (indeed Ottawa has insisted since 1977 that constitutional matters and claims matters be addressed in separate forums). However the final agreements which will set the terms for the several negotiated settlements in the North will necessarily extend the locus of indigenous political control. As authoritative claims institutions assume a place in wildlife management, they can shift the locus of political control to the advantage of northern interests.

The pattern of settlements to date suggest that this will take at least two main forms. First, a variety of "harvesting rights" will be conferred on aboriginal claimants. To the extent that aboriginal people obtain fee simple ownership to surface lands, they will enjoy the property owners' control over access to wildlife thereon. Another set of terms will define exclusive or preferential access to wildlife on lands or waters within the settlement region which remain in crown hands. Secondly, the agreements have defined rights of participation in public management regimes.

Harvesting Rights

In so many respects, their hunting, trapping and fishing activities shaped native peoples' approach to claims. In the years before 1973, when the native groups were still struggling to win formal recognition of their position, the legal strategy aimed to demonstrate that certain rights arising from traditional occupancy had never been extinguished. Once Ottawa recognized the existence of outstanding comprehensive claims, one condition for entering negotiation was that the claimants document their land use and occupancy. Thus it was hardly surprising that wildlife harvesting activities figured fundamentally in all of the northern claims.

A more difficult question concerns how best to *define* these rights. Harvesting rights specify the terms on which wildlife will be brought into personal possession. Although the *Indian Act* guaranteed the right to harvest for food on unoccupied crown land, claimant groups looked toward the settlements to strengthen and clarify their rights of access. This could be done on the basis of species, land class, or type of user. The rights of harvest could be exclusive, thereby preventing non-claimants from taking part in a harvest. Such designations could apply throughout the settlement region, to species essential for subsistence or commercial use. Alternatively, the rights could be defined in terms of preference, thus guaranteeing claimants the first right of access. For example, where quotas are required for conservation purposes, the subsistence requirements of claimants tend to be granted first priority, while commercial requirements (again with a native preference) come next, and the needs of recreational users third. Such hierarchies are particularly important in cases of species endangerment or population decline. Here the law authorizes limits on the general aboriginal right to hunt for personal use. Insofar as the preferential and exclusive rules must be respected in any application of conservation measures, they confer a most significant benefit on aboriginal harvesters. A great deal hinges on the exact definition of terms. For example, "subsistence" harvesting is generally defined to include exchange, barter and sale among claimants, while "commercial" harvesting refers to market transactions involving non-claimants.

Insofar as the state retained a resource management responsibility, no harvesting rights could be absolute. For example the courts had long held that the rights of Indians to harvest for food on unoccupied crown lands could be subject to limits on conservation grounds. Even for lands which passed into native ownership by settlement, public laws of general application would continue to apply, thereby preserving for the state a role in wildlife conservation. Moreover, the scope of fee simple ownership could never equal the vast expanses over which traditional title was held. Consequently a second set of rights issues addresses the question of who controls the regulatory levers based in the general law. In part owing to the political controversies reviewed earlier, aboriginal peoples found the existing public management regime unacceptable. In its place, they have advanced proposals to guarantee participation in revised public management regimes.

Public Management Regimes

The concept of entrenched participation rights in claim-based management bodies offered an avenue of control over wildlife policy. The genealogy of this idea is most revealing. It was mentioned first in the CYI proposal of January 1973.[37] However it was not until the Inuit Tapirisat submitted its 1976 Nunavut proposal, that any concrete features were spelled out. This proposal sought to extend the joint management concept by delegating discrete powers of decision under law.[38] To the Nunavut Game Council (NGC) fell three main roles. The most important concerned the "sub-allocation" of harvest quotas, where endangered status required the regulation of species or populations. This entailed parcelling out the total permissable harvests among three classes of user — subsistence, commercial, and recreational — with priority granted to subsistence claimants. Once these "sub-allocations" were made, the NGC would delegate *local* allocation to community HTAs. On all other wildlife issues, the NGC was guaranteed an advisory role.

Similar provisions were found in the Inuvialuit proposal of 1977, covering the western Arctic region. Both the federal and territorial wildlife agencies harboured serious reservations about vesting claims institutions with general policy authority. Nevertheless, the FWS acted as a broker between federal and aboriginal positions.[39] Not only did this revive the stalled talks late in 1977, but it also produced a compromise which carried through to the Inuvialuit Final Agreement (IFA) in 1984.[40] Of particular interest is the policy machinery for decision making. The Inuvialuit sought a single agency to address a panoply of geographical and species issues. They claimed wildlife rights in the Yukon (on its North Slope) as well as in the Mackenzie Delta and Beaufort regions of the NWT. In addition, they sought to merge land and marine wildlife management, which as we have already seen, would require the harmonization of quite distinct administrative philosophies and traditions. In the result, the IFA authorized three joint bodies with parity representation: two Wildlife Management Advisory Councils (WMAC) for terrestrial species in the Yukon and NWT sections of the western Arctic region, and a Joint Fisheries Management Committee (JFMC) for fish and sea mammals.[41] In this, they paralleled the jurisdictional boundaries and the agency domains of the wildlife field.[42] To select and direct the native delegates, the Inuvialuit Game Council emerged as a claimant assembly.

The next signal advance in the design of wildlife bodies occurred at the eastern Arctic claim table, where the Tungavik Federation of Nunavut (TFN) represented the Inuit after 1981. In the fall of that year, the negotiators initialled a Sub-Agreement on Wildlife, which redefined key parameters of the wildlife package. The TFN sought to advance the autonomous power of its proposed Nunavut Wildlife Management Board, by stipulating strict rules of initiative and response in decision making. Consequently, the NWMB would become the first line of decision-making for most of the matters presently exercised by ministers under law. For terrestrial wildlife, this included protective sanctuaries, management zones, species and habitat protection, and education. It also extended to federal regulations for migratory birds, fish and sea mammals. By contrast to the past models, which allowed the Minister discretion in responding to "advice" of the joint bodies, the onus now was reversed. In order to reject or vary a decision of the Board, the Minister was now obliged to take specific action setting it aside. Otherwise, administrative implementation of Board decisions would be expected.

The initialling of this sub-agreement immediately triggered a complex bureaucratic conflict within the federal negotiating team. Officially, Ottawa questioned the finality of the draft agreement. Ottawa's co-ordinating agency, the Office of Native Claims, argued that the federal chief negotiator, "agreed to include certain provisions that had not been fully approved by the Departments of the Government concerned."[43] The problem was attributed to the excessively detailed terms of the text, and Ottawa further pointed out that the necessity of further review was explicitly acknowledged in the document. The Inuit denied that these terms exceeded Ottawa's negotiating mandate, and charged the departments of Fisheries and Oceans and Environment with attempting to overturn the federal position after the fact.[44] The TFN resisted Ottawa's efforts to re-open negotiations on this agreement, with the result that it remained in limbo until 1986.

In this fashion, the concept of the advisory board with consultative input was being stretched into a quasi-autonomous decision-making forum. It illustrates a salient quality of claims negotiations as a political process. For native groups, the process of defining concrete and lasting benefits in wildlife was cumulative. Each new claim proposal added to the domain of negotiable items. With several claims "tables" in operation for most of the last 15 years, a dialectical sequence ensued, whereby each new concept or newly initialled sub-agreement rebounded on all other tables.

While the Western Arctic Settlement had passed into the implementation phase by the summer of 1984, negotiations at the Dene and Métis claims table were just beginning to accelerate. An interim agreement on Land and Resources was initialled in July of 1985, but a separate wildlife agreement remained on the table, again blocked on the "disallowance" issue. The resemblance between the Dene-Métis approach and that of the Committee for Original Peoples Entitlement (COPE) for the western Arctic and of the TFN can be seen from the terms of a 1984 discussion paper. It proposed an integrated management system in which governments and harvesters would co-operate in joint decision-making forums. Conceding that governments would retain the ultimate responsibility for management, a Central Wildlife Management Board would be "the primary wildlife management authority in the claims area." To it fell the tasks of setting total allowable harvests and sub-allocations, stipulating the seasons and permissible methods of harvesting, and otherwise advising government agencies on any wildlife matters. The Dene and Métis clearly stressed the executive rather than the advisory nature of the Board: "Through the delegation of regulatory and administrative authority, Dene/ Métis and government appointees should jointly participate in the development and implementation of regulations, policies, and programs related to all aspects of wildlife management."[45]

In working toward an interim agreement over the next two years, the precise statement of powers proved difficult. Consistent with its position at the TFN table, the DFO resisted any substantive delegation of authority to the Board, countering with a purely advisory structure. Ultimately a compromise was struck, whereby the relevant ministers retained the freedom to accept, vary or reject Board decisions. In the TFN sub-agreement, this was subject to a procedural requirement that ministerial rejections be referred back to the Board for reconsideration, after which the Minister could vary or reject the decision. In the case of species sub-allocation, ministerial disallowance could only be invoked on designated grounds. Ministerial discretion thus remained unqualified.[46]

The Department of Renewable Resources harboured its own reservations on the delegation question. It favoured a narrower focus on policy principles, to the exclusion of management plans and statutory orders. Recalling its reservations on the IFA, the Department feared lest the constitutional protection of such delegated powers would have the effect of "taking back" legislative powers given to the GNWT under the *Northwest Territories Act.* The general theme here was the protection of ministerial government against the blurred accountability of the joint bodies. Not limited to the Dene-Métis claim, this found increasing voice in Yellowknife as the implications of the total settlement process became more clear.

While the government agencies staged a defence of public legislative power, the Dene-Métis wildlife deal illustrated another complication in conferring public policy mandates on claims bodies. During the winter of 1985-86, press coverage of the ongoing negotiations led to a protest by non-claimant hunters. Organized as the NWT Wildlife Federation, they denounced their loss of harvesting rights under the preferential status and sub-allocation provision in the agreement. Since the GNWT defined its role at the table in part by the need to represent non-claimant citizens, it took the issue in hand, holding clarification meetings with the critics.

In the evolution of these wildlife agreements, we see once again a set of native interests articulated against the existing management framework. After several early experiments, something of a model emerged, combining special harvesting rights for beneficiaries and guaranteed participation in public wildlife management authorities. While the precise terms may vary (and much depends on these terms), the general outline has now been accepted as part of all four comprehensive claims north of 60°.[47] On this basis, several comments can be made about their prospective impacts on the management system. Clearly the boards will enjoy much greater leverage than any other joint bodies to date. One advance, which might only have been possible at the claims table, is to bring non-territorial agencies and programs under the boards' umbrellas. This will dramatically expand the scope of these authorities.

The prospective impact on at least two interests is less clear. Non-beneficiaries' rights to wildlife are clearly affected by the settlements, both in their relative priority in the licensing hierarchy, and in their place in the public boards. Neither issue is entirely new, since the resident hunting license has always been subject to conservation imperatives, and the non-native hunter-fisherman interest has been recognized on past advisory bodies. Similarly, questions may be asked about the future role of the NWT legislature. As in the past, it will play an important role in providing direction to the Minister and the Executive in setting the general policy framework. But it will presumably share this role with the wildlife boards.

This highlights an unresolved tension deriving from the exact role of the boards. From a reading of the formal agreements to date, one could view them either as executive bodies whose decisions feed in to the existing management bureaucracy, or as the core of a new system, which entails its own administrative support in fields such as research and education. This obviously critical distinction has yet to be resolved. The experience of the Inuvialuit wildlife committees indicates the contrasting expectations which will inevitably emerge. This points in turn to another unresolved dilemma, associated with the implementation phase of the settlements. As the Coolican Report pointed out, the costs of implementation have in the past been grossly underestimated and under-budgeted.[48] Not only has this slowed the pace of implementation, and generated predictable frustrations and resentments. The lack of resources has been so extreme as to raise the spectre that certain agreed terms of settlement are being effectively nullified or even taken back by the indefinite postponement of funding.

In the wildlife field this is particularly disturbing, not only because of the centrality of these issues to the claims, but also given the prospective advances which settlements might bring to management programs. High among these is the greater degree of program integration which may result. By cutting across jurisdictional boundaries in fashioning the wildlife settlements, the claims tables have produced the first bodies that can contemplate the entire wildlife field. This opens possibilities for a more holistic approach, in which a full range of species and harvester interests could be addressed in a single co-ordinating forum. At the same time, it is important to observe that a contrasting tendency of territorial segmentation emerges by the fact that three distinct wildlife settlements will co-exist within the NWT. This could pose challenges to the management of widely distributed species or migratory populations. Thus certain questions of co-ordination remain to be addressed.

The Freshwater Fisheries Delegation

To this point in the study, we have identified several paths for the devolution of wildlife authority to the North. Indeed it is the tension among alternative routes, each supported by its own political constituency, which has made new jurisdictional transfers so controversial. This is nicely illustrated in the case of the inland or freshwater fishery transfers which have been pursued over the past five years. Of all the wildlife policy sectors, it represents the closest parallel to the other devolution cases covered by this book. While the political dynamic of the fisheries devolution will be explored in its own terms, it must also be assessed against the broader canvas of wildlife policy. This yields some surprising conclusions. Since only the *inland* share of the fisheries sector was eligible for transfer, the success of this initiative will have the direct effect of further *fragmenting* the management regime for fisheries, and by extension for wildlife as a whole. One further point deserves to be made on the fisheries transfer. Although it would be wrong to underplay the potential significance of this transfer, it will be evident just how modest an advance it constitutes, relative to the major powers and instruments at stake in the wider political contest over wildlife management.

This focus on freshwater fisheries devolution derives from the past century of constitutional accommodation. As was pointed out earlier, the 1867 grant of fisheries jurisdiction to the central authority gave way, under the force of judicial review, to a limited provincial proprietary power based on river and lake bed ownership of inland waters. This led in turn to Ottawa delegating its regulatory and administrative role for freshwater fisheries to the provinces, beginning with Ontario in 1897. Further to formalizing such arrangements, intergovernmental agreements authorize the financing of research and management projects within each province.[49] Accordingly, such arrangements define the horizons of territorial ambition in the area of fisheries. They set out the limits of what federal politicians are willing to concede if not what territorial politicians want to acquire.

Despite these parallels, it is important to note that the territorial case for control of inland fisheries cannot rest on a proprietary claim similar to the provinces, since Ottawa's crown claim to land north of 60° is unqualified. However once a provincial-style delegation became possible, the prevailing arrangements south of 60° formed the operative precedent.[50] Further distinguishing the case of fisheries, the difference between a delegation of management responsibility and a statutory devolution of powers should be borne in mind. The Department of Fisheries and Oceans (DFO) will not completely vacate the inland field after transfer, but will continue to be involved as it is in the provinces. Northern interests may not always share this subtle distinction, particularly as the fishery is being presented and perceived as one element in a broader set of transfers.

The Federal Fisheries Mandate in the North

In contrast to the considerable prominence given to game policy, the fisheries field has been at best a secondary concern to the state in the North. Despite the potent authority of the *Fisheries Act*, Ottawa's record has been largely one of neglect. While conservation regulations were periodically issued for fish or marine mammals, their significance lay more on paper than on the ground, given the absence of field personnel.[51] The native domestic fishery was never seen as a candidate for management, due in part to its open rights of access, and in part since its annual volume did not threaten sustainable yield. Following the Second World War, the DFO's attention turned to the inland commercial fishery, particularly for Great Slave Lake in the Mackenzie region. The Fisheries Research Board sponsored scientific surveys of most major inland lakes, while the DFO established a regulatory framework to allocate permissible catches.[52]

While these efforts betray certain political and managerial priorities, they must also be set within the context of the low priority attached to Arctic and other northern fisheries. One relevant measure is organizational. An area office in Hay River monitored the lake fishery, while policy was handled by the Department's Inland Directorate headquartered in Winnipeg. Likewise in Yukon the Whitehorse area office fell under the Pacific Directorate located in Vancouver. Given the wider responsibilities of each division (the prairie freshwater for Winnipeg, the Pacific coast for Vancouver), the northern Territories were marginal both in terms of geography and productivity. Given that the Department was so thin on the ground in the North, it relied on game management and Royal Canadian Mounted Police officers as ex-officio field staff.

In this sense the Department could be described accurately as a "two-ocean" program. Indeed, a 1966 Fisheries Strategy paper aptly captured these operational priorities. After according 15 pages to plans for the Atlantic region ("the most dynamic sector"), and 11 pages to the Pacific coast, the inland and Arctic sector merited a bare one page. This was confined to the creation of the Freshwater Fish Marketing Corporation, and it altogether begged off a discussion of the Arctic sector.[53]

It was against this backdrop that the territorial governments launched their devolution demands in the late 1960s. In 1969, the NWT Council passed a resolution calling for the transfer of the fisheries program to Yellowknife. The Council tended to view the fishery as a potential instrument of economic growth, whose maximum exploitation required territorial government control. After all, the GNWT was already involved in the provision of economic infrastructure, including marketing. Particularly in the era when the GNWT was on the rise, it resented the absentee control of a major resource by the Fisheries Department. Winnipeg (the regional headquarters) and Ottawa were not only physically distant, but also lay beyond the Council's capacity to scrutinize.

The absentee theme was reinforced further in 1969, when the Freshwater Fish Marketing Corporation became operational. With jurisdiction over freshwater fish from the prairie provinces and the NWT, the Corporation was designed as a marketing agency which could bring advantages of scale to many small and rather isolated fisheries. Almost from the outset its operating procedures drew criticism from the commercial fishermen of Great Slave Lake.[54] The Council consistently provided a sympathetic hearing to the Great Slave Lake fishermen, particularly in their critique of the Corporation's pricing policy. Indeed, the NWT Federation of Fishermen was treated by Council in much the same manner as the HTAs in their respective domain, as the expert voice of the harvester. Councillors whose constituencies bordered on the lake regularly brought the fishermen's concerns before the Council, which frequently passed motions censuring the federal agencies.[55]

Quite apart from the Council's agenda, the management regime was coming under scrutiny from other directions. Aboriginal groups were proposing a set of harvesting and management rights for fish. The lodge-owner portion of the tourist sector was equally concerned with the impact of management policy on its clientele. In 1972 a federal-territorial committee undertook a review of the complete fisheries management framework. Although its recommendations were never enacted, the review continues to offer a set of sound proposals on which to base policy. Challenging the premise that northern waters offered unlimited commercial opportunities, the task force advocated extremely conservative quota-setting, since "sustainable yield from these stocks is small in spite of what appears to be an abundance of fish."[56] Furthermore, it advised that the aboriginal fishery be designated the primary sector, while suggesting caution in opening up any new commercial ventures. It documented extensive potential for new sports fisheries which could be tied to tourist programs. Above all lay the need for accurate information as the basis of a management system.

Given this multiplicity of competing political claims, it would be tendentious to suggest that a territorial fishery service would ever have implemented the full agenda. Yet the evidence from game management suggests at the very least that both legislature and bureaucracy would have been forced into more responsive and innovative designs. As it was, the federal minister offered only to transfer sports fish licensing, an offer accepted by the YTG in 1972 and by the GNWT in 1976.[57] The order-in-council clearly spelled out that the commercial fishery, the ocean fishery and the research responsibility remained in federal hands, while:

> the Commissioner of the NWT will be responsible for printing, distribution, sales, revenue and accounting relating to administration of the licensing system for the sport fishery in the Territory, and any revenue therefrom shall accrue to the NWT consolidated revenue fund, and the Commissioner of the NWT recommends to the Department of Environment, Fisheries and Marine Service, any changes or amendments in the sport fishery regulations that the Commissioner deems necessary.[58]

While sports licensing was more significant in the Yukon than in the NWT, it was a minor consideration in the federal frame of reference. With the advent of the northern gas pipeline, the Department's mandate was rapidly evolving beyond species management toward the challenge of habitat protection.[59]

It would be more than a decade before the question of inland fisheries devolution was seriously addressed again. During this time conflict over basic harvesting and management issues continued to grow. Either implicitly or by design, the state has always sought to regulate those who fish, with a concern for limiting the total harvest as well as the means by which it is taken. This has meant distinguishing the harvesting constituency according to type of use, acknowledging the fact that the behaviour, not to mention the needs, of fishermen varied widely. This also pointed to one of the most intractable problems of fisheries management, namely determining the respective shares of the harvest to be allocated to the different sectors. The subsistence sector includes both native fishermen and non-native "domestic" users, who utilize fish for their household needs (food and dog rations). The commercial fishery involves harvest for sale on the market, while the sports fishery was a recreational pursuit for anglers (those who fish with a hook, line and bait). Since the late nineteenth century, regulations issued under the *Fisheries Act* have required the licensing of all northern fishermen under one of these categories. Within them the volumes and instruments of harvest can also be controlled.

Increasingly the DFO found itself politically on the defensive in the North. A series of incidents offers evidence to this effect. We have already seen how the Department blocked the endorsement of the TFN Wildlife Sub-Agreement, with its controversial clauses on disallowance. The DFO represented the hard-line opposition to anything more than advisory roles for joint management boards. Ottawa's reluctance to accept managerial changes within its own renewable resource jurisdiction contrasted sharply with the rather liberal concessions it was willing to contemplate in the territorial wildlife field. A telling critique of the DFO's northern policy emerged from a workshop convened by the Canadian Arctic Resources Committee. The Department was urged to abandon a bureaucratic culture of distance and detachment, and recognize instead the creative roles which partnership with northern interests could bring to management and research. Notable among the many recommendations was the suggestion that "the DFO must pursue the devolution of federal responsibilities through both territorial governments and land claims negotiations. Of particular concern to the workshop participants is the management of inland waters and fisheries."[60]

The "hard-line" period for northern fisheries administration began to pass by 1986. The DFO released a proposal on marine conservation late in 1987, which endorsed the principle of "shared responsibility for decision making" involving all user groups as well as integrated resource planning and knowledge.[61] Even earlier the Department had taken the initiative in establishing the Great Bear Lake Fisheries Management Committee (GBLFMC). This brought together representatives of the full range of users (the Fort Franklin Dene Band, the sports lodges) and government agencies (DFO, GNWT-DRR, GNWT-Economic Development).[62] While this Committee is quite distinct from a user-based management system under a decision-making board, the fact that it exists at all attests to the change in DFO perspective. Yet the fact that it lagged a decade behind territorial government thinking on such matters not only served to retard the land claims process, but also to lend support to the advocates of jurisdictional devolution.

Negotiating the Freshwater Fishery Delegation

When the freshwater delegation surfaced again, in the context of Ottawa's 1985 devolution strategy, the YTG was the first to commence negotiations.[63] Although the federal offer was open to both Territories, this section will focus on the Yukon transfer. The process began in 1986, with an exchange of letters between federal and territorial ministers, setting out a framework for negotiation and specifying the issues eligible for discussion. Ottawa stipulated, for example, that the range of negotiable issues could not exceed those already transferred to the provinces. It also followed that the instrument of agreement would closely resemble the federal-provincial umbrella fisheries agreement, with separate sub-agreements covering discrete project work. The framework also excluded any discussion of anadromous fish or marine mammals. With the framework in place, each side proceeded to examine and document the existing level of federal freshwater programming. This included the study of personnel and budget levels, capital expenditures and accumulated real assets.

Given a relative consensus on the substance of jurisdiction, it was clear that the financial terms of transfer would prove to be the most contentious issue. An added complication flowed from the fact that only part of the northern fisheries program was at stake. Considerable administrative energy was devoted, on both sides of the table, to sheltering, uncovering and discovering potentially relevant expenditures and assets. Indeed it often proved difficult to separate that portion of a field job or office position which was devoted to freshwater subjects from that involving anadromous fish, marine mammals, or administrative tasks in general. In the case of the Yukon, Ottawa contended that 99 percent of its previous work had been directed to the salmon (anadromous) fishery. In the end, the initial DFO financial package consisted of three fifths of one person-year, plus $25,000 for operations and maintenance.

For its part the Yukon Territorial Government sought to establish the resources necessary to mount an adequate fresh-water program. This served two purposes. In the first place it could highlight the deficient level of past federal effort, and introduce the issue of catch-up provisions. Secondly it provided a standard of comparison, enabling the Yukon Cabinet to judge the acceptability of any settlement, while acknowledging the residual costs to the YTG of assuming the freshwater responsi-bilities. The extent of the "gap" was apparent from the estimate that an establishment of eight civil servants, an annual Opera-tions & Maintenance budget of $650,000, as well as $1 million for "catch-up" inventory research, would be required.[64] The Yukon position was that Ottawa was delegating not only the *manage-ment responsibility* for the freshwater sector, but also the *fiscal resources* for its reasonable prosecution. Consequently, any past neglect by Ottawa in meeting its statutory responsibilities could not be ignored in establishing a floor for the future. Given the distance between opening positions, it is not surprising that movement was slow. Indeed, much of 1987 and early 1988 was taken up by a "Mexican hat dance of the drafts," as proposals bounced between Ottawa and Whitehorse.

The negotiating framework specified that the value of existing commitments at the time of transfer should determine the floor for Ottawa's budget obligation. This led the YTG to search for ways to remedy the obvious deficiency in the fiscal capacity conveyed with the transfer. In the end, a compromise emerged by negotiating a separate one-shot allotment, which could be applied against the start-up costs of the new program, without committing Ottawa to additional permanent base fund-ing. The Yukon proposed an envelope of $900,000 over five years, while Ottawa opened with a $300,000 figure. Ultimately an agreement was secured at $750,000, accelerated over three years, with Ottawa dropping any conditions on the use of this "Conservation Fund." The final terms were settled at the minis-terial level in June 1988. The Yukon Minister of Renewable Resources, David Porter, met the federal Fisheries Minister,

Thomas Siddon in Vancouver on the occasion of a Canadian Wildlife Federation convention. Their letter of intent, which served as the basis for finalizing the agreement, called for $85,000 in base (continuing) funding, the $750,000 enhancement allotment, and a commitment by the YTG to triple its fish licensing fees within three years.

After the financial roadblock was passed, a series of secondary issues was then resolved. Much of this pertained to the range of policy matters to be referenced in the agreement. From the outset it was understood that a "non-prejudicial" clause relating to aboriginal claims negotiations was essential. Other matters were less consensual: the nature and number of issues to be worked out after the main agreement had been signed; the formal acknowledgement of the YTG role in the North Pacific Salmon negotiations; the reference to fisheries research and to fisheries inspection; and the establishment of an oversight committee for the agreement and an annual reporting procedure on its progress.

In the final agreement which received Cabinet approval at both levels, the transfer date was set for April 1, 1989. Given a lag in staffing the new Fisheries Section in the Yukon Department of Renewable Resources, the formal transfer of administrative operations from the DFO District Office in Whitehorse was delayed. Similarly, the first instalment of the three-year enhancement fund was postponed until April 1990. Once the administrative transition is complete, discussions can be expected to begin on two sub-agreements dealing with aquaculture and habitat protection.

Given the ramifications of this issue for the land claims process, the question of native involvement was important from the outset. The Council for Yukon Indians (CYI) was invited to participate in the discussions along with the two governments. CYI officials did attend the initial meetings. However, following the lengthy hiatus associated with the financial deadlock, native participation was not resumed. Nonetheless, a considerable level of informal consultation appears to have taken place throughout the negotiating period. In addition, the Yukon

Minister, Mr. Porter, is an aboriginal person, and was well positioned to deal directly with the CYI leadership. It is significant to note that the period when the talks resumed in 1988 coincided with a renewed peak of land claims activity. In this context, there is no question that the claims table commanded overriding priority. On its own, the non-prejudice clause could not completely assuage the CYI's political concerns about the freshwater delegation. Yet in the end, the CYI did not adopt a formal position either supporting or opposing the final transfer agreement.

A brief consideration of the parallel events unfolding at the land claims table helps to put the fisheries transfer into context. Although the Yukon Indians presented their first claims proposal in 1973, the current round of talks began in the mid-1980s.[65] By 1988 the discussions had reached particularly critical and complex stage. The three parties (Ottawa, Whitehorse and the CYI) had organized their talks by discrete subject areas, to be negotiated one by one and then consolidated to form the basis of the final agreement. Leading items on the negotiating agenda included land ownership, use and administration; renewable resource harvesting and management; financial compensation; taxation; royalty sharing; and Indian self-government.

As in all of the northern claims, the provisions affecting Yukon fish and wildlife were regarded as fundamental to a successful settlement. In the cumulative *Framework Agreement* released in February 1989, the wildlife sub-agreement emerged as the most comprehensive and detailed of the 24 components.[66] On the one hand, it defines a set of aboriginal harvesting rights for hunting, trapping, fishing and gathering, which on implementation of the Agreement will enjoy constitutional status. At the same time, it establishes a joint (aboriginal-government) management regime under public authority. A brief description of its scope should illustrate the key departures in decision-making and power sharing relationships. At the centre of the proposed system is the *Fish and Wildlife Board*, with First Nations and Government sharing equal appointment powers. In addition to its comprehensive policy advisory mandate, the Board exercises certain decision-making powers as part of the management program, most notably in setting the "total allowable harvests" for various species. Operating parallel to the Board, but reporting to the Federal Minister of Fisheries, is the *Salmon Sub-Committee*, whose mandate covers anadromous fish. Each of these bodies addresses the Yukon as a whole. Within the traditional territory of each of the 14 First Nations, a *Renewable Resources Council* is established. The RRCs are similarly constituted to address local wildlife and fishery issues. While they advise the Board and Committee on policy matters in general, the Councils also determine the top priority "basic needs levels" for aboriginal harvesters, and (where conservation requires) allocate harvest quotas to local users.

To put this system in perspective, it is important to note that on all "advisory" matters, the ministers ultimately retain the power to accept, vary, set aside, or replace recommendations from the Board, Committee and Councils. On a more limited range of issues involving harvest levels, basic needs and sub-allocations, the joint bodies would appear to possess full decision-making authority within the legislative framework.

By creating these new structures, and guaranteeing aboriginal participation at all levels, it is clear that the successful conclusion of the Yukon claim will transform the terms of fishery and wildlife management. In effect, this highlights an alternative vision of devolution, not as intergovernmental jurisdictional transfer, but as power sharing between the state and organized groups and communities, opening new channels of resident and local control. Even while a final agreement remained to be formulated, pressure mounted among the CYI leadership and among Band Chiefs for the "pre-implementation" of the Wildlife Sub-Agreement provisions, particularly those involving the Renewable Resources Councils. This point was posed sharply during the summer of 1989, during a controversy over policing the native food fishery. After an Indian elder was charged with a net violation, the Band Chief, Robert Hagar, convened a "fish-in" protest at his river camp near Mayo. By taking salmon without reporting the catch, the organizers sought to withdraw their support for the management process until First Nation involvement was firmly institutionalized.[67] Against the wider political canvas of land claims settlement, the fishery delegation assumes rather modest dimensions for Yukon natives. This contrasts with the far greater stature it holds for Yukon government officials and other exponents of provincial status.

Turning to an assessment of the fishery transfer agreement, it is important to consider not only the financial terms, but also the symbolic and substantive stakes of both governments. On the financial side it is clear that concessions were significant on both sides. While Ottawa refused to expand the base funding for the freshwater program, its enhancement funding went a considerable distance toward closing the research component of the gap as defined by Paish. For its part, the YTG was obliged to scale down its staffing projections from eight persons to five, and rely on contract services for the balance. In addition, its trebling of licensing fees stood to generate several hundred thousand dollars which could augment the base budget for fisheries.

It is evident that the building of a freshwater program will carry a considerable added monetary cost to the YTG. It may yet bring sound value if it meets additional policy goals. From the perspective of the Yukon's broad constitutional strategy, the delegation of freshwater management puts the Territory on a similar footing to a province. There are also advantages to the Yukon in controlling a positive management program. It constitutes one further step toward the desired integrated renewable resource portfolio. It allows the fisheries program to be co-ordinated with tourism and economic development priorities, and with habitat protection requirements. Given the importance of the freshwater component to the overall Yukon fishery, resident political control opens the way to a more sensitive management regime and a more publicly accountable policy framework. Perhaps it is in this broader context that one territorial wildlife official judged that three quarters of the original Yukon objectives for this transfer had been realized. Another perspective emerges from the Devolution Office which serves to co-ordinate the wider YTG strategy of jurisdictional transfer. The fisheries case is regarded as one of the pioneering issues, with much to teach the subsequent process. From the standpoint of co-ordination, the sequence of events was far from ideal, since the fisheries negotiations were virtually complete before Whitehorse formalized its devolution strategy (in a Memorandum of Understanding on Devolution in September 1988.) As a model case it also falls short on the grounds of the net financial cost which falls to the Yukon government.

At the present stage of its resolution, the case of the inland fisheries delegation is as instructive for the light it sheds on the wider questions of wildlife management, as on the particular fisheries outcomes in their own terms. How positive and creative a development is the fisheries transfer likely to be? The discussion thus far points to several conclusions. To begin, the differential significance of this transfer in the two Territories is amply evident. Except for the salmon resource, the Yukon will acquire virtually the entire fisheries field as a result of the transfer. It will extend its administrative control beyond sport fishing and will acquire a major research mandate. Moreover, by obtaining a prospective role in habitat protection, it will be able to address all aspects of the freshwater jurisdiction. This includes a capacity to implement new management schemes with the opportunity to co-ordinate all three fisheries sectors. In the NWT, the control of inland fisheries represents a smaller share of the total fisheries field, since it leaves marine mammals and fish in federal hands. In one sense, the immediate result of the transfer will leave the fisheries jurisdiction *more* fragmented than before. The fisheries policy field will be skewed in another respect, since the expanded capacities of the GNWT will be of much greater consequence to harvesters in the Mackenzie region than in the Arctic region. For the Dene/Métis, the resident sport fishermen and the commercial fishermen, the freshwater jurisdiction will be politically closer to home, hence, presumably, more responsive when it shifts to Yellowknife. However, despite its future freshwater prospects, the Inuit fishery will remain sea-based and therefore federally controlled.

Despite their partial character, each of these delegations offers an advance over past management by the DFO. Given the low priority attached to the administration of northern fisheries, and the program's weak claim on departmental resources, *any* enhanced territorial focus for management and legislation can be positive. Moreover, if the GNWT record in terrestrial game management is taken as a standard of what is politically possible, the prognosis for a devolved freshwater fishery program is again favourable.

On the other hand, the delegation of freshwater jurisdiction *per se* clearly runs contrary to the cause of integrated wildlife management regimes. The latter theme, so evident in the thinking of both aboriginal claims settlements and conservation strategies, is not furthered by fragmenting a hitherto unified jurisdiction. Interestingly, these delegations could prove to be neutral to the question of joint management arrangements, since all jurisdictions appear now to accept some version of this practice. In any event, it seems clear that the overriding foundation for joint management will come from completing the claims settlement process north of 60°. In this sense, the fisheries transfer might be viewed as a way station to more extensive integration of wildlife policy. Only with the collapse of comprehensive claims settlements would the fisheries delegation take on more than modest significance.

Conclusions

There is no question that the two dimensions of devolution which are considered in this paper are analytically and politically distinct. To invoke the cause of jurisdictional transfer is to advance an agenda quite different from the community control version of devolution. In this study we have seen how the two strategies originated with separate constituencies. The most persistent champions of "provincial" type development have been closely associated with territorial governments, either within the civil service or among the resident politicians in the legislature. The early advocates of local control and self-management came from the native movements, harvester organizations and elected native politicians. In contrast to the situation of the 1970s, however, a fragile consensus may have emerged over the past few years. This has developed to the point that a creative search for new institutional forms now drives the policy process. There can be little doubt that whatever management regimes are produced, with or without further jurisdictional devolution, a strong element of harvester participation will be included.

The territorial wildlife management agencies have, since the mid-1970s, occupied something of a middle ground. Far from opposing the participation of the harvesting public, the Wildlife Service facilitated this trend. It supported local involvement in the management regime under law, and seized the initiative in decentralizing the delivery of assistance programs to the community level. The FWS also explicitly affirmed the primary place of native harvesters among those with a claim on wildlife resources.

At the same time, the FWS moved cautiously, and with more than a little ambivalence, on the wildlife provisions of land claims. Faced with the prospect that the settlements could define entirely new regimes for management, the FWS was not categorically resistant but neither would it abandon or minimize the advances already achieved. Part of this betrayed a reluctance to contemplate a system which seemed to be founded on legal harvesting rights as distinct from conservation programs. There were also fundamental differences of perspective between the scientifically oriented managers, the harvesters, and the native leadership. This reflected complex questions of the design, application, and even possibility of management. It is evident in the debate over research models and knowledge bases, alternative models for enforcing regulations, and recognition of the several relevant publics in the wildlife field.

In this light, perhaps it is possible to appreciate both the potential and the limitations of devolution defined in the jurisdictional sense. One tendency has been to dismiss the relevance of transfers for a field such as wildlife, since the more powerful instrument of claims settlements can establish a new regime with constitutional status. Despite the understandable optimism that the wildlife provisions will transform the field, we have seen that the essence of the emerging wildlife regimes is their joint basis. What future transfers might determine is whether a public authority based in Yellowknife, Whitehorse or Ottawa forms the governmental partner. Put this way, there are grounds to suspect that territorial jurisdiction offers distinct advantages relative to Ottawa. Our evidence suggests that this goes well beyond the fact of shorter or longer lines of communication. It also determines the type of political process bearing on wildlife issues. The degree of legislative oversight of game issues in the NWT far exceeds that available in Ottawa. This includes the major statutory overhauls as well as securing day-to-day administrative accountability. Contrast the legislature's record on the *Wildlife Ordinance,* its monitoring of wildlife service operations, and its impressive commitment of funds to key research programs, with the virtual absence of parliamentary attention to northern fishery and bird issues in both the House of Commons and its standing committees. Similarly, the considerable growth in GNWT financial commitments to wildlife research contrasts with the encumbrances on federal agencies saddled with national mandates.

A related but distinct question concerns the prospect of a more unified and integrated future wildlife regime. If this implies the gathering of wildlife programs under a single government authority, it would seem that the limits of territorial development may be reached with the completion of the inland fisheries delegation. On the other hand, integration may well be advanced in the future in ways other than jurisdictional transfer. The latter is not the only way to achieve greater management coordination. Here the broad trends of postwar Canadian federalism are especially instructive. Faced with relatively fixed jurisdictional boundaries, governments at both levels sought bridging devices of an administrative type. This gave rise to the federal-provincial financial arrangements, cost-shared programs, administrative delegations and other practices broadly described as "executive federalism." In the field of northern wildlife, the bridging mechanism may well be the management authorities mandated by the final claims settlements. These are the only bodies which bring together representatives of all major sectoral interests, with the power to reach authoritative decisions. By so doing these joint management bodies gain the unique opportunity to consolidate information, control overlapping issues, and even harmonize policy standards and practices at a working level. It is much too early to judge such possibilities. However, should this come about in the northern wildlife field, it would carry a decisive advantage over the federal-provincial parallels cited above. This stems from the participation of native (and by political necessity other wildlife user) interests in the deliberations. This pre-empts one serious limitation associated with contemporary federalism, namely that the procedural machinery serves to insulate decision making from wider political representation and accountability.

Thus one final irony may characterize devolution politics in wildlife. Despite the evident antagonism between the two competing tracks considered here, it may be in the end that each track may be needed to perfect the aspirations of the other.

NOTES

1   C. Gordon Hewitt, *The Conservation of Wildlife of Canada*, New York: Scribner's, 1921, p. 2.

2   G.V. LaForest, *Natural Resources and Public Property Under the Canadian Constitution*, Toronto: University of Toronto Press, 1969, pp. 176-182.

3   See Robert G. McCandless, *Yukon Wildlife: A Social History*, Edmonton: University of Alberta Press, 1985.

4   It should be noted that Ottawa has retained one very important lever over northern game. The *Northwest Territories Act* authorizes the Governor-in-Council to designate any species deemed in danger of extinction. In such cases, the GNWT can regulate any form of harvest in that species.

5   Section 2 of the *Fisheries Act* specifies "shellfish, crustaceans, marine animals, marine plants and the eggs, spawn, spat, and juvenile stages of fish, shellfish, crustaceans and marine mammals."

6   For a discussion of developments to 1914, see Richard W, Parisien, "The Fisheries Act: Origins of Federal Delegation of Administrative Jurisdiction to the Provinces," Department of the Environment, Ottawa, 1972.

7   For historical details on these regulations, see *Brief on Inuit Rights in Relation to Fish and Marine Mammals*, Submitted by the Inuit Tapirisat of Canada to the Government of Canada, September 1974.

8   For the federal regulatory framework, see the *Migratory Birds Convention Act*, Chapter M-7, *R.S.C. 1985*; and the *Migratory Bird Regulations, C.R.C. 1978*, Chap. 1035 with amendments. The text of the Convention is printed as a Schedule to the *Act.*

9   Dan Gottesman, "Native Hunting and the Migratory Birds Convention Act: Historical, Political and Ideological Perspectives," *Journal of Canadian Studies*, 18(3) (Autumn, 1983), p. 70.

10   For the history of the Convention and the Act, see Janet Foster, *Working for Wildlife*, Toronto: University of Toronto Press, 1978, chap. 6,7.

11   A permanent closed season was declared for insectivorous birds, while natives could take migratory non-game birds for their own use.

12   For details on the structure and mandate of the Department of Industry and Development, see *Annual Report of the Commissioner of the Northwest Territories*, beginning in 1968.

13   *News of the North*, September 18, 1974, p. 1.

14   The complete text of Assistant Commissioner Hancock's report appears in the *News of the North*, September 25, 1974, pp. 3-4.

15   The many reorganizations of the wildlife service between 1967 and the present pose problems for consistent identification. The service was known as the Game Management Service (GMS) until 1975, when it became the Fish and Wildlife Service (FWS). Following the establishment of the Department of Renewable Resources in 1979, the research and policy functions were vested in the Wildlife Management Division, while the field structure fell under the Field Services Division.

16   Northwest Territories Council, *Debates*, 51st Session, 7th Council, January 29, 1974, p. 508.

17   Northwest Territories Council, *Debates*, June 12, 1973, p. 35.

18   *Annual Report of the Commissioner of the Northwest Territories*, 1974, p. 50.

19   *Annual Report of the Commissioner of the Northwest Territories*, 1977, p. 67.

20   Frank S. Bailey, *Consultations on the Proposed Wildlife Ordinance*, 27 November 1976; and *Further Report*, February 23, 1977.

21   Northwest Territories Council, Debates, January 24, 1977, p. 55.

22   Fish and Wildlife Service, "A Review of the Proposed Wildlife Ordinance," Department of Natural and Cultural Affairs, April 1977, p. 6.

23   Northwest Territories Council, *Debates*, 66th Session, October 1978, p. 58.

24   Norm Simmons, Superintendent of Wildlife, in Northwest Territories Council *Debates*, 63rd Session, 8th Council, October 21, 1977, p. 241.

25   See the NWT Fish and Wildlife Service, "1977 Statement on Sub-Objectives" in *Goals, Objectives and Policies*, Government of the Northwest Territories, Yellowknife, 1977.

26   Government of the Northwest Territories, *Estimates*, 1986-1987.

27   A discussion of the challenges in building an effective field structure can be found in Hugh J. Monahan, "Renewable Resource Management in the NWT: A Proposal for Change," Practicum, Natural Resource Institute, University of Manitoba, 1980.

28   Fish and Wildlife Service, *Devolution Plan for Wildlife Service Programs*, Yellowknife, n.d., p. 4.

29   For a general discussion of joint management bodies in the North, see Gail Osharenko, *Sharing Power with Native Users: Co-Management Regimes for Native Wildlife*, Ottawa: Canadian Arctic Resources Committee, 1988.

30   Thomas R. Berger, *Northern Frontier, Northern Homeland*, Vol. 1, Ottawa: Supply and Services Canada, 1978, p. 107.

31   Parks Canada, *National Parks Program*, Ottawa, 1979, p. 40.

32   National Parks System Division, "Joint Management Regimes: A Proposed Management Guideline for Native Peoples' Participation in Planning and Management for Northern Parks," Parks Canada, September 1982, p. 5. For an account of subsequent developments in the NWT, see Ken East, "Joint Management of Canada's Northern National Parks," mimeo, 1988.

33   It could be argued that caribou have been the single most influential object of northern wildlife policy since the War. For an account of an earlier "caribou crisis," see Peter Clancy, "Native Hunters and the State: the Caribou Crisis in the NWT," SNID Occasional Paper 87-101, Program of Studies in National and International Development, Queen's University, 1987.

34   N.M. Simmons, D.C. Heard and G.W. Calef, "Kaminuriak Caribou Herd: Inter-Jurisdictional Management Problems," Progress Report No.2, Yellowknife, NWT Wildlife Service, n.d., p. 18.

35   The history of the joint-management concept in the NWT is a story in itself. It combines precedents from Alaska, the logic of the Berger report, and the policy brokerage by the FWS in the Joint Working Group on Wildlife at the COPE claims table in 1978. One proposal prepared for the GNWT was J.P. Kelsall, "Report on Co-operative Management Systems," for the FWS, Department of Renewable Resources, Victoria, 1981.

36   Its mandate was "to co-ordinate management of the Beverly and Kaminuriak herds in the interest of the traditional users and their descendants...to establish a process of shared responsibility

for the development of management programs...[and] to establish communications amongst the traditional users and the parties hereto, and amongst the parties hereto in order to ensure co-ordinated caribou conservation and caribou habitat protection." "Beverly-Kaminuriak Barren Ground Caribou Agreement," 3 June 1982, published in the *Caribou News*, 2(1), June 1982.

37   Council of Yukon Indians, *Together Today for Our Children Tomorrow*, Whitehorse, 1973. For a comprehensive analysis of the subsequent negotiations on this claim, see Jonathan L. Pierce, "Indian Land Claims in the Yukon: 1968-1984," M.A. Thesis, Carleton University, 1988.

38   The wildlife proposals appear in Section 5 of the *Nunavut Proposal*, Presented to the Government of Canada by the Inuit Tapirisat of Canada, February 1976.

39   B.A. Hubert, "Commentary on Events Leading to the Agreement-in-Principle between the Minister of DIAND and the Inuvialuit of the Western Arctic," Boreal Ecological Services, December, 1983.

40   COPE - Government Working Group, "Joint Position Paper on Wildlife," December 2,1977. The 1978 Agreement-in-Principle was released as "Inuvialuit Land Rights Settlement Agreement-in-Principle" in Government of Canada, *Communique*, Ottawa: Indian and Northern Affairs, October 31, 1978.

41   For the exact provisions, see section 14 of *The Western Arctic Claim: The Inuvialuit Final Agreement*, Ottawa: Indian and Northern Affairs, 1984.

42   For details on these operations, see Nancy C. Doubleday, "Co-Management Provisions of the Inuvialuit Final Agreement" in Evelyn Pinkerton (Ed.), *Co-operative Management of Local Fisheries*, Vancouver: University of British Columbia Press, 1989.

43   *Nunavut Newsletter*, "Guest Editorial by the ONC," June 15, 1982, p. 5.

44   "Guest Editorial: Geoff Lester," Ibid., 6.

45   "Wildlife Harvesting and Management: Dene-Métis Discussion Paper," Dene-Métis Negotiating Secretariat, April 17, 1984, p. 2.

46   Government of Canada and Tungavik Federation of Nunavut, *Sub-Agreement on Wildlife*, Ottawa: 1986.

47   While this section has not addressed the parallel developments in the Yukon, the wildlife provisions of the CYI claim can be found

in Sub-Agreement 13 of the *Yukon Indian Land Claim Framework Agreement*, Whitehorse, February 1989.

48 Task Force to Review Comprehensive Claims Policy, *Living Treaties: Lasting Agreements*, Ottawa: Indian and Northern Affairs, 1985, pp. 94-98.

49 See, for example, the *Canada-Ontario Fisheries Agreement*, 1987. Under these agreements, the actual project work is authorized by subsidiary agreements which spell out the specific undertakings.

50 For a comprehensive review of the freshwater sector across Canada, see Peter H. Pearse, *Rising to the Challenge. A New Policy For Canada's Freshwater Fisheries*, Ottawa: Canadian Wildlife Federation, 1988.

51 For a detailed survey of the application of the *Fisheries Act* to native peoples in the NWT, see Inuit Tapirisat of Canada, "Brief on Inuit Hunting Rights in Relation to Marine Mammals," Ottawa, September 1974.

52 For a description of the research program, see Fisheries Research Board, *Studies in Canada's Arctic*, Ottawa, 1970. The regulatory framework is described in "Expansion of the Fisheries in the NWT," Pamphlet, Department of Fisheries, 1961.

53 Department of Fisheries, *Trends in the Development of the Canadian Fisheries*, Background Document for Fisheries Development Planning, April 1977.

54 See Department of Economic Development, Government of the NWT, "Task Force on Great Slave Lake Fisheries," Yellowknife: June, 1975; and Great Slave Lake Fisheries Task Force, "Interim Report," May, 1984.

55 Of perennial concern was the tight monopoly position of the FFMC which prevented the sale of fish to private buyers in the North, and the Department's application of quota and net restrictions on Great Slave Lake.

56 *Where To Now?* A Federal-Territorial Task Force Report, Volumes 1 & 2. Yellowknife: Government of the NWT, 1972.

57 This was done by regulation under the *Fisheries Act*. See P. C. 1972-1756, August 24, 1972; and P. C. 1976-535, March 9, 1976.

58 P. C. 1976-535, March 9, 1976.

59   One description of this new mandate can be found in the Department of Fisheries and Oceans's "Brief to the Special Committee of the Senate on the Northern Pipeline," September 1982.

60   T. Fenge, P. Jacobs, R.F. Keith, and S.J. Woods, "Toward a Northern Policy for the Department of Fisheries and Oceans," (Report of a workshop sponsored by the DFO, November 17-19, 1985), Canadian Arctic Resources Committee, n.d., p. 26.

61   Department of Fisheries and Oceans, *Canadian Arctic Marine Conservation Strategy*, Discussion Paper, Ottawa: December 1987, pp. 14-15.

62   Corresponding to a relatively well-defined area of interest, the Committee functions in an advisory capacity. To date it has addressed the need for an information system on harvest levels and stock size. It has designated the subsistence sector as the first priority, with the sports fishery secondary.

63   Much of the discussion in this section has also been advanced in another setting. See Peter Clancy, "The Freshwater Fishery Delegation: The Politics of Jurisdictional Transfer," *The Northern Review*, 5, Summer, 1990.

64   Howard Paish and Associates Ltd., *Transfer of Responsibility for the Administration and Management of the Yukon Freshwater Fishery from the Government of Canada to the Government of Yukon: A* Discussion Paper on Program Requirements. Prepared for the Department of Renewable Resources. Vancouver: April 1985.

65   For the initial presentation see *Together Today for Our Children Tomorrow*, 1973. For a comprehensive analysis of the Yukon claims process, see Jonathan L. Pierce, "Indian Land Claims in the Yukon, 1967-1984," M.A. Thesis, Carleton University, 1988.

66   Yukon, Executive Council Office, Land Claims Secretariat. *Yukon Indian Land Claim Framework Agreement*, February 1989. Sub-Agreement 13: Fish and Wildlife Conservation and Use, pp. 67-92.

67   See *Whitehorse Star*, July 20-28, 1989.

4 The Devolution of Health Care to Canada's North

Geoffrey Weller

Introduction

The concept of devolution in the Canadian context involves processes of both constitutional and administrative development for the Yukon and the Northwest Territories. However, the term "devolution" often conjures up the wrong imagery. It is often thought of as implying a greater regional control or influence within a fully established state structure. In fact, the process taking place in Canada might be more appropriately thought of as one of "decolonization", for Canada's northern Territories have long been internal colonies.[1] In short, Canada is a country still in the process of completion, not in the process of decentralizing to a northern "region."

Devolution in the Canadian context has a constitutional aspect. This is the effort to increase the span of control possessed by the governments of the two Territories and to give them greater freedom from the control of the political centre, that is, Ottawa. It was often assumed that this process of constitutional development would eventually lead to the formation of two additional provinces. It was only a question of time before the population levels and the degree of economic development would lead to two additional units in Confederation much like the ones already part of it. However, the existence of large numbers of native peoples in the two northern Territories and their affinity for operating not as isolated individuals in the liberal–democratic context but as part of social collectivities led to the possibility that the additional political units might not be like the ones already a part of Confederation. Moreover, the relative cultural homogeneity of the Inuit north and east of the treeline in the Northwest Territories has meant that there is the possibility that it might be divided into two.[2]

Devolution in the Canadian context also has an administrative aspect. The process of devolution, or decolonization, involves the need for institution-building to ensure that there is something to replace the central authority when it withdraws. Administrative units have to be established with the necessary financial resources, facilities and personnel. These units have to have control over both the level and the type of services they deliver and the operations they conduct. The process of decolonization cannot take place — or certainly cannot take place smoothly — if adequate consideration is not given to such administrative concerns. In Canada's northern Territories the finances, personnel and physical facilities all belonged to an "outside" power, namely the federal government, and could have been unavailable to any new administrative unit within the Territories.

This paper analyses one of the largest and most critical elements of administrative devolution or decolonization, namely that of the health care delivery system. It was one of the largest elements simply in terms of the number of people involved, the amount of money dealt with, and the number and dispersal of the physical facilities used. Certainly if the two Territories were to eventually develop into provinces their health departments would account for nearly one third of all expenditures and be the single biggest administrative units within their provincial bureaucracies. The health care devolution was one of the most critical because health is a field of public policy which not only touches a vast proportion of any given population, but it is one about which most people have strongly held views. It was also one of the most critical because clearly the institutions in place had very nearly reached the limits of their effectiveness and yet were not bringing about the desired results in terms of morbidity and mortality statistics.[3] While there had been vast improvements in some areas, the pattern of illness and death in Canada's northern Territories resembled that of a Third World nation.[4]

This chapter begins by discussing the likely advantages and disadvantages of the devolution of health care. This is followed by an examination of the policy context in which the issue was discussed and, in the case of the Northwest Territories, effected. The actual process of devolving health care in the case of the Northwest Territories is then analysed in detail. This is followed by a discussion of the content of the health care devolution process in terms of finances, facilities, personnel, and structures. An examination is then made of whether or not the anticipated advantages or disadvantages can be detected in the policy outcomes of the devolution of health care. The chapter concludes with a discussion of the likely future for health and health care services in the territorial north.

Health Care Devolution:
Advantages and Disadvantages

The advantages and disadvantages of any devolution process relate to both political matters and to matters specific to the policy field in question, in this case health. The emphasis here is upon the second category of advantages and disadvantages, namely those related to the health policy field. The possible advantages will be discussed first followed by the possible disadvantages.

The major advantage of devolving health care services from the federal government to the territorial governments would be that the system should be closer to the people served and be more likely to be sensitive and responsive to their wishes. The system established by the Medical Services Branch of the Department of National Health and Welfare to deliver health care to native people was certainly not established to serve the specific interests of the Territories either singly or jointly. The system was established to cover the whole nation and was indeed operated on a uniform system nation–wide that paid little or no attention to political boundaries or the varying needs of different ethnic groups. This is revealed in the consistency of its units across the nation, both in the Territories and the provinces, and in the north–south system of connectors.[5] Clearly, the system was established with administrative convenience uppermost in mind, not consumer satisfaction or participation.

The system established across the entire nation, both territories and provinces, was developed largely in the 1950s and 1960s. The Department of National Health and Welfare, which had been established in 1944, had the responsibility for native health transferred to it in 1945. In 1954, the Department created the Medical Services Branch (MSB) to oversee this responsibility and this marked the true beginning of what became an extensive network of health care facilities and services across the nation.[6] The MSB divided Canada into several major regions and established a system of north to south corridors. Within each corridor three levels of care were linked. The first level of care was a network of nursing stations that had basic medical supplies and drugs, x-ray and basic laboratory equipment, an examining room and a few beds. They were staffed by up to six nurses depending upon the size of the station, and this in turn was dependent upon the size of the community they served. The secondary level of care consisted of small "zone" hospitals serving a number of communities with nursing stations. Typically, they had 20–30 beds, more elaborate equipment, a more extensive nursing staff and four or five general practioners. They dealt with minor surgical matters, more complicated childbirth and more elaborate diagnosis than the nursing stations. The third or tertiary level of care was provided by major hospitals in the southern cities of Montreal, Toronto, Winnipeg, Edmonton and Vancouver. The MSB also came to arrangements with the Health Science centres at the major universities in these cities to provide some visiting staff to the zone hospitals and nursing stations. In addition, the MSB developed an increasingly sophisticated system of communications among the elements in its system, including an air evacuation system.[7]

At one level this system was markedly successful. When it was established, the health care status of Canada's indigenous and northern peoples was appalling.[8] The system was the curatively oriented southern system adapted to northern conditions. It was clearly intended to have as rapid and dramatic an effect as possible on health status. The incidence of infectious diseases and infant mortality rates did rapidly decline. The situation now, while by no means as good as it is for southern Canadians, is a vast improvement. However, the system was very costly, and it was not one that was particularly sensitive to the needs of its clientele. Its imperative was really one dictated by one group's criteria being applied to services for another.

A second major advantage of devolving health care services, at least in theory, is that the services would be delivered by people who are less likely to be "outsiders" and, therefore, are likely to be a reflection of either the population make up of the northern Territories or, at least, of the values of northern residents. One of the major criticisms of the health system established by the MSB was that it was delivered by the people of one race to the people of another. Moreover, the federal authorities were criticized for putting relatively little effort into training health care workers among the aboriginal peoples, except at the very lowest levels. In addition, there was a high turnover rate among those who did serve in the North (among nurses in some regions it was more than 100 percent per annum)[9] and clearly the motivation for service in the North was in most cases either monetary or a search for adventure, not a long–term commitment to either the North or to native peoples.

It is certainly the case that the aboriginal organizations in the Northwest Territories were motivated to support the idea of health care devolution because they believed it would allow them to have more direct control or influence over the health care system. They wanted a health care system that would be responsible, both organizationally and programmatically, to the needs of native peoples. This is why they were so concerned to have native groups directly involved in the transfer process.[10]

A third advantage is an essentially administrative one, namely that a single administrative region would replace a dual one. This should result in a greater consistency of approach and efficiency of operation. The dual system was the consequence of some services being delivered to territorial residents by the MSB and others by the territorial governments. After the creation of the MSB, territorial health systems developed steadily. In 1960 the Yukon Hospital Insurance Services and the Northwest Territories Hospital Insurance Service Board were founded. At that time both Territories delivered insured services in some hospitals of their own. The YTG then slowly transferred its hospitals to federal control but the GNWT continued to operate its own facilities, and in 1988 it operated four hospitals (Yellowknife, Hay River, Fort Smith and Iqaluit), the Inuvik long-term care facility, 12 nursing stations and one public health centre. In 1970 the NWT joined the national medical insurance plan which ensured that all residents, both native and non-natives, could receive doctors' services without direct cost to the patients or their families. The Yukon followed in 1972.

The desire to avoid a split administrative regime was evident when the federal authorities argued for a consolidation of services to their system in the Yukon in the late 1950s.[11] It was also evident when the GNWT argued for a health transfer to itself in the 1980s. The GNWT was motivated to push for such a transfer because it believed a single system would administer financial matters more effectively, would eliminate the effects of federal policies, such as hiring freezes, being imposed in the North and would allow for the introduction of programs that would be more specifically suited to the needs of the NWT and not all of Canada. The GNWT also thought a single administrative regime would be able to respond more speedily to new health issues as they arose.

Fourthly, devolution, from the point of view of the Department of National Health and Welfare, had the advantage of allowing them to easily meet down-sizing targets imposed by the federal government without significantly affecting the number of jobs available. Moreover, devolution also fitted in not only with down-sizing, which was partly the effect of the Nielson Task Force,[12] but also to the principle espoused by that Task Force in relation to the Territories, namely that there should be increased devolution of authority to the territorial administrations if only to simplify and rationalize the administrative structure.

A fifth and truly major advantage is often held to be that devolution would increase the likelihood of there being a reorientation of health care services away from the curative, high technology approach favoured by the federal authorities, and which many agree has nearly reached the limit of its effectiveness, to a more preventive low technology approach likely to produce better health outcomes, especially among the aboriginal peoples. While the MSB's operations did succeed in markedly reducing the rate of infectious diseases and improving health care status on the usual indicators of morbidity and mortality, the rate of improvement has slowed substantially in recent years. Doubts have arisen as to the usefulness of pouring additional amounts of money into a system that is experiencing diminishing marginal returns. In addition, it is argued that the pattern of illness and death has changed significantly and in a way that the current system is not equipped to deal with.[13] Infectious diseases have been replaced as the major killers by suicide, accidents and violence, many of which are alcohol or drug related and all of which are a reflection of a life of poverty, hopelessness and, indeed, desperation. A curatively biased, highly technological, doctor-dominated system is not well equipped to deal with such problems. In fact, no health care system is likely to be, as these are not "health" problems but problems (or more accurately symptoms) of social and economic disorder. However, a preventively oriented health system, involving its clientele and linked to social services as well as conducting extensive educational programs directed at affecting lifestyles, is likely to have somewhat greater success.

Associated with the possible reorientation of the health care system from a curative to a preventive emphasis was the additional hoped-for advantage that local control would lead to a greater integration of health care services with other local agencies such as those dealing with housing and welfare. The new pattern of illness in the North indicated that such linkages were increasingly necessary as it reflected generalized social problems rather than health problems per se. Experience in the NWT and elsewhere has been that such linkages tend not to occur in the higher reaches of the various systems and that, therefore, a better approach might be to try to link them at the community level. As far as the GNWT was concerned, this also fitted in well with its concept that each local community constituted what it called the "prime public authority."

One of the disadvantages of health care devolution might be that it would result in a health care system that would be too small to be efficient. It would have to cover a small, widely scattered and variegated population, and would be unable to achieve economies of scale or a significant research capacity. It must always be remembered when discussing the Territories that they have small populations in small communities scattered over vast tracts of land. Moreover, the population is extremely diverse and each segment tends to have widely differing health care needs and expectations. However, this having been said, it should be noted that this is not a condition specific to health care services; it is true of nearly all areas. But the fact remains that being part of a nation–wide system had economies of scale unlikely to be achieved with either one of the Territories.

A second disadvantage of health care devolution could flow from the first. That is, the system's small size would make it easier for it to become controlled by a dominant professional group such as physicians or administrators. It might then become responsive to their wishes and not to those of the clients, thus detracting from one of the possible advantages, namely greater responsiveness to the population served. All areas of public policy are liable to penetration and control by a profes-sional group rather than by a client group or by politicians. Very clearly health care systems in most of the world — and certainly in Canada — have been dominated by physicians. The structure of the system and the kind of services it concentrates upon are a clear reflection of this. Even if the physicians do not have predominant influence it could well be exercised by the health administrators who, even in the south, seem to be achieving greater relative prominence. The likelihood of real control being exercised by lay clients is slight as they have, by definition, little expertise. Even if they had a degree of direct control, it is likely that they would be influenced by others because of their lack of expertise.

A third potential disadvantage of health care devolution is that the resulting system might be less able to reorient itself from a curative to a preventive approach even if it is more responsive to the client population. This is because the client population has yet to be convinced that it needs a more preventive approach. There are clear indications that, as elsewhere in the nation, high quality care, which is what is wanted (but may not be needed) is associated with curative not preventive approaches to health care. Thus it is quite likely that the client group will pressure for what they want, namely more of the curative services they see southerners getting in greater abundance than themselves.[14]

The Policy Context of Health Care Devolution

The policy context in which the idea of health care devolution is discussed can determine whether or not it actually takes place, and if it does, the speed of the process and the precise content of what is devolved. Clearly, the policy contexts were quite different between the two Territories as health care devolution has already taken place in the Northwest Territories and has not yet done so in the Yukon. This reflects very different situations and policy agendas. In this section the different policy contexts will be discussed beginning with a brief discussion of the differential experience in the two Territories with areas of authority previously devolved. This will be followed by analyses of the other devolutions going on at the same time in each Territory, the different nature of approaches to provincial status and to the concept of regional government, and the different nature of the land claims process. Finally, there will be an analysis of another important contextual factor, namely the belief among many observers that the largely federal health care delivery system had reached the limit of its effectiveness.

The devolution of health care services should be briefly placed in historical context. Firstly, it should be noted that there had been changes in the federal system after its establishment in 1954 which, while not devolution as such, set the stage for it. In 1974 the northern region of the MSB was divided into the Yukon Region and the Northwest Territories Region. Then,in

1980, the headquarters of the Northwest Territories Region was relocated to Yellowknife from Edmonton. Secondly, experiments in partial transfer did occur in the NWT before the full transfer in 1988. These preliminary stages will be discussed in greater detail later. Here it will just be noted, firstly, that in 1982 the federal hospital in Iqaluit was transferred to the GNWT, which created a regionally representative Board of Management to operate the hospital and, secondly, that in 1986 all the nursing stations and public health in the Baffin region were transferred to the GNWT, which created a Regional Board to deal with these issues. These preliminary transfers were followed on April 1, 1988 with the full transfer which involved two more hospitals (Inuvik and the cottage hospital in Fort Simpson) and the remaining nursing stations in the central and western Arctic.

Administrative devolution has been ongoing over the past several decades in both the Yukon and the Northwest Territories. The rate of devolutions or transfers has varied over the years. The periods of most rapid expansion were between 1959 and 1962 and between 1975 and 1979. However, the tendency towards devolution received a boost in 1985 with the election of a Progressive Conservative government more sympathetic than its predecessors to the granting of more province–like powers to the Territories. The GNWT no doubt thought it had a four-year opportunity to move through several devolutions and if the government should change thereafter a new government would have difficulty reversing the trend. The GNWT thus gave priority to devolution[15] and had discussions with a sympathetic new DIAND Minister, David Crombie, which resulted in a method of jointly identifying eligible areas for transfer, a manner of negotiating the transfers, and central co-ordinators within DIAND and within the GNWT. In 1985 the GNWT set up a Devolution Office as part of the Executive Council Secretariat to co-ordinate its side of the devolution process. The GNWT gave assurances to the native organizations by preparing a Memorandum of Understanding which stated that no agreement would be concluded in an area likely to affect land claims without their consent, and which offered the native organizations a role in the transfer process itself.[16] This led to the transfer of all remaining health care services (after the Baffin transfer) in 1988.

The attitude of the Yukon Territorial Government (YTG) to devolution in general was and is different from that of the Government of the Northwest Territories. Both constitutionally and politically, the Yukon considers itself to be in advance of the Northwest Territories and has, therefore, paid less attention to specific program transfers. The current attitude of the YTG to health care devolution is also very different from that of the GNWT. This is because there was an abortive attempt at health care devolution in the Yukon in 1978. Throughout the 1970s the YTG grew increasingly critical of the federal government's handling of health care. It argued that a chronic shortage of public health nurses had developed, that there had been too much attention paid to the health of Indians and that the YTG had little influence over the nature of the health care system. By the mid-1970s the federal authorities came around to agreeing to organize a transfer of all health care services on the condition that the Yukon Native Brotherhood was a party to the agreement. In October, 1977 the YTG gave approval in principle to a transfer and the target date was established as April 1, 1978.

As was noted above, this call for devolution on the part of YTG came after it had previously transferred some responsibilities in the other direction, that is, to the federal government. The population of the Yukon expanded rapidly during World War II and for a time thereafter. This led to an expansion of territorially delivered health care services. In the 1950s the federal government made the point that it would be more rational to have a single health care delivery system for such a small total population rather than a federal one for the native population and a separate territorial one for the non–native population.[17] Resources could be pooled and overlap eliminated. A polio epidemic in 1953 revealed the weaknesses of the dual system and in 1954 the Yukon Territorial Council gave approval for a unified health service under federal control.[18] On April 1, 1957 some territorial services were transferred to the federal government. In 1959 the federal government largely financed a new hospital in Mayo. In 1962 all remaining territorial services were transferred, and in 1970 both the Mayo and the Dawson hospitals became federally administered.

The reverse transfer scheduled for April 1, 1978 began unravelling in February of that year. This was because the Yukon Native Brotherhood indicated to the federal government that it would no longer agree to the transfer. The YNB gave several reasons for its change in position. It stated that there was not widespread support for the transfer in the Indian communities. It argued that the YTG was not a sufficiently mature government and might not be able to fairly administer a health care system.[19] It also feared that most health care personnel would not want to join a territorial public service and would leave the Yukon, thereby leading to a deterioration rather than an improvement in health care services. The YTG argued that it would offer certain guarantees to the natives and design programs specifically for native communities, but to no avail. Because the YNB would not agree to a transfer the federal government withdrew from any further discussions on the matter.

The policy context between the Yukon and the Northwest Territories was also different in terms of the way in which provincial status was being pursued. The Yukon was clearly more advanced politically than the Northwest Territories and did not suffer from the possibility of division. Thus the YTG had no reason to push the devolution process. In the Northwest Territories there was a possibility that attempts to divide the Territory between Denendeh and Nunavut might be revived. This possibility was a clear motive for the GNWT to push for the rapid devolution of areas such as health which affect many people. The GNWT wanted to be seen as a unit that could efficiently provide useful services to the population. It wanted to enhance its legitimacy in the eyes of the population in case the issue of division again came to the forefront. In fact, many of the native groups regarded the push for devolution on the part of the GNWT as precisely a rush to get responsibilities in the hope that it would help stave off the possibility of division.

A further complication affected the policy context in the NWT, but not in the Yukon. This was the move to enhance regional government in the NWT. This had a direct effect on health devolution because it affected to whom powers would be devolved. Would they largely be devolved to the GNWT in

Yellowknife or to regional bodies? The native organizations saw regionalization as a mechanism by which money and responsibility would be channelled through the GNWT to the regional bodies where the native organizations would have a great deal of influence. Thus they were suspicious of the GNWT's development of the concept of prime public authority because it implied a direct dealing between the GNWT and each community thus by–passing the regional organizations.

At the time that health care devolution reached the policy agenda in the Northwest Territories and was being mooted in the Yukon there were a number of other policy areas also being devolved. Although health was a large transfer it was only one of many going on at the same time. However it, along with the forestry transfer, was so time-consuming that it did detract from the others. The GNWT, in fact, was able to complete fewer transfers than originally anticipated because of this.[20]

Another element in the policy context at the time of health care devolution was the prominence, if not pre–eminence, of land claims issues. Certainly in the Yukon, land claims issues were pre-eminent and that is the reason that the health transfer has not yet occurred. The YTG has said clearly that it is more concerned with settling land claims issues and dealing with economic development than it is with the whole process of devolution. The attitude of the Council for Yukon Indians (CYI) matches that of the YTG. They have simply been too busy with land claims issues to pay a great deal of attention to devolution. Moreover, they seem to be more concerned with natural resource issues in general than with health care issues. Even though the attitude of the GNWT and the aboriginal groups there was somewhat different, neither really wanted the devolution of health care to detract from ongoing land claims discussions but they were able to come to an accommodation.

The Process of Health Care Devolution

The health care devolution process in the NWT worked relatively smoothly. Unlike the earlier abortive attempt in the Yukon, the support and participation of aboriginal groups was maintained, though at varying levels of enthusiasm throughout. The process was relatively slow and was carefully staged in three parts over the better part of a decade with each of the first two stages being evaluated before the next stage was begun. Thus the process was participatory, piecemeal and prolonged. Steering committees formed in the final stage worked deliberately and with care. The central devolution offices of both levels of government offered these committees and others useful assistance. This having been said, the role of personalities should not be forgotten. Key individuals in the GNWT, the aboriginal groups and the federal government thought that devolution would produce not only a more efficient and responsive health care system for all northern residents but better health outcomes as measured by the usual indicators.

It should be noted at the outset that the process of health care devolution was performed within the context of purely administrative change. There was no legal change of status between the federal and the territorial authorities, nor were there any legal changes specific to the health policy area. In view of the fact that the territorial governments are themselves emanations of federal legal authority, the federal government was essentially shifting administrative responsibility for health from one element of its administrative structure to another. This observation is not to make light of the difficulties of such a switch or to deny the significance of the action but merely to place the parameters of the change in context.

It should also be noted early on that the process of health care devolution and, indeed, of devolution in general was piecemeal and evolutionary. There was no detailed overall agreement between either or both territorial governments and the federal government. Moreover, there was no timetable agreed upon between the parties. This was acceptable to all the parties. None showed any signs of wanting to establish a detailed plan for devolution with a similarly detailed timetable. It was also clear that although all of the interested parties in the GNWT were in favour of the devolution of responsibility for health care they wanted to "feel" their way towards the goal.

This having been said, both levels of government did eventually establish devolution offices, although these offices were not in charge of the process. They were essentially advisory to the various units at each level of government that were involved in, or were likely to be involved in devolution. Moreover, they had responsibility for all of the devolutions and not just health. The GNWT Devolution Office, established in 1985, was technically advisory to the Assembly and Cabinet but it also provided detailed advice and some administrative support to individual departments, such as Health. The GNWT Devolution Office even produced a fairly detailed guide or handbook for GNWT staff involved in transfers.[21] While opinions differ as to the value of the handbook, there seemed to be general agreement that the role of the Devolution Office was a valuable one, especially with regard to matters that affected all departments to some degree. Matters pertaining to a specific policy area such as health had to be dealt with in greater detail by members of the line departments. Much the same can be said of the federal officials who advised the various federal government departments involved.

It was critical to the process of devolution that it have the support of aboriginal groups. Not only was this a common–sense requirement given the policy context, but it was also something the federal government erected as a stipulation, given that it had the responsibility for non–insured benefits for Inuit and status Indians in perpetuity and given the prior experience of the abortive devolution of health in the Yukon. In the case of the Northwest Territories the support of the aboriginal groups was forthcoming and was largely maintained throughout, despite some reservations at times on the part of the aboriginal groups. Indeed, the initial support for the health transfer in the NWT came from the Inuit Tapirisat of Canada (ITC) in 1980. That year the organization passed a motion calling for each community to have its health services provided by the GNWT. The GNWT was certainly not averse to this idea and approached the federal authorities concerning the matter.

The ITC's desire to have authority for health devolved led to the process of transferring just one small part of the system, the Baffin Regional Hospital in Iqaluit (Frobisher Bay), to the GNWT. The detailed negotiations for this transfer began in January 1981 and, in the summer of the same year, the GNWT established a Board of Management that would assume responsibility for the hospital after the transfer. The Board of Management would operate the hospital on behalf of the GNWT and ensure a great deal of local input. By this means it was hoped that local needs would be met. By December, 1982 the transfer was complete. The hospital then operated for two years and was evaluated. The evaluation was a positive one and stated that the transfer and the board style of management were successful.[22] After these positive results the next stage, the transfer of the nursing stations in the Baffin Region, was implemented by September 1986. These two stages were known as Baffin Phase I and Baffin Phase II. Although Phase II was a much larger operation, the principle of maximum participation by aboriginal groups and those affected was preserved. This was done by creating a broadly representative steering committee and three broadly representative working committees that practised wide-ranging consultation.

The steering committee was the key organization whose large membership included the ITC, the Native Women's Organization, the Baffin Regional Council and the Baffin Regional Hospital Board, as well as representatives of the GNWT and the federal Department of National Health and Welfare. This ensured that the native groups felt that they had involvement in and, indeed, ownership of the process and the outcome. The three working committees reported to the steering committee and dealt with the nuts and bolts issues of personnel, operation and finance and capital. Various departments of the GNWT advised these working committees on their specialized areas and all were helped by the GNWT Devolution Office.

Another important aspect of obtaining and preserving the support of aboriginal organizations for health care devolution was agreement ahead of time on a regionally representative organizational structure to which authority for health would be passed by the GNWT when health care was devolved. In short, the aboriginal organizations had to be convinced that local and regional control was a real possibility. It became clear that the concept of regional control was the main reason that aboriginal organizations supported health care devolution at a time when they were also deeply involved in land claims and other issues. They gave their support at a difficult time as they believed they would benefit directly.

The experience of the Baffin Phase I and Phase II exercises led aboriginal organizations across the NWT, by and large, to support the transfer of health care throughout the NWT. The primary reason for their support was that the Baffin experience led them to believe that the Regional Boards to be set up in each region by the GNWT and the broadly participatory nature of the steering committee would give reasonable assurance that they and regional residents would have a large say in the fully devolved health care system. This idea of local or regional control over health care services also fitted in well with their concepts of self–government. The ITC gave full support to the transfer as did the Keewatin and Kitikmeot Inuit Associations and the Committee for Original People's Entitlement (COPE). The Dene Nation and the Métis Association of the Northwest Territories wanted written guarantees concerning the process and the outcome and argued for a formal participation agreement. The Dene Nation signed a Participation Agreement[23] on February 13, 1987 but the Métis withdrew from discussions concerning the agreement and never did sign. Thus after Baffin Phase II, most of the aboriginal groups in the NWT gave their support either warmly or with reservations to the third stage of health care devolution, namely full transfer.

The Dene Nation and the Métis Association insisted on a Participation Agreement largely because they did not trust the GNWT. They wanted to ensure not only that they would be consulted and that responsibility would be further devolved to Regional Boards but also that the health devolution came within the Memorandum of Understanding on Devolution that they had signed with the GNWT and that it would not interfere with or prejudice the ongoing discussions concerning self–government and land claims.

The fact that health care devolution in the NWT was a staged process was critical. Every one of the participants in the process was nervous about the intentions of the others and the staging allowed each to observe both the nature and the result of the transfer process. The native organizations were able to judge whether or not the GNWT would permit significant native participation in the devolution process, and whether the hospital Board of Management and the Regional Board would be given significant powers. The staging of the process also gave the GNWT and the federal authorities an opportunity to observe and evaluate whether or not a highly representative transfer process and management approach would lead to a reasonable degree of efficiency of operation. The demonstration effect of the successful smaller transfers in one region also enabled interested parties in other regions to see how it could be adopted or adapted elsewhere.

Another critical factor in the health devolution process was the interest and participation of individuals within a decentralized system. To be effective, such a system needs reasonably active Community Health Committees (CHCs) in each community. These committees would not only be important elements of the system, but would also form the units from which many of the representatives to the Regional Boards would be selected. The nature of the relationship between the CHCs and the health facilities and staff in each community would be very different from that which had existed prior to transfer, and would give the CHCs a greater influence and say. However, there was not a very strong network of CHCs before the transfer. In fact, many that had been formed under federal jurisdiction had become inactive. This was because little attention was paid to them by the federal government and because they had a purely advisory role largely related to matters of environmental health. Therefore, the GNWT Department of Health mounted a campaign prior to the full transfer to reactivate or re-establish CHCs where necessary. A series of workshops was held for the CHCs that did exist, and efforts were made to establish new ones where they were needed.[24]

One of the aspects of the devolution process that should be briefly noted was that once under way it involved remarkably little input from politicians at either the federal or the territorial level. At the federal level, Mr. Jake Epp, the Minister of National Health and Welfare, was supportive and his support was clearly important, especially for the freedom of action it accorded the Director of the MSB. At the territorial level few of either the territorially elected federal MPs or the members of the territorial legislature had much to say about the health care. Most of the public statements in the course of the health devolution process were made either by the leaders of native organizations or by senior bureaucrats, with only a few coming from the two ministers involved and very few from politicians generally. However, the politicians were largely sympathetic to health care devolution.

Although the views and actions of most politicians were not critical to the health care transfer, the importance of other personalities to the process should not be underestimated. In fact, the officials within both the GNWT Department of Health, the MSB, and other affected agencies such as the Devolution Office worked well together. In addition, despite many political and other differences among the members of the steering committees by and large they managed to put aside most of their differences in their efforts to reach the general outcome that they all wanted to see achieved.

While not without difficulties, as the next section will detail, the health care devolution process worked relatively well. In part this was because of the lessons learned in the earlier abortive Yukon health care transfer. The key lesson was that it was absolutely vital to retain the support of aboriginal organizations. To do this they had to be assured that the devolution process was a participatory one and one that would, therefore, likely result in the creation of a new health care system that would treat all territorial residents fairly. Another lesson learned from the Yukon experience was that the devolution of health care should be accomplished by a process that was slow and staged.

The Content of Health Care Devolution

The content of the health care devolution involves those topics that were discussed and resolved by the three sets of working committees, (Finance and Administration, Personnel, and Operations) and the three steering committees. The topics dealt with by each will be analysed in turn.

The three steering committees established to discuss the detailed content of devolution were the Arctic, Inuvik and Western Steering Committees. The Regional Director of the MSB and the Deputy Minister of Health of the GNWT were on all three steering committees, and an official of the GNWT Devolution Office, Mr. Lee Horne, acted as the Secretary to all of the committees. Each steering committee was otherwise representative of the major groups within each of the three regions. For example the Inuvik Health Transfer Steering Committee included representatives of the Inuvialuit Social Development Fund, the Dene/Métis Mackenzie Delta Regional Development Council, the Beaufort Delta Conference Group, the Shihta Regional Council, the Inuvik Hospital Advisory Board and the Town of Inuvik.

The steering committees were responsible for guiding and negotiating the preparation of all the appropriate documentation, co-ordinating the efforts of the working committees that reported to them and making the final decisions on issues that arose.[25] The work of these steering committees was obviously vital. It is fortunate that the prior Baffin transfers had set the pattern for discussions because there was the possibility of a variation in approaches that might have made the production of a single transfer document difficult. In the final result a single transfer document was drawn up. The discussions of the steering committees concentrated upon the broader issues, as would be expected. Prime among these were the issues of the degree of autonomy and the degree of authority that the Regional Health Boards would have. To focus these discussions the GNWT Department of Health developed a model Regional Health Board framework based upon the Baffin example.

The three Finance Committees had to identify all of the financial resources that should be transferred and assess their adequacy. In addition, they had to identify all of the properties affected, inspect them and value them.[26] In terms of the finances, everyone was reasonably confident that they could obtain an accurate estimate of the sums involved. This was done by analysing a five-year history of the finances of a particular region, provided by the federal government. This document was used as a base line and it was assumed that staff costs were the authorized person-years whether or not particular positions were actually filled and expenditures made. To this base a wide variety of adjustments were then made for all the likely reasonable cost variations. For example, it was clear that the Regional Board structure would entail additional expenditures and thus estimates were made to cover them.

Although the sums involved were large (the full transfer added $58.6 million or 7 percent to the total GNWT budget for 1988–89) everyone was confident that their estimates would turn out to produce adequate finances. This was largely because the Baffin Regional Hospital transfer ($3.1 million to the 1985/86 GNWT budget) had been accurate.[27] In addition, a special audit of the transfer of the nursing stations in the Baffin region (which added $3.8 million to the 1987/88 GNWT budget) indicated that the estimates made prior to that transfer had also been accurate. It should be noted that of the $58.6 million involved in the full transfer, $49.9 million was added to the expenditure base of the GNWT used for the calculation of formula funding from the federal government. The remaining sum was a payment to the GNWT for the administration of Indian and Inuit health care and is negotiable annually. Discussions in the working committees on facilities were lengthy and complicated. For each building the cost of construction at the time of construction was obtained and the cost of any renovations added to produce the current cost of the building. Every building was then inspected by a team comprising members from both the GNWT and federal Department of Public Works to obtain an estimate of the number of useful years of life left remaining, using the assumption that every building had a life span of only 25 years. The useful life left for each building was then averaged by region. The cost of replacing all the buildings at the end of their useful life was then estimated. This figure was then divided by the years remaining to get the yearly amount required, and this was then transferred.[28] It should be noted that the property on which each building stood was also transferred to the GNWT. Any buildings that were in the process of renovation or construction at the moment of transfer would remain the property of the federal government until the work was completed and then additional calculations would be made and the buildings and property transferred. In addition to the buildings and land upon which they stood, all of the public property listed in the Health Public Property Register had to be taken into account. This included vehicles, equipment, food, linen, drugs and supplies on hand at the time of transfer.

The three Personnel Working Committees had to re–classify all the federal jobs to the GNWT system, counsel all affected employees and liaise with the unions involved.[29] This proved to be the most contentious and problematic area in the lead-up to transfer, despite the fact that both the federal government and the GNWT went to considerable lengths to assure employees that they would be treated fairly. Both said that one of their major concerns was employee well–being. All those who did not want to be transferred from the federal public service to that of the GNWT were to be given every opportunity for re–employment with the federal civil service. All those who wanted to be transferred were assured by the GNWT that every precaution would be taken in relation to such matters as levels of responsibility and pay in the process of job reclassification. It should be noted that the task of reclassifying all the jobs to the GNWT's personnel system was a lengthy and complicated process. In addition, the federal government and the GNWT agreed that all those transferred had the opportunity to return to the federal public service with priority status for re–employment if they did not want to remain with the GNWT. Clearly this was offered as an inducement to federal employees to make the switch.

At the time of transfer most of the federal employees did change employers, including 85 percent of the nursing staff —

the single largest group. This was a pleasantly high percentage as far as the GNWT was concerned, especially in view of the fuss created by nurses just prior to the transfer. The idea of changing employers quite naturally created a lot of uncertainty, despite the assurances provided by both governments.[30] The problems involved tended to focus on the issue of union membership. Many nurses said that they would not sign on with the GNWT if they had to drop membership in the Professional Institute of the Public Service (PIPS) and become members of the Union of Northern Workers (UNW). In fact, a group of nurses even took the matter to court but their arguments were rejected by Justice M.M. de Weert.[31] However, despite these concerns, most of the nursing staff did change employers as previously indicated. It should be noted that just prior to the date of transfer the federal government had difficulty replacing those who left because of the impending changes, although it has been suggested that the federal government did not try very hard to replace them knowing that transfer was in the offing and the hiring problem would soon become one for the GNWT.

It is likely that most of the nursing staff eventually made the change because, despite all the problems and uncertainties, employment with the federal government was becoming less attractive and employment with the GNWT more attractive. The MSB was undergoing rapid change and with the Northwest Territories transfer, a possible Yukon transfer as well as the possible transfers south of 60° to native self-government, the MSB was obviously likely to pass out of existence almost entirely at some point in the future. Thus there was as much, if not more, uncertainty with employment with the MSB as with the GNWT Department of Health. At the same time the career path possibilities were getting better with the GNWT as it expanded in size. Moreover, it was also becoming a more sophisticated and responsible employer as the various transfers proceeded.

The difficulties with the nurses appeared to be the only major problem in personnel terms until just a few months prior to the April 1, 1988 full transfer. However, in February of 1988, the GNWT announced a Transfer Policy that caused a great deal of upset.[32] The newly announced policy called for those people who worked in the fields of personnel, public works and the like within the federal health care system to be transferred not to the GNWT Department of Health but to the appropriate functional department, such as Personnel or Public Works. The members of the Regional Boards and the major native organizations saw this as a move deliberately undertaken to reduce the significance of native participation and to reduce the span of control of the Regional Health Boards. Some of the native organizations said the policy indicated bad faith on the part of the GNWT, especially since the policy was not going to be applied *ex post facto* to the Baffin Region.[33] The GNWT said the policy was not intended to reduce the influence of the Regional Health Board and was, in fact, intended to help them since they would not have the capability of dealing with a wide range of personnel when only very small numbers would be involved in each category. However, officials of the GNWT did agree that the timing of the announcement, though they said it was accidental, was not the most appropriate.

The three Operational Working Committees had to identify the level of health services to be transferred, define the residual responsibilities of the MSB and identify the monitoring data for non-insured health benefits.[34] This was not a particularly easy set of tasks. The two levels of government possessed different types of programs prior to the transfer. The federal government's services such as community health programs in relation to nutrition, careers, environmental health, dental health and communicable disease control had to be blended at an appropriate level with the GNWT'S medical and hospital insurance programs and programs in the area of family life education, health information and promotion, physician recruitment and covering the costs of prescription drugs. This adjustment was made with little rancour although some personnel were not happy that some of their programs were "messed with."

It was not particularly difficult to identify the residual responsibilities of the MSB but it was not very easy to decide exactly how to organize, deliver and pay for them. The residual responsibilities were largely those related to non-insured health services which are drugs prescribed by a licensed physician, prescribed appliances, ophthalmic services, dental treatment, transportation and alcohol treatment. However, they also included health services to federal employees, civil aviation medicine and health services under the *Quarantine and Immigration Act*. It was decided that non-insured health services could not be transferred to the GNWT but could be administered by them under the terms of a *Contribution Agreement*.[35] This agreement stipulated that the staff, offices and services would be provided by the GNWT and paid for by the federal government. In other words, the GNWT would become the administrative agent for the federal government. As such, it would have no role in determining the nature and level of services to be provided. This would be decided by the federal government in consultation with Native organizations. The consultative arrangement was specified in the *Contribution Agreement* and was a committee in each of the regions broadly representative of the native groups but also including a representative of the GNWT Department of Health and chaired by a federal official. It should be noted that the sums involved in the area of non-insured health services were sizable, amounting to $22.3 million in 1989/90.

The Policy Impact of Health Care Devolution

Generally, the policy impact of the health care transfer can be divided into two areas. The first is its impact upon health policy outputs and health status. The second is its impact upon the two governments involved — namely the GNWT and the federal government — and especially upon the two line departments affected, namely the GNWT Department of Health and the Department of National Health and Welfare or, more specifically, its Medical Services Branch. While it is somewhat early to be able to assess some of the policy impacts, it can be observed whether or not the new arrangement is likely to have an effect.

The transfer has created a more unified system and one that should result in a greater focus of attention on problems specific to the NWT. While the federal government still retains real authority in non-insured services, the GNWT does administer them and have some say in what they will be. This means that the focus of the GNWT Department of Health will be upon a broad range of health problems specific to the NWT. Under the previous federal system the MSB had to deliver services to both of the territories and south of 60° in most of the provinces. Clearly then, the MSB's main focus was not just the NWT. The new devolved health care structures incorporate a Territorial Health Board that has the role of ensuring that public partici-pation in both policy and management continues to have a Territory–wide focus, that is, it is charged with maintaining reasonable equity among regions in terms of facilities, services and standards.[36] This is done both for its own sake but also to stop each of the Regional Boards competing with the others over staff and other matters.

This greater NWT focus within a more unified system is to some degree reflected in the stated intention of the Minister of Health and the Department of Health to provide more health services and have more health facilities in the NWT.[37] This is coming to fruition as there is a significant upgrading of facilities and services being undertaken at the Stanton Yellowknife Hospital and a boarding home for Inuit is being built in Yellowknife. Clearly the intention is to replace the multiple north-to-south referral routes that existed before transfer with a referral route that will see most patients going to the Stanton Yellowknife facility. It is likely, therefore, that in time other facilities changes will occur such as the replacement of the use of the Churchill Health Centre in Manitoba with a small hospital in the Keewatin region of the NWT.

The transfer has created the possibility of greater local influence over, and control of, health care services. Implicit within this is also a greater degree of influence or control by natives and native organizations, which is why the native organizations were in favour of health care devolution in the first place. The transfer has set the basis for this because of the regionalized nature of the system to which health care has been devolved. There are five Regional Health Boards in the NWT: the Keewatin, Kitikmeot, Mackenzie, Inuvik and the Baffin. Each Board is broadly representative of the groups within each region and each has major responsibilities in the planning, manage-ment and delivery of health care services, both medical and dental, and the operation of hospitals and nursing stations within their regions. Thus the Regional Boards are important administrative units. The GNWT has stated it is in favour of strong local control via these bodies because this is likely to make health services more responsive to both local and inter-ethnic needs and, thereby, improve the general level of satisfaction with them.

The Regional Boards are very representative of their regions. For example, the Keewatin Regional Health Board is made up of one member from each of the eight communities in the region, as well as a representative each for the Keewatin Inuit Association, the Keewatin Regional Council, the Churchill Health Centre Board, the Department of Health and Welfare (ex officio and non–voting), and the Northern Medical Unit of the University of Manitoba (ex officio and non–voting). The members are appointed by the Minister of Health from nominations made by municipal or band councils and the nominees have generally been members or chairpersons of Community Health Committees (CHCs).[38] Initially the Regional Boards were chaired by the GNWT Regional Directors (who no longer have line authority) but lay chairpersons have now been appointed following the Baffin model.

However, representative membership does not guarantee the desired outcome although it is a precondition. The local representatives also have to be willing to work and gain a degree of expertise in relation to the health care system. Even if a willingness to work is present many board members may have difficulty with actually performing the work as there is a situation of overload on capable local representatives. The general trend to regionalization and local control has placed a considerable burden on many people, especially the most active and able. Indeed, in the Keewatin this was precisely why a number of the CHCs had become largely defunct prior to transfer. Admittedly, the GNWT has recognized the problem and has tried to do something about it. The GNWT tried to revitalize the CHCs before the transfer with reasonable success and established a training program for CHC members in co–operation with Arctic College. In addition, the Department of Health has prepared a trustee manual to help with the training of members of the Regional Health Boards.

On paper, the Regional Boards clearly have significant authority. They will operate as autonomous managers of health program delivery as described in a master agreement between the GNWT and each of the Boards. They will each negotiate separate support service contracts with the GNWT service departments for the provision of direct and indirect services.[39] Each Board has appointed a Chief Executive Officer (called an Executive Director in those regions without a hospital). While this is laudable, the fact remains that an inexpert lay group will be attempting to control experts and, indeed, experts of another race. It is quite possible that the Chief Executive Officers may be able to dominate the Regional Boards because of their expertise. It is also possible that the physicians, or possibly another expert professional group such as the nurses, will come to dominate both the Regional Boards and the CEOs. Another possibility is that the Department of Health in Yellowknife might eventually impose its own administrative expertise, either via the CEOs or via the use of an extensive and uniform regulatory system imposed by the Territorial Health Board.

While local or regional control, if effective, should ensure that there is a much greater degree of native influence and control, all the potential problems just cited could detract from such influence. Moreover, there will be a continual problem if influence or control is exercised by one racial group over those of another. While the structure being put in place is in theory — and hopefully in practice — a better situation than the previous one, it is still inherently unsatisfactory. A satisfactory situation will only result when the services are provided by and administered by people of much the same racial and other background as those who are the clients of the system. Prior to transfer the efforts to train native health care professionals were woefully inadequate both in absolute terms and in comparison to nations such as the USA. However there are hopeful signs in the post-transfer situation. The GNWT Minister of Health, Nellie Cournoyea, has stated "we expect to make inroads into the area of attracting native people into health careers."[40] In the long run the NWT will only have a truly responsive health care system when the composition of that system is reasonably representative of the population it serves.

The health care transfer had a major impact on both the MSB and the GNWT Department of Health. For the MSB and, therefore, the Department of National Health and Welfare (DNHW), the transfer meant a significant downscaling of staff and operations. It was clearly the predecessor of future transfers to the Yukon and to self–government units south of 60°. While the transfer meant that the DNHW could relatively easily achieve its downsizing targets, the future prospects for the MSB led to morale and employment problems. It was clear that employment prospects with the MSB were becoming both uncertain and truncated, thus it became more difficult to attract people and more particularly good people. To some degree the sense of mission was adversely affected. In the early years especially, the MSB attracted some very highly motivated and able people because of its sense of mission. With the onset of the era of transfer, the sense of mission had not gone but was now linked to an obvious process of self–destruction of the unit in a relatively short period of time. As in any field it is especially difficult to find people who are dedicated to working themselves out of a job.

The impact on the GNWT was, of course, almost the reverse of that for the MSB. The transfer meant expansion, an enhanced career path for employees and a chance for some to try to put new ideas or approaches into effect. The GNWT Department of Health was restructured as 500 people were added to its staff.[41] A three-column structure (Programs and Standards, Hospital Operations and Health Insurance Administration) headed up by chiefs[42] was replaced by a two column structure (Community Health and Standards and Institutional Health) headed up by Assistant Deputy Ministers.[43] It was argued that this structure would be better able to cope with a regionalized structure and the new responsibilities, as well as the added staff.

Another significant impact of the transfer may well be in the nature of health policy itself. The concept of a more unified system for the entire NWT plus greater local control via the method of regionalization has always been linked with a desire to effect some program reorientation. Many of those involved in health policy matters believe that the existing curatively biased, doctor-dominated, hospital-based, highly technological form of health care delivery has come close to reaching the limits of its effectiveness and also is not very likely to be able to successfully combat the new pattern of sickness and death in the North. The argument is that emphasis has to be shifted from curing infectious diseases to tackling chronic illness and a variety of essentially social pathologies, and that this shift will require a more preventive set of measures and closer links with other social services. Such a shift is often advocated for Canadian society in general but it has greater applicability in the North given comparative morbidity and mortality statistics.

Some effort is being made to effect a change in orientation in the post–transfer period. The nursing stations have been renamed Community Health Centres which, while it may not be of much practical significance, is of some symbolic importance. Here it should be noted, however, that the change of name was accompanied by the requirement that nursing staff would henceforth live in the community and buy food there like everyone else, rather than live in the nursing station and have their supplies provided separately. In addition, visiting specialists and the like will now stay in the community, not at the nursing stations. Also the GNWT has stated that it intends to place a greater emphasis on health promotion and health education than was the case under the MSB. A new health education program is being developed and efforts are being made to increase the number of certain types of health care workers such as Community Health Representatives. While these are relatively small beginnings, the stated intention is to build upon them and gradually effect a significant reorientation via the mechanism of enhanced local input in a regionalized system.

However, there are forces which are likely to impede progress toward such a shift in orientation. These forces are much the same as those likely to impede progress towards a greater degree of local control. It is quite likely that there will be professional resistance to a significant reorientation. As in the South it implies a change in the pecking order or power structure among the health professionals and the currently dominant professionals — the physicians — are bound to resist. Many residents of the NWT have long been conditioned, as we all have, to think that the only true form of health care is that provided by doctors in hospitals. Consequently, there is a tendency to think that if such services are not readily available one is being short-changed. Thus even many tiny communities in the NWT feel they are being hard done by or discriminated against if they don't have a resident physician. It will take a lot of effort in the North, as in the South, to reorient peoples' attitudes and expectations. In addition, the GNWT Department of Health and the Regional Boards have taken over the facilities and programs developed under the older way of thinking. These long standing features of the health care system will be expensive and difficult to change.

Conclusions

The health care devolution process in the NWT has set the stage for a potentially valuable reorientation of the health care delivery system and it has indicated that even in a policy field with a great many potential difficulties, reasonably efficient transfer can be effected. As such, it sets the stage for the future transfer of health services in the Yukon and may even provide useful lessons for how to deal with health care transfers south of 60°.

The health transfer in the NWT has also set the stage for positive developments in health care. A more integrated system with a high degree of local input and input by native people has resulted from the transfer. This, in and of itself, is a positive outcome but one which, as has been observed, is fraught with difficulties that could lead in time to the erosion of public or consumer input and its replacement by the dominance of "experts" or professionals of one kind or another.

The health transfer has also resulted in a system which may be able to reorient itself to better tackle the current pattern of health care problems in the North. However, that reorientation is also fraught with difficulties. Despite decades of fine phrases generally in Canada about the need to reorient the health care system, very little has actually changed, as indicated by the fact that no greater a percentage is spent on broadly preventive approaches than was the case several decades ago. As has been observed, even greater local or native control is no guarantee that the needed reorientation will occur as the association of "health" with "curative" rather than "preventive" health services is widespread at all levels and among all groups in society.

In purely procedural terms the transfer worked remarkably smoothly given the potential pitfalls. The explanation for this in part resides in the fact all the interested groups involved were convinced that a devolved health care system was likely to further their interests and, in so doing, improve health services and health status for all residents of the Northwest Territories. The slow, staged and experimental or fluid process managed to retain the support of most of the major policy participants largely by giving them a considerable say in both the process and the outcome and allowing them to observe in the first stages that what was intended did, indeed, result.

NOTES

1   K. Coates, *Canada's Colonies*, Toronto: James Lorimer, 1985.

2   See Geoffrey R. Weller, "Self–Government for Canada's Inuit: The Nunavut Proposal," *The American Review of Canadian Studies*, Vol. XVIII, No. 3, Autumn 1988, pp. 341–358 and Gurston Dacks, "The Case Against Dividing the Northwest Territories," *Canadian Public Policy*, Vol. 10, No. 11 pp. 202–223.

3   See Geoffrey R. Weller, "The Delivery of Health Care Services in the Canadian North," *Journal of Canadian Studies*, Vol. 16, No. 2, Summer 1981, pp. 69–80.

4   See John O'Neil, "The Politics of Health in the Fourth World: A Northern Canadian Example," *Human Organization*, Vol 45, No. 3 Summer 1986, pp. 119–128.

5   See Geoffrey R. Weller, "The Delivery of Health Care Services in the Canadian North," *Journal of Canadian Studies*, Vol. 16, No. 2, Summer 1981, pp. 69–80.

6   Canada, *Establishment of Northern Health Services*, Memorandum to Cabinet by Paul Martin. Ottawa: Department of National Health and Welfare, October 12, 1954.

7   This structure is described in A.P. Ruderman and Geoffrey R. Weller, *Report of a Study of Inuit Health and Health Services in the Keewatin Zone of the Northwest Territories 1980*, Ottawa: Department of National Health and Welfare, 1980.

8   See R. Quinn Duffy, *The Road to Nunavut*, Kingston and Montreal: McGill–Queen's University Press, 1988, Chapter 2 "Looking After Health" pp. 51–94.

9   See P. Ruderman and G. Weller, op. cit, p. 30.

10   See *Healthbeat*, Vol. 9, No. 2, Summer 1987, p. 2.

11   See Janet Moodie Michael, *From Sissons to Meyer: The Administrative Development of the Yukon Government, 1948–1979*, Whitehorse: Yukon Education, Libraries and Archives Branch, June 1987, p. 29.

12   Canada, Task Force on Program Review, *Improved Program Delivery: Health and Sports*, Ottawa: Supply and Services Canada, 1986.

13   See John O'Neil, op. cit.

14   This tendency is discussed in A.P. Ruderman and Geoffrey R. Weller, "Health Services for the Keewatin Inuit in a Period of Transition," *Inuit Studies*, Vol. 5, No. 1 Spring 1981, pp. 49–62.

15   See Government of the Northwest Territories, *Annual Report, 1985.*

16   Government of the Northwest Territories, Dene Nation and Métis Association of the Northwest Territories, *Memorandum of Understanding on Devolution of Power and Authority to GNWT from Canada with the Involvement of the Dene and Métis.* Yellowknife, April 24, 1986.

17   Janet Moodie Michael, op. cit., p. 29.

18   Ibid, p. 28.

19   Ibid, p. 99.

20   Interview with Mr. Horne, Manager, Devolution Office, GNWT, February 13, 1989.

21   Government of the Northwest Territories, *Planning for Devolution: Principles, Process and Guidelines,* Yellowknife: Devolution Office, 1987.

22   Lynn Elkin Hall and Associates, *A Recommended Outline of the Devolution Process Based on the Baffin Health Phase II and Forestry Transfers,* Yellowknife: Lynn Elkin Hall and Associates, December, 1986, p. 10.

23   Government of Canada, The Commissioner of the Northwest Territories, and the Dene Nation, *Participation Agreement on the Devolution of Health Services within the Dene/Métis Settlement Area in the Northwest Territories,* February 13, 1987.

24   Interview with J. McGraw, Department of Health, GNWT, February 14, 1989.

25   Government of the Northwest Territories, *Steering Committees, Transfer of the NWT Region, Terms of Reference,* Yellowknife: GNWT, January 14, 1987.

26   Government of the Northwest Territories, *Administrative and Finance Sub-Committee, Transfer of the NWT Region, Terms of Reference,* Yellowknife: GNWT, January 14, 1987.

27   Government of the Northwest Territories, *Audit Report, Baffin Regional Health Board, Transfer of Health Care Responsibilities,* File 91–04–31–800, no date.

28   Interview with Mr. Horne, Manager, Devolution Office, GNWT, February 13, 1989.

29   Government of the Northwest Territories, *Personnel Sub-Committee, Transfer of the N.W.T. Region, Terms of Reference*, Yellowknife: GNWT, January 14, 1987.

30   See Hon. Jake Epp, *Notes for an Address at a Ceremony Transferring Responsibility for Health Care to the Government of the Northwest Territories*, Yellowknife, August 25, 1988, p. 5.

31   See *News North*, April 25, 1988, "Most Nurses Accept Job Offers."

32   Government of the Northwest Territories, *GNWT Transfer Policy*, Yellowknife: GNWT, February 24, 1988.

33   See, for example, Inuvialuit Regional Corporation, *Press Release on Transfer Policy*, Inuvik: Inuvialuit Regional Corporation, March 30, 1988.

34   Government of the Northwest Territories, *Operations Sub-Committee, Transfer of N.W.T. Region, Terms of Reference*, Yellowknife: GNWT, January 14, 1987.

35   Government of Canada and Government of the Northwest Territories, *Contribution Agreement*, Tabled Document No. 127–88(1), April 7, 1988.

36   See Government of the Northwest Territories, *Institutional Structures, GNWT Health System*, Yellowknife: GNWT, July 6, 1987, pp. 9–10.

37   The Hon. N. Cournoyea, *Address at the Health Transfer Ceremony*, Yellowknife, August 25, 1988, p. 4.

38   See Hon. J. Epp, op. cit. p. 6.

39   See Government of the Northwest Territories, *Institutional Structures, GNWT Health System*, Yellowknife: GNWT, July 6, 1987, pp. 7–8.

40   N. Cournoyea, op. cit. p. 4.

41   See Hon. Jake Epp, op. cit. p. 5.

42   See Government of the Northwest Territories, *Main Estimates, 1989/90*, Yellowknife: GNWT, 1989, p. 14–04.

43   Ibid. p. 15–02.

5 The Impact of Devolution on Health Services in the Baffin Region, NWT: A Case Study

John D. O'Neil

Introduction

Since their introduction in the 1950s and 60s, government administered health services in the Northwest Territories have been distinctly colonial in character.[1] The aboriginal population had previously relied during times of sickness and distress on local practitioners — shamans, medicine men, herbalists and midwives — but now became increasingly dependent on non-native professional nurses and doctors working for the federal government. Typical of other federal bureaucracies, most decisions about northern health problems or issues were made at senior administrative levels, far removed from northern community interests. Colonial attitudes permeated the system, from policy decisions which fostered cultural assimilation and dependence on southern medical institutions, to patient care which ignored individual preferences and cultural concerns.[2] One example of this colonial approach to providing medical services was the imposition of an obstetric system which required all women to give birth in southern hospitals, separated from family and community.[3] Another example was the lack of attention given to language differences in the clinical setting, which often resulted in loss of patient rights.[4]

This is not to say that technically, the medical care provided was not of high quality and comparable to that received throughout Canada. Given the immense communication and transportation problems associated with the Arctic climate and geography, the federal system was reasonably successful in ensuring that southern standards for patient access to medical care were provided to northern communities. Although nurse-practitioners rather than physicians provided the first point of contact with the medical system for most northerners, many independent evaluations of this system concluded that the basic medical care provided was nearly equal to physician services in southern Canada.[5,6] An elaborate and expensive support system of flying doctors, travelling consultants, and air ambulance services ensured that few people suffered from the *technical* quality of services available. During the 1950s and '60s when tuberculosis and other infectious diseases were prevalent in the North, there is little doubt that the federal system had a significant impact on improving the health status of northern people.[7]

By the mid-1970s however, changes began to occur that eventually left the federal medical system behind, ineffective in meeting new health challenges, and increasingly the target of frustration and anger for northern residents. Northern political institutions began to mature and northern people exercised increasing local control over many sectors of community life such as housing, education, commerce, and municipal services.[8] Settlement populations grew, and improved transportation and communication facilities contributed to opportunities for expansion of community facilities and service infrastructures. Increasing numbers of native people received the necessary education and training to meet the requirements for local occupations including professional positions such as teachers, town managers and social workers.[9]

Health care however, remained singularly independent of this trend towards local control, particularly at the community level. Attempts by the federal government to establish community health committees or para-professional occupations were superficial and rarely successful.[10] By the early 1980s the growing level of dissatisfaction among clients of health services contributed to morale problems and high turnover rates among professional staff. Many community nurses felt unappreciated by their clients and unsupported by their supervisors (and probably unfairly criticized by academics). In some communities, confrontations between residents and health service administrators were characterized by anger and frustration.[11] Most observers argued that fundamental changes were required in the structure of health service delivery, and concluded that territorial authority over the system was an essential first step towards implementing change.[12]

The issue of self-determination in health care is more than a political or administrative issue however. The quality of the relationship between providers and clients of health services can have profound implications on several dimensions of personal well-being. The fundamental premise of the contemporary approach to health promotion is that individuals must have confidence in their ability to influence their life circumstances if environmental or lifestyle changes are required for improved health.[13] Of critical importance to achieving this confidence is a relationship with health care providers characterized by trust and mutual respect — a relationship which is difficult or impossible in a colonial system where all authority resides with the health professional, and decisions about patient treatment are made paternalistically.[14] If individuals are alienated from their own illness experience, empowerment necessary for effective health promotion is impossible.

However, changing the colonial medical relationship is a fragile and complex process. The rhetoric on health promotion and empowerment often assumes that superficial institutional changes are all that is required to motivate individuals to take greater responsibility for their own well-being. In the North, the creation of Community Health Committees (CHCs) by the federal government is a good example of this attitude. CHCs had only advisory status but were expected to provide for community input into health policy and planning. In most northern communities, health committees have been politically ineffective.[15]

It is precisely for these reasons that Inuit Tapirisat passed a resolution at their annual general assembly in Coppermine in 1980 requesting that responsibility for health services be transferred to the territorial government and ultimately to the Inuit themselves. This resolution was particularly significant because it came in the context of sensitive discussions concerning the relationship of devolution to the land claims and aboriginal self-government proposals. Aboriginal political organizations were generally resistant to the concept of devolution because of the potential impact it might have on aboriginal efforts for self-determination. Although the territorial government in Yellowknife was "closer" to the people, in the late 1970s it was still considered a "foreign" government by aboriginal political organizations. From the aboriginal perspective, devolution threatened to strengthen the Yellowknife government at the possible long-term expense of aboriginal political organizations.[16]

Inuit political representatives were aware, however, of the depth of resentment and frustration towards the federal health system that existed at the community level. Representatives from the various regional Inuit associations expressed these concerns at the Coppermine assembly and the resolution was carried. Other regional organizations such as the newly formed Baffin Regional Council (BRC) also supported the transfer of authority for health services and entered into direct negotiation with the federal government to bring about this transfer. In 1982, operating authority for the Baffin Regional Hospital was transferred to the territorial government and this authority was delegated to the Baffin Hospital Board (BHB). In 1986, operating authority for all Baffin health services (including all nursing stations and health personnel in addition to the hospital) was transferred to the Baffin Regional Health Board (BRHB) which was an expanded version of the hospital board. In 1988, all federal health care services and administration of non-insured health care services were transferred to the territorial government and five regional health boards were established to administer this responsibility.

This paper will describe the Baffin transfer in detail and assess the extent to which the devolution of health services in the Baffin region has resulted in the decolonization of the health service system. As described above, the rationale for devolving health services was to achieve a system in which local residents assume greater responsibility for the health services provided and the health status of the population.

The central question being asked in this case study is whether devolution has made the health care system more accountable to the people served, and if so, what changes have occured or are occurring in the development of community health programs and the relationship between providers and clients.

Devolution of health services will be examined in terms of changes in the various relationships identified in Figure 1 below. The primary set of relationships is among government, health care workers and patients (or clients). Within this larger framework there are secondary relationships that may also be affected. As authority and resources for any given service are transferred from one level of government to another, relations between the federal, territorial and regional and local governments will be affected. Within the health care worker corner of the triangle, the respective interests of medicine, nursing and ancillary health workers (e.g. community health representatives, native midwives, mental health counsellors, etc.) will be affected. Finally, the client community itself is structured by interests associated with class, ethnicity and gender. The question posed here is how does devolution affect these different relationships and how do these changes affect the practical questions of quality of health services and improvements in health status?

Methodology

This paper is a case study of the Baffin region's experience with health services over the period 1981-1988. Field work for the study was conducted in the fall and winter of 1988-89. As such, it is both retrospective and subjective. I made no attempt to quantify the impacts of devolution on either health status or people's understandings of the process. This decision was made after preliminary discussions with people in the region where it became obvious that insufficient time had elapsed to measure quantitative changes in these areas. The more important issue that emerged was whether the process of devolving health services was meeting the expectations of the various interested parties; a question best answered through open-ended, unstructured interviews.

Figure 1
Health Service Relationships
Affected by Devolution

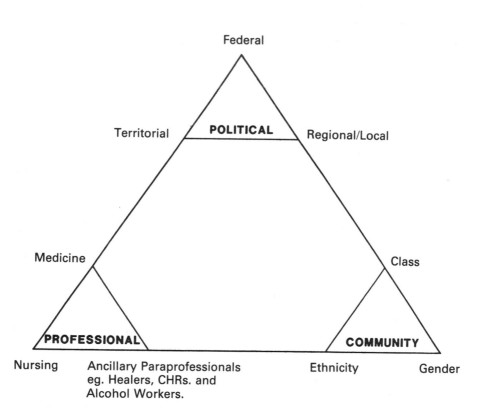

To this end, I interviewed senior officials in the Medical Services Branch of Health and Welfare Canada, and the GNWT Department of Health in Yellowknife, Edmonton and Ottawa. I attended BRHB meetings and interviewed board trustees and administrative staff. Finally, I visited three Baffin communities and conducted key informant interviews with a variety of people with interests in health such as mayors, hamlet councillors and administrators, social workers, medical interpreters, nurses, physicians, Inuit traditional healers, members of alcohol and mental health committees, and other members of the communities identified by the hamlet councils.

The process of identifying respondents utilized the technique of snowball sampling. Initial discussions with hamlet administrative personnel identified key individuals in each community known to have active interests in the health field. "Interest" was defined as including everything from providing a service either historically or presently, involvement in administrative planning, or having chronic health problems requiring frequent contact with the health care system. Each individual identified was also asked to suggest others who fit these parameters until the "sample" was saturated (i.e, no further persons were identified). Interviews with local residents were conducted with the assistance of a research assistant/interpreter who also assisted in identifying potential respondents.

Interviews were open-ended but followed a proto-typical structure. Respondents were first asked to describe their personal involvement in health care and comment on the extent to which they are presently able to perform or receive relevant services. Respondents were then asked to comment on health care historically and to identify strengths and weaknesses of previous systems. Questions next addressed respondent awareness of recent (devolution-related) changes in the structure of health services and visible changes at the community level. Finally, respondents were asked to predict the future direction of health services in the context of community and regional development. Respondents were encouraged to illustrate their comments with case examples wherever possible. When case examples were mentioned which involved other community members, other respondents were also asked to comment on a relevant case. All interviews were tape-recorded, transcribed and analysed for thematic content and details of case examples.

Devolution of Health Services in the Baffin Region

The Baffin region was a testing ground for both the federal government and the GNWT. When the case was made to the federal government for the broad transfer of health resources to the GNWT, the Baffin region was cited as a success story.[17] Ironically however, the devolution process in the Baffin region did not begin on the initiative of the federal or territorial levels of government, neither of whom felt ready for the transfer in the late 1970s. The primary initiative came from organizations in the Baffin region such as the Regional Council and the Regional Inuit Association. In 1980, the Baffin Regional Council (BRC) began to lobby the Medical Services Branch of Health and Welfare Canada for the direct transfer of health services for that region. This initiative was supported by the Baffin Regional Inuit Association (BRIA) and its parent organization, Inuit Tapirisat of Canada (ITC). This support was somewhat surprising, since the national aboriginal organizations were generally opposed to devolution in principle, arguing that transfer of power to the territorial government threatened the land claims and self-government objectives. However, ITC representatives recognized that politics had to give way to resolving some of the pressing health policy and program concerns inherent in a colonial medical system. This appeal for greater local control over health care was given formal status at the ITC annual general assembly in Coppermine in October, 1980 where a motion was passed requesting the transfer of federal health services to territorial jurisdiction.

The federal response was surprisingly quick. In 1981, the Baffin Hospital Board (BHB) was formed. A steering committee was struck with federal, territorial, regional and ITC representatives. At the time there were other hospital boards operating under the jurisdiction of the GNWT in Yellowknife, Fort Smith and Hay River. These boards, however, did not have regional or "political" representation and consisted essentially of prominent members of the local community appointed by the Commissioner.[18]

Prior to the creation of the BHB, the Baffin Regional Council and ITC insisted that the board provide broad Inuit representation including Baffin communities, regional government and aboriginal organizations. As a result, the initial Baffin Hospital Board had representation from the BRC and the BRIA, as well as representation from some of the Baffin communities. It was also initially chaired by the Regional Director who was the senior regional government official responsible to the government in Yellowknife.

The first hospital board consisted of eleven members — seven Inuit and four non-Inuit — appointed as follows:

GNWT (2)	- Regional Director (Chair) Deputy Minister (Health)
BRC (3)	- Executive Director Two Mayors
MSB (1)	- Zone Director
BRIA (1)	- Board Member
Frobisher Bay (1)	- Prominent Citizen
Members at large (3)	- Chairpersons of Health Committees from: - Frobisher Bay - Hall Beach - Arctic Bay

The GNWT insisted however that board members be appointed by the Commissioner rather than elected by the local communities. Regional organizations were asked to put forward a list of names, and hamlet councils were also asked to submit a list of names. These lists usually included the chairpersons of the local health committee (if operational), and all community appointments to the board were initially chairpersons of these committees. Although ITC was represented on the steering committee, it was not represented on the BHB.

Subsequent to the creation of the hospital board, two new administrative structures were created in 1982. The first was responsible for hospital services and patient transportation and reported to the Baffin Hospital Board and ultimately to GNWT through the Territorial Hospital Insurance Services Board. The other was a downsized version of the MSB Baffin Zone office with jurisdiction over community health facilities. Several administrators came over from Medical Services Branch to the BHB, while others came from other territorial departments or were recruited directly from the South.

As a result, for several years, there were two health service administrative structures in Iqaluit (Frobisher Bay) which operated relatively independently. Extensive communication provided for patient co-ordination, but the administrative staff of the Baffin Hospital Board remembers the period as somewhat difficult and tense.

Since the BHB administrative structure was established as a pilot project, subject to external evaluation, members and staff felt vulnerable to MSB scrutiny. Medical Services staff apparently had expressed little confidence in the ability of the board to manage the hospital successfully and were resistant to further transfers of health services. Indeed, most informants indicated to me that the primary resistance to the transfer of health services in general has come from health professionals in the region, and community nursing staff in particular.

In 1983, a steering committee was established to evaluate the hospital transfer and determine whether further transfer should occur. The steering committee consisted of the Medical Services Regional Director from Yellowknife, the Assistant Deputy Minister of Health from GNWT, and representation from the BHB and ITC. This process was again somewhat unique because community-based representation was a structured part of the steering committee in addition to professional administrators. Baffin representatives on the steering committee also played a prominent role in negotiations. Although the process was essentially a government-to-government (federal to territorial) transfer, regional interests received primary attention. The prominence of regional representation was due partially to the lack of resources in the GNWT Department of Health. Prior to devolution, the GNWT Department of Health was one of the smaller departments in government. It lacked both manpower and resources in comparison to Medical Services Branch representatives from the federal government. As a result, all participants agreed that in retrospect, representatives from the Baffin Regional Council and the Baffin Hospital Board were responsible for protecting much of the territorial interests in the negotiation process.

In 1986, the Baffin Regional Health Board (BRHB) was established to replace the BHB. The new board was expanded to 15 members and was now responsible for both the hospital in Iqaluit and nursing stations (or health centres) throughout the region. The new administrative structure reflected this dual responsibility, with both administrative arms reporting to a central executive office. Board representation was also redefined to emphasize community input. Thirteen members represented all Baffin communities; one of these representatives was appointed because he also represented the Baffin Regional Inuit Association. The remaining two board seats were filled by representatives from the territorial government (Regional Director) and the Baffin Regional Council (Executive Director). Although the Regional Director was initially appointed to the chair, the board elected a community representative as chair in 1989.

Formal Properties of the NWT Health Care System and the Baffin Regional Health Board

Subsequent to the full transfer of health services from the federal to the territorial government in April 1988, the new health care system was structured as illustrated in Figure 2. The Baffin case varies significantly from this general structure in that many of the services now provided by other government departments to health boards in other regions (i.e. personnel, finance, public works) are provided directly by the BRHB. Implications of this important structural difference will be discussed later in this chapter.

Responsibilities of the various participants are briefly outlined in Figure 3 below. Again the principal difference in the

Baffin region initially was the absence of a contracting relationship with other government service departments and the addition of administrative staff reporting to the health board through the CEO in areas such as finance and personnel.

According to the NWT Health Board Trustee's Handbook, each participant in the system has the following responsibilities and obligations:[19]

1. *Minister of Health (and elected government)*

   - decides total annual health care expenditures
   - determines major priorities of the health care system
   - initiates health care legislation
   - appoints health board trustees
   - has final authority on health care matters

2. *Territorial Health Board*

   - is appointed by government
   - maintains, funds and monitors all health boards
   - ensures that NWT residents have an equal opportunity to participate in the management and development of their health care delivery system

3. *Department of Health*

   - assists Minister of Health with overall control of health care delivery system
   - sets health care standards
   - evaluates and regulates key participant performance
   - administers health insurance benefits
   - provides consulting services to health boards

4. *Regional Health Boards*

   - define broad policies for their health services in relation to community needs and internal organization
   - protect patients including appointing all health care staff, providing secure and safe facilities, and ensuring patient reputation and rights to privacy
   - set long range health service development plans

Figure 2
NWT Health Care Structure

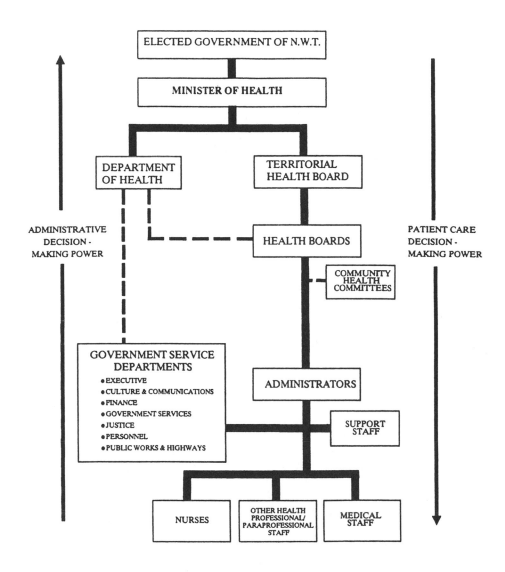

Source: NWT Health Board Trustee's Handbook

Figure 3
Roles of Health System Participants

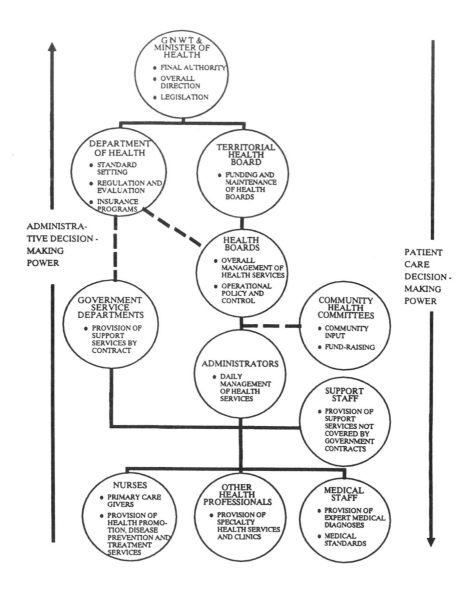

Source: NWT Health Board Trustee's Handbook

- develop and adopt suitable by-laws and organizational plans
- appoint administrators and evaluate performance
- appoint, evaluate and ensure professional standards for medical and nursing staff
- obtain and administer adequate financing of health services
- provide adequate personnel, equipment and facilities to meet needs for patient care, health education and health research
- ensure that public is fully informed on health service activities and needs
- monitor and evaluate performance of board members

5. *Health Trustees*

- are appointed by the territorial government (Minister of Health)
- are responsible and trusted members of the community who represent patient interests in the operation of the health care delivery system
- ensure that health services meet needs of community and are of the highest reasonable quality for the lowest reasonable cost
- assumes liability of owners of health service facilities and custodians of sick and injured people
- represents authority for the conduct and operation of all activities within the health region or health facility

6. *Community Health Committees*

- are advisory groups on health issues
- are associated with local government
- work with local health staff to promote community health
- undertake fund-raising activities for health related projects
- have *no* financial or health management authority
- nominate members to the health board

Significant among these responsibilities are the ambiguities concerning authority in policy development and planning. While health boards are expected to "define broad policies in relation to community needs," the Department of Health "sets health care standards" and "evaluates and regulates the performance" of the health board. The THB and ultimately the Minister maintain final authority over the actions of the health boards. Both the trustee and regional boards are expected to "represent, protect and provide for" the health needs of people in each region, but all of these responsibilities are subject to "monitoring, evaluation, and maintenance" by various government structures and offices in Yellowknife. These structural ambiguities are a prime source of tension between the regions and Yellowknife as will be described below.

Structural Analysis of Changes in Health Services

In order to fully understand the effects of the devolution of health services, it is necessary to view recent changes against the pre-devolution colonial structure. Figure 4 graphically represents the lines of accountability in the old federal system. For example, the thick line between "H & W" and "MSB" indicates a direct hierarchical and accountable relationship of one government branch to its ministry. In contrast, the dotted line between "MSB" and "Health Services" indicates a consultative, horizontal relationship where neither structure is responsible or accountable to the other.

This diagram depicts the health care delivery system as a separate administrative system headquartered in Ottawa, operating through a hierarchical structure into the nursing stations at the community level. Attached to the nursing station was an advisory health committee that was generally initiated at the request of the nurses. Members were elected but most communities have had uneven success in motivating people to serve on the health committee and/or to attend meetings.

The health care structure was also quite separate in either a hierarchical or horizontal sense from any of the aboriginal interests represented by ITC, the Regional Inuit Associations, or community organizations. The relationship between health services and the GNWT was also limited to an advisory/consultative basis.

The current post-devolution structure is a system in transition, despite the formal model described earlier in this paper. The system is transitional because the political system in the North is still transitional with various competing aboriginal, territorial, regional and community interests, as other chapters in this volume will attest.[20] Figure 5 illustrates clearly that not only has devolution resulted in significant change in the hierarchical structure of the system, but that horizontal connections between different interests and agencies have begun to emerge. The Baffin Regional Health Board is situated in an emerging structure that involves aboriginal representation through the Baffin Regional Inuit Association, and regional representation through the Baffin Regional Council. Indeed the emergence of cross-representation at the regional level is a most significant product of the devolution of health services. Nonetheless, these regional links are largely consultative with hierarchical authority centred in Yellowknife. The ambiguity inherent in the current structure is best exemplified by the "trustees" position in the system.

Trustees are nominated by their local hamlet councils (and/or health committees) and appointed by the Minister of Health in Yellowknife. As previously discussed, some provide dual representation for both their communities and other regional organizations. Trustees have consultative relationships with both the community health centre and the health committees in their home communities. They are also accountable in a general sense to the Department of Health in the GNWT.

The other service agencies that operate at the community and regional level are accountable to the territorial government through the Regional Director, (a territorial government senior administrator) who also sits on the health board. The Regional Director's office administers other government programs such as social services, and these programs all have local offices in the

Figure 4
Pre-Devolution Health Service Structure

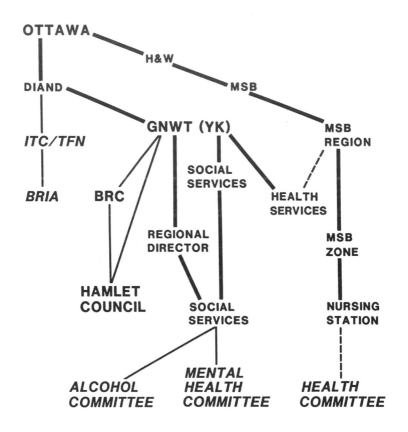

Indicate decreasing levels of structural authority, accountability, responsibility and vertical hierarchy.

＊ "Services" are distinct government departments.

a) **ELECTED GOVERNMENT**

b) **BUREAUCRACY**

c) ***ELECTED ORGANIZATION**

d) *GOVERNMENT APPOINTED*

communities that are independent of either the health centre or the municipal governments.

One of the objectives of health service devolution was the development of consultative links between the various health-related committees at the community level. These committees have emerged over the past 10 years in all northern communities and have varying degrees of responsibility for issues such as mental health, alcohol education, youth justice, etc. In the past, committees have been formed in communities essentially to reflect territorial or federal government departments and they have been brought into existence in response to programs initiated in either Ottawa or Yellowknife. By and large, they have operated independently, although the same people may sit on several committees. However, prior to devolution there was generally a lack of consultation among committees, and there was little attempt to develop a comprehensive community health and social service policy. The growth in number of these committees has also contributed to difficulties in finding qualified and motivated people to serve.

Although consultative relationships are beginning to emerge, these relationships often still depend on individual associations in communities. There is as yet no structure that encourages collaboration, nor is there comprehensive policy that promotes collaboration on health programs which overlap in all these different areas.

In some Baffin communities the Alcohol Education Committees and/or Mental Health Committees are quite active. Some have little trouble achieving quorums for meetings and some have mental health counsellors on staff who have histories of involvement in traditional counselling. There are people for example, who had been active in the churches and are called upon by various people at different times to assist in family conflicts such as mediating between parents and teenagers. However, in one community many of the members of the Alcohol Education Committee did not know who was on the Mental Health Committee, or more importantly, who their local representative was on the Baffin Regional Health Board. In another

Figure 5
Current Transitional Health Service Structure

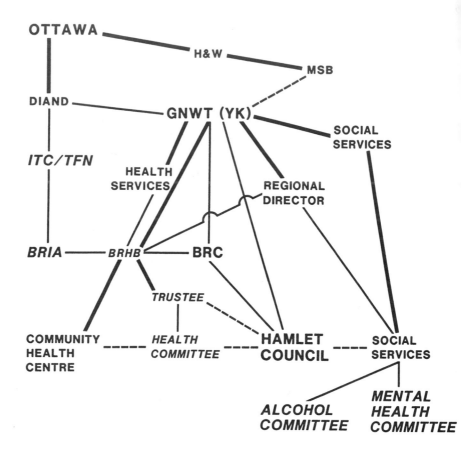

Indicate decreasing levels
of structural authority,
accountability, responsibility
and vertical hierarchy.

* "Services" are distinct
government departments.

a) **ELECTED GOVERNMEN'**

b) BUREAUCRACY

c) *ELECTED ORGANIZATIO*

d) *GOVERNMENT APPOINTED*

community, however, the Mental Health Committee was meeting regularly with both the local nurse in charge of the health centre, and with the board trustee. Trustees in both communities indicated that some effort was being made now to increase consultation and they were attempting to consolidate some of this effort at the community level.

Although some structured changes are evident as a result of devolution, perhaps the more important question is: What future changes are likely to occur as the political structure of the Territories continues to evolve? These questions are particularly important because of several controversial policies adopted by the territorial government which have sparked debate at the regional and community level, and because the settlement of the land claims and the territorial division issue are likely to radically restructure the organizational framework for the provision of services. Based on discussions with key informants at both the regional and territorial levels, I propose the following scenarios as a description of the current tension over future directions for health services between territorial and regional levels of government.

It would appear that the territorial and regional levels of government hold different visions of what the end point of devolution may be for the region. More importantly, these different visions will have distinct health service structures at the regional and community level. The tension between these visions is absorbing much of the creative energies of both levels of government.

The *territorial scenario* is based on the concept of prime public authority being vested in municipal government structures such as hamlet or band councils. This policy is best expressed in a document entitled "Directions for the 1990s " which was released in 1988 by the House Leader.[21]

> As prime public bodies, community governments will gradually absorb most NWT sponsored community bodies and territorial government programs transferred to the local level. A new policy will identify community governments as a primary tar-

get for transfer of government programs. While there may be an exception such as housing programs because of the joint ownership of public housing with Canada Mortgage and Housing Corporation, our government will work towards integrating even housing programs with the prime public body concept. Emphasizing community government requires a review of regional structures including both the governments regional administrative structures and the role of regional bodies, such as regional and tribal councils and divisional boards of educations, health boards etc.

This statement expresses a clear vision that ultimately the primary government-to-government relationship will be between the government of the NWT in Yellowknife and the hamlet council or equivalent municipal structures. Informants further indicated that there is an interest in creating a health commission in each community which would be a sub-committee of the hamlet council. The health commission would consolidate all the various health committee activities at the community level, such as the Alcohol Committee, Mental Health Committee, Health Committee, etc.

The eventual relationship of the health centre to the hamlet council has not been clearly defined as yet. However, the spirit of the prime public authority concept suggests that the municipal government structure should ultimately have direct control over all community services including health care. This vision has obvious implications for the future relationship of health professionals to communities and most importantly, to the long-term development of regional health boards. The most likely scenario would be for the regional boards to become administrative co-ordinators for services requiring regional administration (e.g. visiting medical specialists).

The *regional scenario* is based on the attainment of political goals that are not necessarily compatible with devolution. These goals are the division of the NWT into Nunavut and Denendeh and the successful settlement of land claims based on the principle of self-government. In this scenario, regional governments would become the primary focal point of government services. The Nunavut government would serve a co-ordinating role for regional governments and act as a central agent in relations with the federal government. Accordingly, GNWT is now considered an interim government which would essentially disappear, except possibly to co-ordinate relations with a western Arctic government. The regional level of government would be an amalgam of the BRC and the BRIA which would emerge as a product of the creation of Nunavut and the settlement of the land claim.

The BRHB would continue to operate as a substructure of the Baffin Regional Government and would likely remain responsible for operating community health centres. A similar consolidation of local committee activities into a community health commission might also occur, but the relationship of this commission to the local health centre would likely remain consultative.

The difference between these two scenarios is obvious. The GNWT scenario essentially suggests that the regional structures between Yellowknife and the communities. Alternatively the regional scenario suggests that the regional government would become the primary administrative structure with various fiscal and administrative relationships with local communities, Nunavut, Ottawa, and possibly Yellowknife.

The AIDS Issue

Some of the tensions created by these alternative models for political development and service delivery are illustrated by an issue that gained public attention in the Baffin region in November 1989. In 1987, the Department of Health in Yellowknife hired a family life educator to initiate and run an AIDS educational program throughout the NWT. The family life educator met with the various regional boards and community committees, in order to improve their understanding of AIDS; its transmission, prevention and treatment, and related ethical questions. Issues of individual rights versus public protection were discussed.

These discussions implied that there are standard procedures for responding to communicable diseases such as AIDS in Canada. However, although there are Canadian laws regarding the reporting of communicable disease, AIDS has created some disagreement as to whether these laws are universally applicable.[22] In southern Canada and elsewhere in the world, there is considerable debate as to whether individuals who test positive for HIV should be identified in order to protect those with whom they have contact (particularly if they are sexually active); or whether doctor-patient confidentiality and the rights of the individual to privacy override the public concern. In cross-cultural situations, these ethical issues are even more complicated because of different moral standards and ideas about individual versus collective responsibilities and rights.

The native response to this issue has generally been more concerned with collective rather than individual rights than the mainstream Canadian response. Some native leaders have stated that they would prefer that people with AIDS or HIV are identified in their communities. They argue that prevention of further spread may require infected individuals to be ostracized and isolated.[23] In the North, some Inuit leaders have argued that the best strategy for preventing the spread of AIDS is to ensure that everyone is aware of infected individuals in their community. These issues had been discussed by the members of the Baffin Regional Health Board with the (non-Inuit) family life educator from Yellowknife and not resolved.

It is important to recognize however that the Inuit response to this issue is inherently cultural. There are certain principles of Inuit justice and social organization that apply. Traditionally, if someone was dangerous to the community, they were either ostracized or executed. Although individuality was valued, the well-being of the individual depended on the well-being of the group. On the other hand, sick or disabled individuals were cared for and supported by the entire community as long as resources were available. In interviews, Inuit leaders told me that this last principle — public support of the sick — is an equally important component of their position on identifying AIDS patients as are concerns about protecting the public.

Figure 6
Territorial Scenario for Health Service Structure

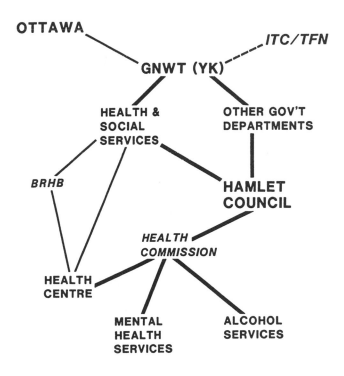

Indicate decreasing levels
of structural authority,
accountability, responsibility
and vertical hierarchy.

✳ "Services" are distinct
government departments.

a) **ELECTED GOVERNMENT**
b) **BUREAUCRACY**
c) *ELECTED ORGANIZATION*
d) *GOVERNMENT APPOINTED*

Figure 7
Regional Scenario for Health Service Structure

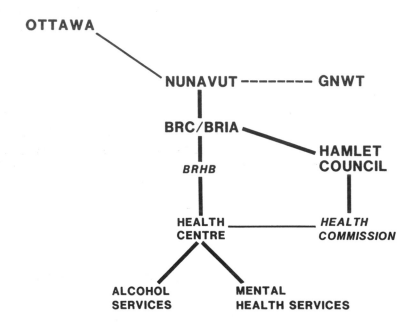

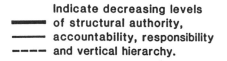

▬▬▬ Indicate decreasing levels of structural authority, ―――― accountability, responsibility ‐‐‐‐ and vertical hierarchy.	a) **ELECTED GOVERNMENT**
	b) **BUREAUCRACY**
	c) *ELECTED ORGANIZATION*
✳ "Services" are distinct government departments.	d) *GOVERNMENT APPOINTED*

At the BRHB meeting in November 1989, the Chief-of-Staff for the hospital reported to the board that there was one case of AIDS and two cases of HIV infection in the Baffin region.

The Health Board discussed this issue in depth throughout the day. There was an awareness of the potential threat to Inuit survival that this disease entailed, given epidemiological predictions that for every detected case there may be 15 to 30 undetected cases. The administrative staff argued that the names of these three cases had to be kept confidential. The medical officer did not report the names but the Inuit representatives on the board wanted the names of cases, and their home communities. The administrative staff, who are generally non-Inuit health professionals and professional health administrators, argued that this did not meet Federal or territorial ethical guidelines for the reporting of communicable diseases such as AIDS.

The outcome of this discussion was that the board decided to publicize the names of the communities where these cases were, but they would protect the confidentiality of the individuals. They argued that people in the smaller Baffin communities might continue to assume they were not at risk; that is to assume that such risks were only present in larger centres like Iqaluit.

The medical officer asked for the opportunity to report the cases to the territorial epidemiologist before the board took action. It is important to note that under the previous colonial medical services system, this type of consultation between a health professional and a group of community leaders would never have occurred. There would not have been public discussion of an important or controversial issue at the community or regional level prior to reporting to Ottawa.

The board waited half a day and then sent a FAX message to the Department of Health in Yellowknife outlining their proposed plan of action. They indicated they were going to provide the media with the names of communities where there were infected individuals. They also indicated they would like to initiate an AIDS educational program in the identified communities. They immediately received a FAX message back from Yellowknife stating that the issue was being discussed at the ministerial level, and to please wait. Two days went by and there was no further word back from Yellowknife. In the interim, the board meeting had ended and trustees had returned to their communities.

The next thing the board members heard was an official press release on CBC radio that there were now cases of HIV infection and AIDS in the NWT. There was no explicit reference made to the number or location of the cases. The board then held a conference call and decided to take action without the approval of the Minister of Health and announce over CBC radio that there were three cases in the Baffin. They decided not to specify the communities. The Minister of Health in Yellowknife then made a public announcement that the Baffin Regional Health Board would be disciplined for breaking confidentiality.

This case study is significant on several levels. First of all, it illustrates the problematic nature of culture in relation to policy development. While there is a consensus in the North that health policy and services must be culturally appropriate, this principle has not been subjected to critical analysis. Moral and ethical standards vary significantly from culture to culture, and native approaches to issues such as confidentiality, informed consent and public protection may be contrary to standards acceptable to the Canadian majority (which are also culturally determined). If a primary goal of devolution and the transfer of health services to local control is to facilitate the development of a health care system sensitive to local cultural expression and needs, planners must be willing to consider some cultural principles with which they disagree.

Secondly, this case illustrates the ambiguity which exists in determining who has authority in setting health policy. While the formal statements on the respective responsibilities and obligations of the various participants in the health care system indicate that final responsibility rests with the Minister, they also state explicitly that Regional Health Boards are responsible for setting "broad policies on health services in response to community needs."[24] This is exactly what the BRHB attempted to do in the AIDS case and their authority was overridden by the Minister. While the Minister's decision may have been the correct one, the Board's experience of the incident reaffirmed a growing perception that Regional Boards are administrative in function only.

Provider-Client Relationships

As I mentioned previously, there was a common perception among all those involved in the devolution negotiations that the primary resistance to devolution or transfer came from health professionals and particularly community nurses. Health professionals indicated that many of their colleagues felt that it was too early for devolution to go ahead, that GNWT did not have the administrative expertise, or that there was insufficient job security. Those involved in the negotiations also suggested that many nurses were concerned about rumours circulating in the Baffin region that community health centres were going to be administered by the hamlet councils. Community nurses particularly were worried that community control might be the emergent structure and expressed these concerns to their supervisors. Their supervisors then argued to the negotiators that if devolution went ahead, nurses would resign en masse.

There were attempts by the negotiating committee to alleviate these concerns. Teams of administrators representing all levels of government travelled to each of the communities and tried to apprise people of the progress of negotiations but there were other processes that conspired against clarification of the issue. First of all, it seemed the GNWT was not entirely clear that in fact the rumours of hamlet authority might not be true; the implications of the "prime public authority" policy for hamlet control of health services had not been fully resolved. Various statements from aboriginal organizations added to the confusion because they also appeared to support the principle of community control. Finally, because the negotiations were occurring *in camera*, due to confidential discussions over the magnitude of resources to be transferred, the negotiating team could not report accurately on the negotiations to the public.

The negotiations had to be complete before the final structure could be reported.

As described in the introduction, relations between health care providers and clients in northern communities are a bellwether for the overall quality of community health services which ultimately affect the health status of the population. This is not to say that local nurses or doctors are entirely responsible for local health conditions; as many scholars have demonstrated, the health of a population is more determined by socio-economic and environmental conditions than by medical care.[25] However, if broader health promotion efforts are to succeed in small northern communities, local health professionals must be able to work co-operatively and effectively with other community organizations and individuals. If the health care provider-client relationship is strained or embattled, not only is clinical medical care compromised, but the larger issue of community health is unlikely to be addressed effectively.[26]

Relations between health care providers and clients at the community level are sometimes solely the result of personalities. Nurses and physicians who are sensitive and open to cross-cultural differences, and who have a high degree of commitment to community development issues, generally find it easier to develop productive relationships with their client communities. Similarly, health care providers with rigid ideas about their role in the community, or who have limited interests in community life generally, find it difficult to establish satisfactory relationships with either individual clients or the community at large. However, these individual personality quirks and orientations are enhanced or inhibited by the social and political characteristics of the health care delivery system.

Under the federal system, the colonial structure tended to have the opposite effect; sensitive and committed individuals were frustrated and inhibited in their efforts while those with a more "colonial" approach (i.e. oriented to remaining aloof and detached from community life) were rewarded.[27]

Since one of the primary goals of the devolution of health services was to alter the structure of health services so that provider-client relations improved, it is important to examine this issue in some detail.

Relations between health care providers and clients in post-devolution communities can be examined through an analysis of the trustee's role in resolving conflicts. Prior to devolution, conflicts between community nurses or doctors and community residents often festered until a major crisis occurred. Since a significant dimension of the trustee's role at the community level is to mediate relations between providers and clients, several trustees were interviewed to determine changes in this area.

Case Study #1

In one Baffin community, the trustee initiated monthly, Friday afternoon visits to the health centre which were intended to provide an opportunity for the trustee and nurses to discuss public health concerns and patient satisfaction. The trustee indicated that these meetings served two purposes. First of all, they helped the trustee to collect information on community concerns to report to the monthly regional board meetings. They also provided an informal mechanism to enact his liaison function and resolve any tensions between nurses and patients before they escalated into major conflicts. In the trustee's words, "I wanted to just drop in, have some coffee, get to know the nurses and talk about things. If I don't know the nurses, how can I help with health problems in the community?"

Unfortunately, this particular Baffin community had experienced considerable turnover in nursing staff and some of the new staff members had not received adequate briefing on administrative relationships and the particular role of the health trustee. Some of the nurses expressed concern to me that they were unclear as to the extent of the trustee's authority over the health centre.

The nurses indicated that they felt community control over the health centre was inappropriate in terms of local administrative competence and issues of professional autonomy. These attitudes translated into a general suspicion of the trustee's motives; some nurses indicated they understood the trustee's job was to observe the nurses' activities and report on their competence to the regional Health Board.

As a result, the trustee's attempts to maintain monthly meetings with the health centre staff were rebuffed. The trustee often found the nurses "too busy" or openly hostile during these meetings. In a later interview, the trustee indicated that he thought the nurses were unwilling to discuss health issues with him because he was native. He perceived that racial prejudice was a major impediment to the effective functioning of a health trustee.

Case Study #2

In a second Baffin community, the senior nurse had instituted a program of producing monthly reports on all local health programs, including information on patient utilization and nurse staffing. These reports were addressed to the local health trustee and copied to the Regional Health Board, the Baffin Regional Council and the Department of Health. Prior to regional Board meetings, the trustee met with the senior nurse to discuss issues relevant to the meeting.

The trustee had also been asked by health centre staff to mediate several cases where conflicts had occurred between nurses and patients. One such case involved an elderly person who died while in a Montreal hospital. The death occurred on a Friday and a staff nurse in the community health centre was notified immediately.

In this community, the normal procedure for notifying a family of a death is for the nurse to contact one of the local ministers. Various elders and church officials constitute an informal committee who then accompany the nurse to the home of the bereaved family. In this instance, the nurse attempted to contact a local minister on Friday afternoon but was unsuccessful. The nurse then waited through the weekend before attempting to contact the minister again, and the family was not notified until Monday afternoon.

Needless to say, both the family and religious leaders were outraged and immediately contacted the trustee. The hamlet council was also contacted and requests were made to have the guilty nurse banished from the community. The trustee arranged a meeting between the family, the religious leaders and nurses at the health centre. A formal apology was made to the family and the trustee explained that since the nurse was otherwise competent and new nurses were hard to recruit, perhaps the apology was sufficient. The family accepted the mediation and no further action was taken. The trustee expressed the view that prior to devolution (and the creation of the trustee position), a conflict of this nature might have resulted in severe and long-term damage to the relationship between the health centre staff and the community.

Examples from these two communities indicate that on the one hand, the transitional period may be responsible for some confusion and ambiguity concerning the trustee's role and responsibilities. On the other hand, new nurse-community relationships are emerging where the trustee has a clear role to play as a mediator and patient advocate. The trustee may also be contributing to the emergence of increasing consultation among the various committees responsible for the well-being of the community.

Conclusion

This case study has examined the devolution of health services in the Baffin region, NWT. It has looked particularly at the way in which devolution is perceived at the regional and territorial level; and at the impact that devolution has had on the development of the Regional Health Board and the emergence of a health service system appropriate to the needs of Inuit in Baffin communities. It appears that community-based consultation for policy and program development is limited, largely because regional and territorial approaches to the devolution process are in conflict. This conflict is absorbing much of the creative energy of both levels of government and as a result, little community-based development has occurred.

There is a further irony in the fact that devolution of health services has had only minimal impact at the community level in the Baffin region. Most community spokespersons indicated strong support for the role of regional structures in the administration of services for their communities. They also expressed support for the "prime public authority" concept and the consolidation of health-related committees into a sub-committee of the hamlet council. There is however, significant variation in the extent to which they feel comfortable with assuming an administrative role over health centres.

Government officials in Yellowknife indicated that the primary rationale for focussing political development on the community was to ensure that a sufficient share of increasingly scarce financial resources would be available for community-initiated programs. There was concern that further growth of regional structures would siphon off resources intended for community development. Indeed, a prime concern of community health-related committees is for stable funding to provide support staff and facilities.

Regional spokespersons felt that without strong regional support, community initiatives would be misunderstood and poorly supported by a government in Yellowknife too far removed from community concerns. The controversy surrounding the reporting of AIDS cases was cited as an example of Yellowknife failing to understand the cultural basis of community-initiated health policy.

Clearly, if devolution is to achieve its goal of contributing to the emergence of accountable, community-based health policy and programs in the North, these conflicts in political perspectives must be resolved. Both regional and territorial levels of health administration must commit the resources necessary to foster consultation among various community groups already involved in the health promotion process. Failure to do so will result in loss of confidence at the community level with the result that the various community health "experts" such as the trustees, mental health and alcohol counsellors, committee members etc., may once again move off into different developmental areas. Under the older federal system, a significant number of people received training and experience in health (e.g. medical interpreters, community health representatives , lay dispensers, etc.), but few of these people continue to be involved in community health development. The likelihood that this process may continue to occur despite the creation of a supposedly community-based system is the greatest health service challenge facing all levels of government in the North today.

Acknowledgements:

The author acknowledges the support of the Donner Foundation, the Social Science and Humanities Research Council and the National Health Research and Development Program, Health and Welfare Canada. He is also grateful to the members and staff of the Baffin Regional Health Board; the Department of Health, GNWT; and Medical Services Branch, Health and Welfare Canada. Jackie Linklater provided valuable clerical assistance.

NOTES

1   See John D. O'Neil, "The Politics of Health in the Fourth World: A Northern Canadian Example," *Human Organization*, 45(2):119-128, 1986.

2   See John D. O'Neil, "Self-Determination, Medical Ideology and Health Services in Inuit Communities," in G. Dacks and K. Coates, (eds.), *Northern Communities: The Prospects for Empowerment*, Edmonton: Boreal Institute for Northern Studies, pp. 33-51, 1988.

3   See John D. O'Neil and Patricia A. Kaufert, "The Politics of Obstetric Care: The Inuit Experience," in W.P. Handwerker (ed.), *Births and Power: Social Change and the Politics of Reproduction*, Boulder, Colorado: Westview Press, pp. 53-69, 1990.

4   See John D. O'Neil, "The Cultural and Political Context of Patient Dissatisfaction in Cross-Cultural Clinical Encounters: A Canadian Inuit Study," *Medical Anthropology Quarterly*, 3(4):325-343, 1989.

5   A.P. Ruderman and G.R. Weller, *Report of a Study of Inuit Health and Health Services in the Keewatin Zone of the Northwest Territories*, 1980.

6   Gordon A. Friesen Limited, *Mackenzie River Area Health Services Study*, 1975.

7   Lyall M. Black, "Health Care Delivery in the Arctic," *Nordic Council for Arctic Medical Research Report Series*, 33, 1981.

8   See Gurston Dacks, *A Choice of Futures: Politics in the Canadian North*, Toronto: Metheun, 1981.

9   See Frances Abele, "Gathering Strength," *Komatik Series, Number 1*, Arctic Institute of North America, 1989.

10 John D. O'Neil, "Democratization of Health Services in Northern Canada," *Northern Review*, Issue #5 (Summer, 1990).

11 John D. O'Neil, "The Cultural and Political Context of Patient Dissatisfaction in Cross-Cultural Clinical Encounters: A Canadian Inuit Study," *Medical Anthropology Quarterly*, 3(4):325-343, 1989.

12 See for example, A.P. Ruderman and G.R. Weller, op. cit; G.A. Friesen Ltd., op. cit; and John O'Neil, "The Politics of Health in the Fourth World: A Northern Canadian Example," *Human Organization*, 45(2):119-128, 1986.

13   Hon. Jake Epp, *Achieving Health for All: A Framework for Health Promotion*, Ottawa: Ministry of Supply and Services, 1986.

14   See John D. O'Neil, "Self-Determination....," pp. 33-51, 1988.

15   John D. O'Neil, "Democratization of Health Services..."

16   Letter from Inuit Tapirisat of Canada to Hon. David Crombie, Minister of Northern Affairs, November 21, 1985.

17   Lynn Elkin Hall and Associates, *A Recommended Outline of the Devolution Process Based on Baffin Health Phase II and Forestry Transfers*, Yellowknife; Lynn Elkin Hall and Associates, December 1986.

18   NWT Health Board, *Trustee's Handbook, Volume I*, Yellowknife: Department of Health, no date.

19   NWT Health Board, op. cit.

20   See G. Dacks, "Devolution and Political Development in the Canadian North"; G. Weller, "The Devolution of Health Care to Canada's North"; and K. Graham, "Implementing the Policy to Devolve: Learning by Doing" in this volume.

21   Government of the Northwest Territories, *Directions for the 1990s*, Yellowknife, 1988.

22   See for example, Albert R. Jonsen, Molly Cooke and Barbara A. Koenig. "AIDS and Ethics," *Issues in Science and Technology*, II(2):56-65, 1986; and Dennis Altman, *AIDS and the New Puritanism*, London: Pluto Press, 1986.

23   News/North, May 8, 1987, "ITC Wants More Info on AIDS Victims".

24   NWT Health Board, op. cit.

25   See Kue Young, *Health Care and Cultural Change: The Indian Experience in The Central Subarctic*, Toronto: University of Toronto Press, 1988.

26   See John D. O'Neil, "The Cultural and Political Context of Patient Dissatisfaction in Cross-Cultural Clinical Encounters: A Canadian Inuit Study," *Medical Anthropology Quarterly*, 3(4):325-343, 1989.

27   See John D. O'Neil, "The Politics of Health in the Fourth World: A Northern Canadian Example," *Human Organization*, 45(2):119-128, 1986.

6   Devolution and Local Government

Katherine A. Graham

This chapter explores the interplay between the initiative in the 1980s to devolve powers and program responsibilities from the federal government to the Northwest Territories and Yukon Territory and the evolution of local government in those two places. In this context, local government is taken to mean those community bodies with legislative and administrative responsibilities established under the *Municipal Act* in the Yukon Territory or under one of the various pieces of local government legislation within the purview of the Minister of Municipal and Community Affairs in the NWT.[1]

It is important to understand that any examination of the evolution of settlement, hamlet and village councils necessarily involves examination of their relationship to other community-based organizations (such as local education societies and Hunters and Trappers Associations [HTAs] in the NWT) and to the various regional organizations.

The Northwest Territories has experienced the most significant growth of regional organizations which have implications for life in communities. The Government of the Northwest Territories (GNWT) is decentralized into five administrative regions. Each regional office is headed by a regional director, who has the status of a deputy minister. All important operational departments of the GNWT, such as Transportation, Education, Public Works, Social Services and Municipal and Community Affairs, also have staff working at the regional office level. These are territorial public servants who ultimately report to the headquarters of their respective departments, located in the territorial capital, Yellowknife.

The first regional council of municipalities emerged in the Baffin in 1977. Perhaps because it operates in the region that is the farthest from Yellowknife and because it attempts to represent the interests of communities with relatively homogeneous Inuit populations, the Baffin Regional Council (BRC) has a solid base of support in the communities it represents. It has evolved into a relatively sophisticated operation which has the involvement of territorial politicians representing ridings in the region. It also has the ear of territorial public servants, particularly those serving in the Baffin.

Since the establishment of the BRC, five other regional councils, representing the interests of municipalities and, in some cases, Indian bands have been created under the *Regional and Tribal Councils Act*, which was passed by the legislature of the Northwest Territories in 1983. In addition, one tribal council, representing exclusively the interests of Indian bands in the Dogrib region, has been incorporated under the Act.[2] These regional and tribal councils enjoy varying degrees of interest and support among the communities they serve.

The GNWT has adopted the practice of having community representation on regional boards that it has established to oversee the operation of particular services. The two major instances of this practice are in the fields of health and education. The GNWT established regional health boards after it assumed responsibility for health care from the federal government in 1988. Regional school boards have also been established. Membership on regional health and school boards is by community, although local representatives are not necessarily members of municipal councils.

Regional structures are much less developed in the Yukon, although there is some decentralization of territorial government operations. The federal government has been something of a force for regional devolution in both Territories, through its involvement in the establishment of regional planning commissions.

Analysis of the relationship between local government development and devolution is further complicated by the importance of local governing institutions to the final settlement of outstanding aboriginal claims in the two territories and by the debates and initiatives through which aboriginal peoples might achieve self-government. Although it may be suggested that devolution is not a direct catalyst for the settlement of claims or the realization of self-government, the fact that devolution is proceeding both opens avenues and closes options in these other two forums. This may be particularly true in the area of local government development. The waters are muddy indeed.

The research undertaken for this particular study bears out one of its fundamental assumptions: the two Territories are very different.

The question of the implications of devolution for local government has been much more directly joined in the NWT than in the Yukon. In the Yukon, claims issues have dominated the governmental and public agenda to the point where local government development is now being pursued in the context of finalizing the Council for Yukon Indians (CYI) aboriginal claim.[3] In the NWT, the territorial government has aggressively pursued the establishment of local governments outside the claims process which meet the needs of that Territory's aboriginal and non-aboriginal people. A statement by the Commissioner of the Northwest Territories in his opening address to the territorial assembly in February 1989 emphasizes this perspective on government development:

> At this time our government believes that Northern self government is well advanced within the existing public government system in the Northwest Territories and that many of the goals of aboriginal self government are already in place or potentially in place within the present system.[4]

As a result, this chapter will place relatively more emphasis on analysis of the situation in the NWT. However, an effort will be made to develop thematic comparisons and contrasts.

Subsequent sections of the chapter attempt to link some of the contemporary issues about the implications of devolution for local government to some of the historical concerns about the role and nature of local government in the two Territories.

History suggests a set of ongoing concerns about the evolution of local government. Some of these have emerged from the communities themselves; others have been raised by the territorial or federal governments. In some instances, there has been a unified perspective concerning what issues are important and how they should be dealt with. In other cases, debates are ongoing. In any event, it is important to understand the extent to which the current process of devolution is dealing with these long-standing issues, the extent to which it may be aggravating conflicts over them and the extent to which it is putting new questions about the role and structure of local government in the two Territories on the table.

There are a number of assumptions and important principles underlying this review. Most important is the assumption that local government is important to people in the two Territories and that the desire for efficacious and sensitive local government arrangements will persist. In both the NWT and the Yukon, the geographic isolation of northern communities from each other and from major regional centres or the territorial capital provides a *raison d'etre* for the provision of services at the local level. However, the cultural differences between smaller communities and capitals in Canada's North give rise to a need for systems of local governance which are particularly sensitive to local needs. Accordingly, it is important to distinguish between *decentralization* of territorial government operations and *devolution*, which is the empowerment of local communities to make real choices. This chapter focusses on the potential which federal-territorial transfers raises for further devolution of powers and responsibilities to local governments, and more generally for the development of patterns of local governance that are effective and sensitive to local needs and interests.

This study is based on a review of relevant primary and secondary documents and key informant interviews with community leaders, territorial and federal government officials, and other interested parties. Regrettably, it was impossible to undertake field interviews across the two Territories. Field interviews were conducted in a number of communities in the Baffin and in the Mackenzie area of the NWT.[5]

198

The Baffin was selected because it has been at the forefront of many of the debates about the development of local government and regional structures in the NWT. When one thinks of the role of local government, it is useful to think of it as a vehicle for the articulation of community interests, as well as a provider of local services. The recent regional land use planning exercise which has taken place in the Lancaster Sound area made the Baffin communities selected for field work all the more attractive for exploration of communities' advocacy role in the contemporary political environment.

Whereas communities in the Baffin are overwhelmingly inhabited by Inuit, the majority of the population of most Mackenzie area communities is Dene or Métis. The co-existence of these aboriginal peoples with a non-aboriginal population has presented an ongoing challenge to develop a system of local government which meets the interests of both. In the western part of the NWT, this challenge is exacerbated by the existence of Dene bands, which have their own local governing structure. Government at the local band level is inextricably linked to the federal government, under the terms of the *Indian Act.* Therefore, one objective of field work in the Mackenzie was to find out how communities are dealing with systems of local government that are evolving in these two contexts: municipal government, which is evolving through the territorial, local relationship, and aboriginal self-government at the band level, which is evolving through the federal-aboriginal relationship in the context of discussing the Dene-Métis aboriginal claim and in the context of the relationship between individual Dene bands and the federal government.

Local Government in the NWT: Agent of Service or Cornerstone of Democracy?

The history of local government in the NWT has been both interesting and tortuous since the federal government responded to the recommendations of the Carrothers Commission and set up the first resident territorial government in Yellowknife in 1967. That same Commission recommended that a Department of Local Government be set up as part of the newly restructured

GNWT. This recommendation was also accepted with the result that the Department of Local Government (now known as the Department of Municipal and Community Affairs [MACA]) was one of the original GNWT departments established in 1967.[6]

Carrothers saw the establishment of local governments in communities as an important vehicle for helping northerners to become accustomed to public institutions of government and democratic life. In his view, this was especially crucial for the Inuit, whose social organization did not include explicitly political institutions.

The early local government system in the post-1967 period was largely based on southern models and assumptions. Perhaps one of the most important assumptions behind the system was that communities would "advance" from settlement to hamlet to the point where they would achieve the status of a village, town or city and, hence, be capable of governing with an independent property tax base. Electoral procedures were modelled on southern practices. The emphasis was on local governments providing traditional "hard services" such as water supply, sewage and garbage removal, and road maintenance. Community involvement in other areas, which were often of equal or greater concern locally, was sought through the establishment of a wide range of local committees. These committees were established by other departments of the GNWT to enable territorial-community liaison on such matters as social services, recreation, alcohol and drug abuse, housing, hunting and trapping, and so on. These committees were an efficient vehicle for line departments of the GNWT to use in informing communities of their programs and for inducing community participation in programs and other initiatives largely developed in Yellowknife or in GNWT regional offices. In communities with Dene bands, such as Fort Good Hope and Fort McPherson, there was the added complexity of bands dealing with the federal government to get funding and services for their membership. This fragmentation of the structure of local governance again replicated southern models. This time, however, the approach taken duplicated one which is seen as problematic, even in the southern Canadian context. Critics of the Canadian local government system have long decried the fragmentation of local responsibilities among municipal councils, school boards and numerous other local agencies, boards and commissions.[7]

The result of this situation was considerable frustration on the part of communities. The system of government put in place was imposed and alien, especially since it ignored traditional forms of leadership selection and decision making. The range of services assigned to local councils did not necessarily represent local priorities. Despite various attempts at training local people, the predominant pattern was for the administrative and service arms of local governments to be run by people imported from outside, who often stayed very briefly. Finally, the plethora of committees established outside the orbit of local councils fragmented the communities' ability to deal with issues in a holistic way and placed severe demands on the limited number of people able to serve at the local level in individual communities. Burnout was common.[8]

The overall result was that a decade after its establishment, the system of local government in the NWT was in need of reform. The level of frustration in some communities with the structure of local government, electoral rules and council operating procedures imposed by Yellowknife made the system useful as a teacher of democratic values primarily to the extent that it prompted communities to express their displeasure. In terms of local government's role in the provision of services, the lack of real power for local councils to determine service priorities and the lack of indigenous financial and human capacity combined to alienate people further from the system.

Despite these frustrations with the explicit form of the system of local government in the NWT, the notion that local government might indeed be important had gained wide currency by the latter part of the 1970s. Various aboriginal organizations, including the Inuit Tapirisat of Canada (ITC) were talking about the importance of local organizations in the context of their claims negotiations.[9] Their view was ultimately acknowledged by the federal government in 1982, when it reversed its long-standing position that governmental arrangements could not be discussed in the context of claims negotiation. In that year, local government structures were formally included in the range of subjects eligible for negotiation at the claims table.[10]

C.M. Drury, in his role as special representative of the Prime Minister on constitutional development in the Northwest Territories, also focussed on the continuing need for vital local governments in the NWT. Although his report focussed on many of the specific problems with the existing system referred to above,[11] it is equally important for its strong statement about the democratic value of local government and its particular importance in the NWT derived from the cultural diversity of the territory and the isolation of communities from each other. His recommendations to strengthen the system of local government were based on the premise that "the community will continue to be the base for social and political organization...the acquisition of political and administrative experience at the local level provides the greatest potential for influencing the process and structures of government at the territorial level."[12]

Responses to the perceived problems with the local government system, including the difficulties associated with establishing a strong inter-governmental relationship between local governments and the GNWT, emerged from a variety of sources beginning in this same period. These initiatives can be summarized as follows.

Legislation Review

The GNWT undertook a prolonged revision of its municipal legislation which culminated in passage of revisions to its existing legislation and in the creation of a new *Charter Communities Act* (1987). This act attempts to deal with the long-standing difficulty of establishing a legitimate public government at the local level where a community co-exists with an Indian band or other aboriginal organization that itself has strong political roots. It allows each community to create its own charter, thereby designing a structure of local government that meets the specific needs of all its residents.

Emergence of the Prime Public Authority Concept

The Department of Local Government came to recognize the problem of fragmentation of responsibility at the local level coincident with the work of Drury. Its first response came with publication in 1978 of the document *Department of Local Government - Direction For the 1980s*, which recommended that local governments be strengthened so as to establish clearly the prime importance of local councils in providing the overall direction for the well-being of the community. This marked the beginning of extensive proselytizing about the merits of what came to be called the "prime public authority" (PPA) concept by various territorial politicians, some mayors and officials of MACA. The importance of this concept to current discussions about the development of local government in the context of devolution will be dealt with subsequently.

At the local level, one community, Fort Good Hope, had amalgamated the operation of its band and municipal council by 1980. This initiative influenced the development of policies at the territorial level related to both PPA and the charter communities legislation.

Efforts to Enhance Administrative, Technical and Political Capacity at the Local Level

Concern about the low level of indigenous administrative and technical capacity in communities has emanated from the communities themselves and from the territorial government. Communities have generally sought to have local government jobs filled by local people. However, the barriers to education and relevant training and experience for people in many NWT communities tended to close doors for employment with municipal or band councils. The GNWT has also been concerned about this situation, as well as about the uneven quality of local government personnel recruited from outside. To meet these problems, courses in municipal administration and other technical operations have been developed through MACA and Arctic College. At the political level, the Northwest Territories Associa-

203

tion of Municipalities (NWTAM) has sought more involvement by municipal leaders from smaller communities through the creation of a special caucus for them. This is intended to help leaders of small communities lobby the GNWT about concerns particular to small communities.

Despite these efforts, there are still ongoing concerns about the capacity of local governments to do all that they might want to do or be called on to do, given the limitations of human and financial resources in communities. The GNWT does attempt local training but the low impact of this training and high turnover of political and staff personnel in communities remain problems. Financial resources continue to be tight for the territorial government and for communities themselves, since local revenues are minimal and costs are high.

The Emergence of Regional Councils

As indicated earlier, there has been an initiative by local councils in many parts of the NWT to establish regional organizations to co-ordinate planning and present a stronger voice to the GNWT. The grass-roots nature of this initiative was strongest in the Baffin. In some other areas, the impetus to establish a regional council came more from regional officials of the GNWT. Nonetheless, regionalism is seen as assisting realization of local government needs and interests. The view of regionalism from GNWT headquarters has been much less sanguine. As will be seen, the view from the capital on the extent to which regional governance should be promoted also has implications for the devolution of powers from the territorial to the local level.

Changes in Federal Claims Policy on Negotiating Local Government Arrangements

The 1982 reversal of federal claims policy to permit the discussion of governmental arrangements in the forum of claims negotiations opened up the possibility for discussion of local government development in this important arena. The new policy was reflected in the Agreement-in-Principle for the Dene/ Métis claim concluded between the federal government and the

Dene/Métis in 1988. This Agreement provides for the discussion of aboriginal self-government as part of the final claim agreement.

All of these initiatives had long gestation periods. In the context of the contemporary period of federal-territorial devolution, the process of resolving some of the policy dilemmas they pose has not been completed. However, these contextual factors are important for the review of the specific relationship of federal-territorial devolution in the 1980s to the development of local government in the NWT.

Local Government Devolution in Contemporary Times: Rhetoric Versus Reality

Devolution and Community Government

Since the publication in 1981 of the discussion paper "Our Land Our Future,"[13] the Government of the Northwest Territories has sustained a policy stance on the development of local government that holds much promise. However, this promise is yet to be realized. From the perspective of community leaders with whom the evolution of community government was discussed, the gap between rhetoric and reality in territorial policy is largely related to the hesitation by territorial public servants to devolve further powers to community governments. This perception is important. But the entire policy environment is more complex and is important for consideration.

"Our Land Our Future" set out the important themes which would be reiterated in subsequent policy pronouncements by the GNWT on devolution and local government, made during the most recent round of devolution from the federal government to the territorial level.

Among the policies and principles it set out were: "devolution to community governments...the passing of political authority and responsibility and resources for the delivery of government programs and services from the GNWT to community governments." Devolution was to facilitate community choice in how programs were to be devolved and expand the role of community councils in the delivery of services and programs.

These central themes were strengthened in 1983 with the publication of the discussion paper entitled "A Design For Devolution of Additional Powers and Responsibilities to Communities."[14] It reiterated the GNWT's policy to enhance the role of community government but noted the difficulties in doing so because of legislative confusion over the powers of local councils and the erosion of the authority and accountability of local councils by the establishment of special purpose bodies. The principle and concept of prime public authority was proposed as a possible solution to this problem, especially in hamlets.

The policy of the current Government of the Northwest Territories regarding local government development in the context of devolution was first articulated in 1987, when the government released its keynote policy statement "Direction for the 1990s." This wide-ranging document dealt with the overall priorities of the government of the day. The government indicated it would pursue the PPA concept and develop a framework for public government in the NWT which "includes measures to speed the federal devolution process; clarifies the relationship between our government, regional bodies and community governments; simplifies the form and operation of government; and strengthens ministerial government while enhancing local control."[15] The government announced that it would be introducing a new policy which would target community governments for program and service transfers and that it would also conduct a thorough review of regional bodies and structures.

The prospect that devolution from the federal government to the GNWT would result in an enhanced role for community governments was further reinforced with the announcement of the GNWT policy and directives on devolution, also in 1987. One of the principles for devolution set out in that document is that: "After powers have been transferred, the GNWT may exercise its authorities in any manner deemed to be in the best interests of the people of the NWT including delegation to regional or community bodies."[16] It should be noted that the terminology used was "may," not "would." However, the fact that this principle was articulated in such a specific manner, combined with the creation of the regional boards of health as part of the transfer of responsibility for health to the GNWT, gives one a sense that federal-territorial devolution could well result in the further transfer of power to the local or regional level.

Despite these earlier signs, the reality of the GNWT's stance on devolution to the local level is of a different nature. This reality is evidenced in the rather tortuous course of implementing the much vaunted concepts of prime public authority and charter community.

As indicated above, the need for more coherent community government in the NWT has been under discussion since Drury's work in the late 1970s. As early as 1981, the GNWT promulgated the concept of prime public authority whereby community councils would become the main focus of local decision making. For a variety of reasons, the PPA concept never really advanced beyond the talking stage. The specifics of how it might be implemented remained vague throughout the 1980s. In 1989, the Inuvialuit Regional Corporation (IRC) received funding from MACA to research implementing the concepts in the western Arctic. At the conclusion of its work, the head of the IRC project indicated to the territorial assembly that communities in that region were supportive of the concept, but still lacked sufficient understanding of how it would work. Communities were also seeking training to help them implement PPA.[17]

There were widely different levels of awareness and understanding about the concept in the three Baffin communities where field interviews were conducted. Only one mayor had actually reviewed any government documents pertaining to PPA; another had been involved in discussions of the concept, while the third mayor had only the vaguest notion of the idea as a formal proposal of the GNWT. Despite the rather minimal information among Baffin community leaders about the territorial initiative, there was general support for the idea of giving communities more power and for concentrating that power in local councils. In the Baffin, councils are already seen to be the main public body in the community, for the most part. One concern, however, is that some GNWT departments provide higher honorariums for participation in other local committees that relate to their specific interests in social services, education, alcohol and drug abuse or whatever. This is seen as a drain of the best local talent away from participation on council.

In the Mackenzie communities where interviews were conducted, there was also a general awareness of the PPA concept among local politicians and administrators. In addition, the charter community concept had achieved some prominence. However, the consensus was that the territorial government had not really refined its thinking on PPA sufficiently to permit communities to embrace the idea. Instead, these communities were pursuing an independent course in the development of their community governments. One community, Fort Good Hope continues to work on its concept of a community assembly as the democratic base for community government which includes Dene band council members as well as other members of the community. The other community, Fort McPherson, has adopted the practice of having regular meetings of the municipal council, band council and Métis local. These meetings, plus membership on the municipal council of band leaders and Métis, are seen as facilitating communication and complementing action. There has been an acknowledged division of responsibilities in Fort McPherson: the municipal council looks after hard services, such as water, sewage disposal and the community centre facility, while the band council and Métis local look after the social and cultural needs of their memberships.

The two western communities exhibited differing levels of interest in receiving more power from the GNWT. One was very assertive on its interest; the other took more of a "wait and see if it's important to us and if we can do it" approach. This view was partly conditioned by their perception of what community leaders in a third western community had experienced in taking on numerous additional powers for service delivery from the GNWT. Their sense was that municipal government in that third community did not have the skilled resources to manage properly. As a result, it had floundered under the weight of its new role.

Municipal councils in both western communities had recently assumed new responsibilities from the GNWT. In each case, the community had to enlist political support for the transfer at the ministerial level to move a reluctant bureaucracy to make the transfer. Neither community had received all of the responsibilities it sought. None of the responsibilities trans-ferred relates to the functions devolved from the federal government to the GNWT in the 1980s.

There are a number of reasons why the move to implement the GNWT's policies advocating prime public authority, devolu-tion to communities and the establishment of charter commu-nities has been so tangled and difficult.

At the territorial cabinet level, the concepts of prime public authority and charter community have been subject to different interpretations and different emphases. One view has been that PPA is merely a housekeeping move to consolidate with local councils those responsibilities currently distributed among a variety of community committees. Another interpretation is that PPA enables communities to receive additional powers, and thereby take greater control over matters affecting them. An important question which the GNWT has yet to resolve, if the proponents of this second view are to be satisfied, is whether or not a community seeking charter community status can receive any responsibilities other than those it might be delegated as a municipality by the Minister of Municipal and Community Affairs.

These debates at the political level about the evolution of local government in the NWT reflect the tension that under-standably emerges from the political development of the territo-rial government. One major impetus for political development at the territorial level in the 1980s has, of course, been devolution. Coincident with the devolution of new responsibilities from the federal government to the GNWT has been the move by the territorial cabinet to emphasize the concept of ministerial au-thority.[18] This suggests a conception of government ministers, by those currently in office, as having increased responsibilities and powers. Despite hints to the contrary, devolution of powers and responsibilities from the federal government to the GNWT may not, at least in the short run, result in a parallel shift to greater power or influence to the local level. Cabinet as a whole and individual ministers may seek to consolidate their newly won power. This may be a short term move to assure orderly transition or it may be a stance which lasts at least until the implications of aboriginal claims settlement for the territorial government become clearer.

At the bureaucratic level within the GNWT, there have also been ongoing disputes about what the concept of prime public authority means and about its implementation. In part these have reflected differences of opinion in Cabinet. However, the desire of individual departments to retain their independent links with communities seems particularly strong. Departments such as Renewable Resources, Social Services and Education have consistently fended off efforts by MACA to encourage PPA. At the community level, this has resulted in increased administrative burden. The local administrators interviewed spoke of difficulties as municipalities cope with different accounting and reporting requirements by various territorial departments that channel money through the community for use by specialized committees.

The political and bureaucratic conflicts over the devolution of powers to local governments and the consolidation of powers at the local council level are mirrored in the GNWT Transfer Policy, which was promulgated in February 1988.[19] This policy and its accompanying directives set out the current principles and procedures for the devolution of authority and responsibility for government programs to community governments and for the delegation of more limited responsibilities to community governments or other organizations. This document is interesting for a number of reasons. Although it provides for devolution only to community governments, MACA is not explicitly given a role in the devolution planning process. Line ministries are to take the lead role. Municipal and Community Affairs has an overall mandate to husband the development of community government and ensure probity and effectiveness at the local level. This suggests that, at the very least, it should be acknowledged as an important player in the transfer process. In the case of delegation (which is seen as a more limited form of transfer) the prospect exists that other bodies may take on the role of territorial agent in the delivery of programs or services. This has definite ramifications for promulgation and implementation of the prime public authority concept. Finally, the terms and conditions of delegation are very rigorous in establishing a client-like relationship between any local or regional body receiving new responsibilities and the GNWT itself. In the case of delegation, employees will remain members of the GNWT public service. The GNWT is intended to provide support services to organizations taking on specific responsibilities.

There are a number of other factors inhibiting the influence of federal-territorial devolution on the development of local government, at least over the short term.

Within the immediate orbit of the GNWT and communities, there are the problems of bringing about any change in an area as large as the NWT where regions are so vast and communities so isolated. In addition, both communities themselves and the GNWT have concerns about the capacity of local governments to take on additional responsibilities. The Department of Municipal and Community Affairs is frequently preoccupied with providing basic support services to community government. The continuing need to develop sound administrative and service capacity at the local level is, understandably, a priority both for MACA and individual communities. The idea of overhauling the responsibilities of community councils in the face of ongoing administrative challenges may seem a little daunting, despite the benefits that may result.

At a somewhat higher level is the conundrum posed by the two outstanding aboriginal claims between the Dene/Métis and Inuit of the central and eastern Arctic and the federal government.

As indicated earlier, discussions about local government were recognized by the federal government as a legitimate part of the negotiations between itself and the Tungavik Federation of Nunavut (TFN), representing the Inuit of the central and eastern Arctic. The local and regional management boards for wildlife and other purposes which are part of the TFN *Agreement-in-Principle* have relevance for the possible role of local government institutions.

The Dene/Métis have concluded — but not ratified — a *Comprehensive Land Claim Agreement* with the federal government. They tried to realize their vision of a local or regional system of self-governance in the context of the negotiations which led to this agreement. Indeed, the negotiation of governmental arrangements through the claim was a high priority among community leaders in the Mackenzie communities visited as part of this study. In the end, they received half a loaf. The agreement does not establish any institutions of self-government. Rather, it only commits the governments and the Dene/Métis to negotiate self-government outside the context of the claim, which will already have been settled before the negotiations begin. At the same time, the Dene/Métis can take some comfort from the provision of the agreement that these "...negotiations will address the Dene/Métis desire to have self-government exercised as close to the community level as is reasonably possible."[20]

Although they were not full partners at the bargaining table, the GNWT has responded to the Dene/Métis interest in negotiating self-government by removing responsibility for prime public authority's implementation from MACA and centralizing further work on the development of community government in the Aboriginal Rights and Constitutional Development Secretariat. The Secretariat's work on community government is to be carried out jointly with the Dene/Métis. This initiative, undertaken in 1989, even before the claims agreement was reached, adds another complexity to the evolution of public local government in the NWT. The time necessary to ratify both settlements and to work out their implications for local government seems likely to retard further territorial-local devolution.

Emerging from all of this is a sense that a gap exists between the aspirations of community governments to enhance their ability to take on additional responsibilities and service their residents according to local needs and priorities and the willingness or ability of the GNWT to devolve additional powers to the local level. Very real concerns about local capacity have yet to be allayed. These concerns can, however, be dealt with through training and other forms of assistance. The real question is whether the political and bureaucratic leadership of the GNWT will ever find an appropriate time to undertake further devolution. Aside from their reading of community capacity, a positive decision at the territorial level to devolve will require a sense by territorial leaders that the political timing is appropriate and that the GNWT will retain a role. The government's apparent concern with this latter issue is suggested by its recent initiatives regarding regional councils.

Devolution and Regional Councils

Following the establishment of the Baffin Regional Council, the GNWT acquiesced to the establishment of other regional and tribal councils. Their creation was accompanied by varying levels of enthusiasm in different GNWT regional offices and among communities themselves. Territorial policy statements of the period viewed these councils as the agents of communities in their respective regions.[21] By 1987, seven regional and tribal councils existed under the auspices of the *Regional and Tribal Councils Act* and were receiving funding from the GNWT.

Most recent indications are that the GNWT is about to significantly reduce its support for regional councils and may attempt to eliminate them altogether. The committee to review regional councils, which was established in 1987, presented its report to the Executive Council of the GNWT early in 1988. One of its key recommendations was to strengthen the powers and responsibilities of regional and tribal councils in program and service delivery. After some delay, the Executive Council released the report and responded to it in November 1988. The report was rejected *in toto*. The Government Leader, Dennis Patterson, indicated that the report did not meet all of its terms of reference, that it failed to consider the recent establishment of regional boards for education and health and that it ignored the government's policy on prime public authority. Equally important, the Executive Council's critique indicated that the review committee had failed to consider the evolution of ministerial authority in the NWT.[22] This suggests a conception of government ministers, by those currently in office, as having increased responsibilities and powers. At least in part, this may be associated with the current devolution of powers from the federal to the territorial government.

In at least one region, the Baffin, communities are critical and suspicious of the government's rejection of the review committee's report. The BRC is seen as having developed into a good vehicle for individual communities to work together. Elimination of territorial funding for the BRC and other regional and tribal councils may well result in a reassertion of the role of GNWT regional offices, with the result that the system of territorial-local relations in the regions of the NWT would return to the relationship between GNWT regional offices and communities in the 1970s.

As indicated above, a system of regional boards was adopted for health care following the transfer of that responsibility from the federal government to the GNWT. Given the nature of the health care system, the existence of regional hospitals to supplement local health care services and so on, the establishment of a regional organization with representation from the local level may be an appropriate approach. The one concern with establishing a regional body with specific responsibility only for health is that it may suggest a trend to a fragmentation of responsibility at the regional level which mirrors often criticized fragmented structures at the local level. However, the central point is that a regional approach may be the best way to give greater community control over additional responsibilities. As was indicated earlier, that has been the traditional concept of regional councils espoused by the GNWT. Regional councils were to exist to serve the needs of local communities. It is also the perspective local governments have of regional councils, at least in the case of the longest standing regional body, the Baffin Regional Council (BRC). Individual communities may not have the capacity to take on new program responsibilities and so the sharing of resources and joint efforts at problem solving make a certain amount of sense.

Even the newly established regional health boards have expressed disquiet about their status. Their creation was thought to be a signal that local control over health care delivery would be increased. However, the GNWT Transfer Policy, discussed above, was interpreted by the regional boards as tightening the strings of GNWT control.

In recent years, individual ministers have pushed for communities to be given specific new responsibilities in particular cases. However, this review of formal policy statements and analysis of recent GNWT actions in the contemporary period of devolution suggests that there is a gap between rhetoric and reality. Successive territorial councils have espoused the inherent value of local government and embraced the concept of prime public authority as something of a cure-all to the problems of governance at the local level. However laudable the aim of implementing PPA might be, there are some very real questions about the capacity of community government in the NWT to take on additional responsibilities, at least without the assistance of a representative organization at the regional level. The GNWT's reaction to the regional and tribal council review committee's report and its establishment of special purpose regional boards of health following the devolution of health care responsibilities from the federal government suggest that it is reluctant to support the type of multi-purpose regional body needed to develop and sustain community councils with broad-ranging responsibilities. The functional orientation of the GNWT's Transfer Policy further reduces the likelihood that something akin to PPA will be implemented on a wide scale in the near future.

In part, the GNWT's "second thoughts" about further developing local government through devolution are understandable. Reference has already been made to the problems of capacity at the local level. However, equally, if not more important may be a sense among territorial politicians and officials that the territorial government must retain a range of responsibilities for itself, if it is going to sustain itself as the dominant government in the NWT. Merely passing on long-standing or newly received authority and responsibilities to regional or local councils would beg the question: "Why have a territorial government at all?" This is by no means a new question, as anyone familiar with the debates on territorial division well knows. However, the adrenalin that accompanies a process like the current round of devolution makes posing this question now awkward indeed for GNWT politicians and officials.

All this might suggest that the development of local government in the NWT will go on hold until the GNWT assures itself of a legitimate role in the future governance of the NWT. However, there are other influences being felt: aboriginal claims in the NWT and the movement to aboriginal self-government.

It is possible that developments in these other forums will exert pressure to rethink views of regional and tribal councils and to seriously move the development of strong local government forward. Overall, the danger is that a melange of local and regional structures and governing processes will emerge from different quarters and the system of governance at the local and regional level will become a house of cards. Perhaps this risk can be reduced if the GNWT, communities, aboriginal organizations and the federal government go back to first principles and think about the role of local government in the NWT and what is needed to sustain that role. The pressure to do this will most likely come from aboriginal claims and self-government negotiations, not from devolution of powers from the federal government to the GNWT.

Yukon: On the Verge of a New Era

Currently in the Yukon, there are eight incorporated communities, one hamlet and ten unincorporated communities, which receive local services directly from the Yukon Territorial Government (YTG). Unlike the Northwest Territories, local government in the Yukon was not traditionally seen as a major vehicle for political development.[23] However, there have been some modest developments in recent years. The YTG passed a new *Municipal Act* in 1980 which contributed to the incorporation of five municipalities by the mid-1980s and has enabled creation of the Territory's single hamlet, Elsa. In 1987, the YTG passed a *Municipal and Community Infrastructure Grants Act* which brought in a system of block funding to incorporated municipalities for capital projects. The new act also provides for limited block funding for the operation and maintenance of community infrastructure.

Even in the context of these advances, the YTG itself continues to provide extensive advisory services and plays a supervisory role vis-à-vis incorporated municipalities. This is done through the Department of Community Affairs and Transportation Services. A wider range of Yukon departments provide services directly both in incorporated and unincorporated communities.

Overlaid on this system of public local government are the 14 Yukon band councils represented in the Council for Yukon Indians (CYI) claim. Basically, each Yukon band exists in proximity to a municipal centre.

Settlement of the CYI claim has been a priority of both Yukon Indians and the YTG. The importance of the claim to the agenda of the territorial government has resulted in devolution assuming secondary priority.

The 1989 Framework Agreement for the CYI claim has potentially profound implications for the system of public local government in the Yukon. The next step includes negotiation of the powers and structures of band government, as each Yukon band goes through its own review and ratification process to finalize the claim agreement. It appears that some bands want to discuss the immediate implementation of aboriginal self-government for their members. All bands want to ensure that the final agreement provides the potential for them to implement self-government when they think it appropriate.

These negotiations are still continuing. Some individual communities are participating with particular interest. The YTG is also awakening to the need to ensure that there is some logic to the relationship between aboriginal government at the local level and public local government in the Yukon. So far, the YTG has been quite low-key on where it stands specifically on this issue. It may find that a more evident public position is necessary in order to focus the debate on a territory-wide basis.

One area of particular interest in the Yukon context is the recent establishment of a regional land use planning regime. Responsibility for land use management has not been devolved to either of the two northern Territories by the federal government. However, the long debates over the appropriate role for territorial governments in regional land use planning have resulted in the establishment of a regional land use planning commission structure in the Yukon that may be said to represent partial devolution of the federal authority, in the sense that it acknowledges a formal role for the YTG, through the Minister of Renewable Resources.

On October 22, 1987, an agreement on land use planning in the Yukon was finalized between the Government of Canada and the Government of the Yukon. The agreement provides for the establishment of regional land use planning commissions with members to be chosen by the federal government, the YTG and the CYI. Henceforth, any municipal or community plans in the Yukon are to conform to the regional plans that emerge. The first exercise undertaken is in the Greater Kluane region. The Greater Kluane Regional Land Use Commission was established shortly after conclusion of the federal-provincial agreement. The village of Haines Junction is part of the area under study.

The Association of Yukon Communities and the Village of Haines Junction itself objected to the structure of the commission and the powers of its plan, once it was adopted. They argued that affected municipalities should be guaranteed corporate representation on any regional land use planning commission. Furthermore, they objected to the requirement for local government conformity to regional plans, especially since communities have no corporate status in their preparation. To date, the Yukon Territorial Government has attempted to appease these objections with assurances that there will be adequate opportunity for local participation. It does not appear willing to include communities formally in its hard-won regional land use planning process. The CYI Framework Agreement provisions on land use planning guarantee Indian participation in this process. Presumably Yukon Indian participants in the process will be selected by individual Yukon Indian nations, as the agreement does not refer to a pan-Yukon Indian body. However, the agreement does not indicate whether all nations will be represented and whether the Indian members of planning subcommittees examining particular areas of the Yukon will be drawn from adjacent communities. The agreement, of course, is silent on how the non-Indian participants in the planning process will be selected and, in particular, whether and to what extent local interests will be represented.

On other fronts, the YTG officials are looking to the further decentralization of Yukon government operations to communities. They recognize that eventual devolution in areas such as health care and new aspects of resource management will increase the YTG's visibility at the local level and thereby contribute to the YTG decentralization initiative.

It seems that in the Yukon case, devolution from the federal government to the territorial government will promote administrative decentralization, not devolution of authority to local governments. Claims, rather than devolution, will be the engine of change for local government. Negotiation in the claims forum will require the YTG and communities themselves to think in a concerted manner about the future of public local government in the Yukon.

Concluding Observations

The situations in the Yukon and in the NWT are obviously very different. From different roots and in different ways local government has progressed considerably in the two Territories in recent years. However, devolution has not really the engine of local government development in either case.

In the NWT there is a closer interplay between the current process of devolution and the evolution of local government. Ironically, devolution of powers and responsibilities from the federal government to the GNWT may not, at least in the short run, result in a parallel shift of greater power or influence to the local level, despite hints by the GNWT that this might occur.[24] It would seem that the current trend is for the GNWT to guard key aspects of its newly devolved responsibilities at the territorial level. This may represent an attempt by the GNWT to sustain itself as a government with a legitimate role in the face of a variety of pressures for devolution to the regional or local level.

This thesis is advanced in full knowledge of the GNWT's recent (and repeated) embrace of the concept of local councils as the so-called prime public authority at the local level and its passage of the *Charter Communities Act.* While these two initiatives themselves do much to address some of the long-standing concerns about the role of local councils, they are little known or understood at the community level. Accordingly, the short- and medium-term prospects for resolution of some of the outstanding issues related to the development of local government in the NWT are slight, if devolution is regarded as the engine of change.

It may be, however, that other forces — the push for aboriginal self-government and the settlement of claims — will serve as the necessary catalysts for devolution to the local level. Considerable good faith by all parties will be necessary for the positive future development of local government in the NWT. The danger is that the push/pull of federal-territorial devolution, claims and the move to aboriginal self-government will result in governmental gridlock, as individual aboriginal communities, claimant groups and the federal and territorial governments respond to their perceptions of the desire of communities for power by creating structures and putting in place particular initiatives that give at least the appearance of community involvement. This suggests that some of the basic issues of local government development in the NWT — how it will be structured, how councils will be accountable, how community governments will get the administrative, technical and financial capacity to manage their own affairs — will be incapable of being dealt with, despite much rhetoric and some positive will to the contrary. These basic issues must be dealt with if the devolution of any powers and responsibilities to the local level is to succeed.

In contrast, the Yukon government is letting the CYI claim, as it is linked with aboriginal self-government, drive the local government development process. While the issues may be no less thorny, especially as negotiations proceed on a community-by-community basis to establish new forms of community government, YTG proprietorship of specific responsibilities seems to be less well developed. There is some recognition that the YTG will be faced with the question of how to link public government at the local level to aboriginal government; but a strong territorial initiative has yet to emerge. If the coming era in the Yukon is to be characterized by local institutions with a new sense of mission brought on by the settlement of the CYI claim, the Yukon Territorial Government may itself need to take on a special role.

NOTES

1   These are the *Charter Communities Act, Cities, Towns and Villages Act, Hamlets Act and Settlement Act.*

2   As of November 1988, regional and tribal councils recognized under the terms of the GNWT legislation were: The Baffin Regional Council, Deh Cho Regional Council, Keewatin Regional Council, Kitikmeot Regional Council, Shihta Regional Council, South Slave Regional Council and the Dogrib Tribal Council. See *Report of the Regional and Tribal Council Co-ordinating Committee,* (Yellowknife: Legislative Assembly of the Northwest Territories, November 4, 1988).

3   Coates suggests there is considerable irony in this emphasis, given the original artificiality of Yukon communities as the organizing units for Yukon Indians' social, cultural and political lives. See Ken Coates, "Upsetting the Rhythms: The Federal Government and Native Communities in the Yukon Territory, 1945-1973," in Gurston Dacks and Ken Coates (eds.), *Northern Communities: The Prospects for Empowerment,* (Edmonton: Boreal Institute for Northern Studies, 1988), p. 20.

4   Opening Address of Commissioner John H. Parker to the Fourth Session of the Eleventh Assembly, February 8, 1989. Yellowknife, NWT, p. 3.

5   Communities in the Baffin were: Pond Inlet, Arctic Bay, Pangnirtung and Iqaluit. I visited Fort Good Hope and Fort McPherson in the Mackenzie. I would like to express appreciation to all those interviewed for this study for their time and thoughts. I would also like to thank the community of Sachs Harbour, which welcomed me to visit. Unfortunately, I was unavoidably prevented from doing so.

6   Advisory Commission on the Development of the Northwest Territories, A.W.R. Carrothers (Chairman), *Report to the Minister of Northern Affairs and Natural Resources,* (Ottawa: 1966). See also Gurston Dacks, *A Choice of Futures,* (Agincourt: Methuen, 1981) p. 106.

7   See, for example, T.J. Plunkett and G.M. Betts, *The Management of Canadian Urban Government,* (Kingston: Queen's University, 1978), pp. 120-122.

8   For a review of these problems, see Katherine A. Graham, Anne
      B. McAllister and Marsha George, *Local and Regional Govern-
      ment in the Northwest Territories*, (Kingston: Institute of Local
      Government, Queen's University, 1980).

9   Inuit Tapirisat of Canada, *Political Development in Nunavut*,
      (Ottawa: 1979) and *Parnagujuk* (Ottawa: 1980).

10   *News/North*, August 27, 1982, p. A5.

11   C.M. Drury, *Report of the Special Representative on Constitu-
      tional Development in the Northwest Territories*, (Ottawa: Minis-
      ter of Supply and Services Canada, 1980), p. 37.

12   Ibid, p. 42.

13   Minister of Aboriginal Rights and Constitutional Development,
      "Our Land, Our Future: Discussion Paper on Political and
      Constitutional Development in the NWT," (Yellowknife: Govern-
      ment of the Northwest Territories, 1981).

14   Minister of Local Government, "A Design for the Devolution of
      Additional Powers and Responsibilities to Communities: A Dis-
      cussion Paper on Proposed Local Government Legislation,"
      (Yellowknife: Government of the Northwest Territories, 1983).

15   Government of the Northwest Territories, "Direction for the
      1990s," (Yellowknife: Government of the Northwest Territories,
      1987) "Shaping Public Government."

16   Government of the Northwest Territories, *Policy: Devolution*,
      Yellowknife, October 23, 1987, p. 1.

17   See: remarks by Roger Gruben to the Legislative Assembly of the
      Northwest Territories - Eleventh Assembly, Fourth Session
      (1989), *Hansard*, pp. 2759-2772.

18   See, for example: *Government Response to the Report of the
      Regional and Tribal Councils Review Co-ordinating Committee*,
      Legislative Assembly of the Northwest Territories Tabled Docu-
      ment No. 57-88 (2), November 4, 1988.

19   Government of the Northwest Territories, *GNWT Transfer Policy*,
      Yellowknife, February 24, 1988.

20   Dene/Métis Negotiations Secretariat, Comprehensive Claims
      Branch (DIAND) and Aboriginal Rights and Constitutional Devel-
      opment GNWT, *Comprehensive Land Claim Agreement Between
      Canada and the Dene Nation and the Métis Association of the
      Northwest Territories*, (unrevised, April 9, 1990), Section 7.

21   See for example, "Our Land Our Future" and "A Design for Devolution of Additional Powers and Responsibilities to Communities."

22   *Government Response to the Report of the Regional and Tribal Councils Review Co-ordinating Committee,* Legislative Assembly of the Northwest Territories Tabled Document, No.57-88 (2), tabled Nov. 4, 1988.

23   Dacks, op. cit. 1981, p.108.

24   See Government of the Northwest Territories, *Policy: Devolution,* October 23, 1987, p.1.

7   The Quest for Northern Oil and Gas Accords

Gurston Dacks

"Settlement of land claims, combined with continued political devolution and our new Northern Accord, will create a new climate of certainty, stability and opportunity throughout the North"

Prime Minister Brian Mulroney
Yellowknife, September 6, 1988

In September of 1988, the Government of Canada signed "enabling agreements" with the two territorial governments declaring their commitment to the devolution of responsibility for the management of oil and gas resources north of 60° and for the sharing of revenues to be derived from these resources. These agreements anticipate the negotiation of Northern Accords which will devolve to the territorial governments a jewel in the devolution crown — one of the most important provincial-type powers which has not yet been transferred to the North. This paper will describe the interplay of interests which is shaping the Northern Accords, the process leading to and beyond the 1988 agreements and the issues which will determine the fate of the Northern Accords process.

The Interests at Stake in Northern Accords

It is difficult to overstate the significance of the Northern Accords to the political actors which have interests in them. Should it prove possible to negotiate these Accords, they will radically close the gap between the powers of the Territories and those of the provinces. Indeed, the Northern Accords will give the Territories more powers than Alberta and Saskatchewan enjoyed when they were made provinces in 1905. They may profoundly affect the future revenues of the Territories, particularly the

NWT, and reduce their fiscal dependence on Ottawa. They will also clarify the form of public government which will develop in the NWT and the balance of power between the Government of the NWT and the aboriginal groups of the Territory. Finally, they promise to establish a more coherent and predictable regime for managing these resources than presently exists by dispelling the uncertainty which the prospect of devolution has raised and by committing the territorial governments to establish stable management regimes, familiar to the oil industry.

The backdrop for these prospects is the existing regime for managing oil and gas resources in the Territories. At present all management authority is held by the owner of the resource, the Government of Canada. The *Canada Petroleum Resources Act*[1] and the *Oil and Gas Production and Conservation Act*[2] make the Department of Energy, Mines and Resources (EMR) responsible for energy policy in Hudson Bay and Hudson Strait and the Department of Indian Affairs and Northern Development responsible for the rest of Canada north of 60°, excluding Quebec and Labrador. Together, the two acts define the range of northern energy policy, hence the list of topics which any negotiations leading to a Northern Accord will have to cover. The *Canada Petroleum Resources Act* authorizes the issuing of interests such as exploration licenses, significant discovery licenses and production licenses; establishes the royalty regime; requires that energy companies prepare benefits plans, which ensure that adequate benefits in the form of jobs, sales and contracts for Canadians will result from the companies' pursuit of oil and gas which the government is authorizing; establishes an environmental studies research fund; and requires 50 percent Canadian participation before production can begin. The *Oil and Gas Production and Conservation Act* prescribes the actions which government can take to manage the process by which oil and gas is produced. The concerns of this act include regulating the location, drilling, producing, suspending operations and abandoning of wells; safety procedures; setting rates of production to prevent waste; preventing spills, reporting them when they occur and recovering the damages and costs of cleanup which they create; managing the interests, in particular, determining production shares of several owners of a single pool of oil and gas; and requiring owners to put the resources they own into production in order to prevent waste. The two acts are administered by the Canada Oil and Gas Lands Administration (COGLA). All governmental revenues derived from the production of oil and gas accrue to the Government of Canada. This set of arrangements has important implications for the various political actors with interests in northern oil and gas. These are the Government of Canada, the territorial governments — most importantly the Government of the Northwest Territories (GNWT) — northern aboriginal groups and the oil and gas industry.

The Government of Canada is not a monolith. Indeed, its behaviour at times owes more to relationships among its own agencies than to external factors. The intragovernmental struggle over Northern Accords exemplifies this pattern. For its part, DIAND has come to view Northern Accords as the best means for bringing about future northern oil and gas production. It is concerned that few new exploration rights have been granted to the industry since 1971. As existing permits expire, the amount of land available for drilling has declined[3]. At the same time, officials in DIAND feel that it is inappropriate for a federal government agency to issue new exploration rights in the North, in part because aboriginal claims have not been resolved throughout most of the Territories and in part because of their sense of the legitimacy of the territorial governments and their wish to enhance that legitimacy. Looking to the future, DIAND sees elements of aboriginal claims settlements which will continue to limit Ottawa's ability to issue new exploration permits. Because these elements will be constitutionally entrenched, they will not be easily circumvented or overridden. The resulting unavailability of land for exploration poses a major obstacle to the discovery of new oil and gas resources in the North. Moreover, DIAND has appreciated for a number of years that the claims will create public government agencies — for land use planning, regulating water use and other purposes — for managing the surface of the land. DIAND correctly judges that oil and gas development will proceed more coherently and efficiently if these bodies mesh with the regimes established to manage subsurface resources.

The easiest way to ensure a successful integration of the two regimes is to put them in the hands of a single government. For the reasons cited above, it believes that this should be the government of each territory. In any case, DIAND believes that the territorial governments have the means to obstruct any project being brought into production regarding which they feel that they have been denied their rightful management role. Furthermore, DIAND believes that the territorial governments would be supported in such actions by the bulk of the population of the Territories. To summarize, DIAND does not view Northern Accords as taking power away from the Government of Canada. From the perspective of DIAND, Ottawa's power over northern oil and gas development has already lapsed. According to this analysis, what is necessary is to give northerners the significant interest in northern energy development which will motivate them to allow it to proceed. The time is ripe to fill the jurisdictional vacuum by clearly vesting authority in the territorial governments in that both the extent of existing exploration rights and the level of economic activity relating to northern oil and gas are at low ebb. This means that moving now will have less significant practical implications than would devolving authority over oil and gas at some future time of great activity in the industry.

Other agencies of the Government of Canada, agencies higher on the Cabinet pecking order than DIAND, do not share this consciousness. Officials of the Department of Energy, Mines and Resources and of COGLA view the energy resources of the North as part of the patrimony of Canada. They believe that the 40 percent of Canada's reserves of producible conventional oil and 50 percent of natural gas which the North contains should be managed in the national rather than the regional interest. They believe that the pace of development of these reserves should reflect national energy requirements. They also hold that the governmental income generated by this development should flow to the Government of Canada, which has invested enormous sums of money in northern hydrocarbon exploration, rather than to territorial governments which serve tiny fractions of the total population of Canada. Further, these officials view the territorial governments as so deficient in the administrative capacity needed to manage hydrocarbon development that it is premature to consider devolving jurisdiction over this function to them. Their minister until 1988, Marcel Masse, supported these views. His successor, Jake Epp, is significantly more sympathetic to northern aspirations and committed to delivering on the Accord enabling agreements which his government had signed by the time he was appointed minister.

Other agencies of the Government of Canada have also had their doubts about Northern Accords. A fundamental concern of the Department of Finance is the performance of the Canadian economy. The Department is concerned that any changes which occur should enhance rather than harm the climate for oil and gas development and in this way contribute to, rather than undercut, national economic growth. This concern has led Finance to seek assurances that the oil and gas management regimes which Northern Accords will put in place will be sound and viable from the perspective of the industry. Finance has also been concerned that transitional arrangements will provide for a smooth transfer of authority.

The Federal-Provincial Relations Office of the Privy Council Office may also feel some concern that Northern Accords would give the territories powers which some provinces might feel ought only to be held by provincial (or, in the North, the federal) governments. The Meech Lake Accord reinforced the principle that the provinces have a legitimate interest in the creation of new provinces[4]. Its demise has not necessarily undermined this principle, nor the position some provincial governments may hold that devolving authority over so important a subject as oil and gas might be seen affect their interest in this power being uniquely (except for the federal role on the Canada Lands) theirs.

The federal Department of Justice also has its particular concern regarding the Accord, that whatever its substance, it be established on a firm legal basis. While it would be quicker and more convenient to use an order-in-council based on Section 16 (v) of the *Northwest Territories Act* to transfer management of oil and gas to the Territories, Justice is concerned that some aspects of this responsibility derive from other pieces of federal legislation. If these are not properly accounted for, the territorial governments may find that they lack the full authority they need to manage their resources. Conceivably they could face lawsuits over actions which they may not have the jurisdiction to take. Justice's concern is not a substantive one, but it could lead to delays in negotiating and implementing the Accord.

A number of federal government departments are interested in the Northern Accords. However, it is clear that the major dynamic determining the policy of the Government of Canada has been the conflicting analyses of DIAND, which has actively pursued the Northern Accord process, and EMR and COGLA, which have resisted it.

In the words of the Government of the Northwest Territories, "Having northerners take over control of NWT energy resources and their development from the federal government is one of our major objectives." [5]   The economy of the NWT has always been a high cost, staples-based, hinterland economy.[6] These factors require government intervention to promote economic stability and prosperity. This need is particularly pressing regarding oil and gas activity, whose potential to fuel territorial economic development and also to disrupt northern life in the future is enormous. By controlling the disposition and administration of oil and gas rights, the GNWT will be able to influence the pace and extent of hydrocarbon exploration. The power to regulate exploration, development and production activities will enable the GNWT to ensure that the full range of activities which the oil and gas industry undertakes will meet safety, environmental and other standards that reflect the values of the people of the Territories, rather than the concerns of outsiders. In particular, this power is a crucial component of a comprehensive, integrated system for managing the totality of natural resources in the North. Such a system will manage both subsurface resources, in terms of conservation and revenue maximization, and the surface of the land, in terms of protecting the environment and wildlife. In particular, it will determine the balance which will be struck between the interests of those promoting energy development and the desires of the aboriginal peoples that non-renewable resource related activities will not undercut the pursuit of their traditional economic activities on the land. In other words, the regulatory power can provide the means for deciding one of the fundamental policy questions facing the North — the relative weights which will be attached to the renewable resource and the non-renewable resource based economies of the North. There is no more important issue facing the North because the resolution of this issue will seal the fate of the traditional economy, and with it the cultural integrity of the aboriginal peoples of the North.

The GNWT is particularly interested in setting, administering and receiving the governmental revenues which are anticipated to flow from oil and gas development. The GNWT is sensitive to the relatively short duration of this type of revenue, and sees it as providing the means for establishing a more stable and diversified future territorial economy. The actual economic rent which oil and gas revenues will provide will depend on the relationship between the high costs of northern production and the world price of energy. The current relatively low world price for energy makes substantial development uneconomic for both industry and government. However, these unfavourable economics are likely to change in the future. To the extent that they do and for as long as the GNWT's share of the economic rent is substantial, it will increase the fiscal capacity of the GNWT. This will permit it to more easily finance its activities. In addition, it will prove constitutionally significant by strengthening the GNWT's claim for more of the attributes of provincial status. One of the major objections to granting provincial status to the NWT is that it lacks the fiscal capacity of the existing provinces.[7] Leaving aside judgments about the validity of this objection, significant revenues from northern oil and gas production, particularly if they are projected to last for a number of years, should enable the GNWT to satisfy this fiscal criterion, hence more persuasively to pursue its goal of enhanced constitutional status.

Finally, control over oil and gas will enable the GNWT to negotiate "northern benefits." In other words, it will ensure that the optimal number of northern workers and companies receive jobs and contracts from energy activity in the North. This will strengthen the northern economy by cycling as much energy-related business through it as possible, in contrast to the historic pattern by which energy exploration provided a smaller multiplier effect than it could have because the industry sup-plied itself more exclusively from southern Canada than it would have if government had negotiated effective northern benefits packages with it.

All of these considerations would place a Northern Accord high on the list of GNWT priorities. The importance of gaining an accord is heightened by the predicament in which the GNWT has found itself as the aboriginal claims approach settlement. These settlements will create management and planning bodies on which the aboriginal groups enjoy constitutionally guaranteed representation[8]. They will also confirm aboriginal ownership of substantial areas of the NWT. Both of these factors will add significantly to the role of the aboriginal peoples vis-à-vis oil and gas development. In the absence of a clear grant of jurisdiction over subsurface resources to the GNWT, this aboriginal role regarding the management of the land surface could give the aboriginal peoples a great deal of power over the decisions which will bring — or deny — to the NWT the types of benefits described above. At the very least it could predicate the management systems which will govern northern resource development more on a concern for protection of the interests of the aboriginal peoples and less on mandating the GNWT to exercise provincial-type powers. For the GNWT, a Northern Accord is the means to contain this development and ensure that it, and not the aboriginal groups, controls the impact of hydrocarbon develop-ment on the territorial economy.

In contrast, the Government of the Yukon (YTG) is more cautious about pursuing a Northern Accord. It recognizes the advantages, but gives them less weight than does the GNWT. For example, a Northern Accord will empower the territorial govern-ment and add to its credibility. However, it has less need of this bolstering as it does not face the same challenge to its legitimacy that the GNWT encounters. Party politics, a system of responsible government officially sanctioned by Ottawa and a large non-aboriginal majority in the electorate guarantee that the Government of the Yukon will be a parliamentary government for the foreseeable future. Recognizing that they cannot change the basic nature of the territorial government and more interested in self-government at the local rather than the territorial level, Yukon Indians have opted to seek self-determination through the creation of separate (and local) Indian structures of government rather than — as has been discussed in the NWT — restructuring the public government. This acceptance means that the YTG has no need to acquire new powers in order to defend its essential nature from aboriginal challenges. The Yukon has many fewer onshore hydrocarbon prospects than does the NWT. Thus it stands less to benefit from gaining the power to manage its oil and gas. However, it will have to pay the costs either of developing the administrative capacity to manage these resources or of contracting out this task. These costs could be particularly high in comparison to the financial return which the Territory's modest energy resources are likely to provide if the territorial government were to implement an expensive administrative system. If it operated a simpler system which involved little negotiation with industry about conditions, the cost would be substantially lower.

While there have been some significant exceptions, in general during the devolution process, the federal government has tried to minimize the resources which it transfers to the territorial governments to cover the costs of the activities it is devolving. This pattern will sensitize the Yukon government to the need to weigh carefully the financial costs and benefits of its participation in a Northern Accord, and perhaps to work toward an administrative regime which is relatively inexpensive to operate. In any case, a Northern Accord fits less easily into the Yukon's approach to relations with Ottawa than it does into Yellowknife's. Historically, perhaps because its institutions matured earlier or because its non-aboriginal population is so numerically dominant, the Yukon has pursued provincial status more forcefully than has the Northwest Territories. For example, it met head on the obstacles which the Meech Lake Accord presented to this ambition, emphasizing its desire to gain the attributes of provincehood which Meech Lake denied it. These included, for example, the rights to nominate senators and justices of the Supreme Court and to take part in first ministers' meetings. In contrast, while the GNWT condemned Meech Lake, its strategy emphasized gaining the span of jurisdiction which the provinces exercise. This would enhance the GNWT's administrative capacity, demonstrate its ability to govern responsibly and, in this way, strengthen its argument for enhanced status in Confederation. While the merit of the two strategies can be debated, the consequence is that the Government of the Yukon has pursued devolution more cautiously than has the GNWT. Because this has been especially true of devolution of oil and gas, this paper will emphasize the NWT, and only refer to the Yukon where it has been significantly involved in the accord process.

The aboriginal interest in devolution is clearly the other side of the territorial coin, particularly in the NWT. To the extent that the claims settlements which they are negotiating only partially secure their economic and cultural interests, the aboriginal groups are determined to ensure that the matters which fall outside the claims settlements are arranged in such a way as to complete the comprehensive protection which they desire. Aboriginal-owned lands are relatively well protected; the settlements enable the aboriginal groups to negotiate "access"[9] or "participation"[10] agreements with energy companies which have rights to subsurface resources lying under lands which have been transferred to aboriginal ownership. The right to negotiate these agreements enables the aboriginal groups to ensure that they are fairly compensated for allowing the companies access to their lands. However, aboriginal harvesters need to hunt, fish and trap beyond the boundaries of the lands they will own as a result of their claims settlements. Moreover, the availability of wildlife on their lands may be affected by non-renewable resource development activity taking place on lands which they do not own. An ideal regime from their point of view would enable them to control this development. However, Canada's comprehensive claims policy does not permit control over subsurface resources throughout the total area of land covered by a claim to be a subject for negotiation under aboriginal claims[11]. The best it has provided aboriginal groups has been a role in public government bodies which will plan onshore land use, assess social and environmental impacts and license land and water uses.

The aboriginal groups are taking part in the process of the northward devolution of control over oil and gas because the existing arrangement is insensitive to their concerns. Also, before the Dene/Métis and Inuit settlements were reached, these groups sensed that the process might proceed without their participation, and felt it was better to try to shape the Northern Accord than to wait and oppose whatever deal the governments worked out among themselves. They hoped that their participation in the negotiation of this devolution will ensure that the system of management which the Northern Accord puts in place will complement the provisions of their claims agreements in principle. Above all, they seek to prevent an accord which creates institutions or policies which are not compatible with their tentative agreements . The Inuit Agreement-in-Principle explicitly provides for this, while the "Signed Memorandum of Understanding on Devolution" represents an early effort by the Dene and Métis to gain this kind of security[12].

Each of the aboriginal groups has its own particular reasons for being willing to take part in negotiations towards Northern Accords. The Dene/Métis have negotiated a share in energy royalties, hence would like some say in decisions which affect the setting of the royalties which they will share. They, along with the other aboriginal groups of the NWT, also hope that taking part in accord negotiations will contribute to their goal of maximizing the devolution of power — at least regarding northern benefits — to their individual communities, which are their primary political units, rather than just to central bodies which will make decisions for the entire territory. The goal here is to increase the standard of living in their communities. Indeed, one of the four conditions which they argue a Northern

Accord must include is that "Northern benefits programs should be community-based and should provide economic stability, growth and diversification."[13]

The Inuit also have a very real interest in shaping the accord negotiating position which the GNWT presents to Ottawa. It is true that very little energy-related activity is occurring within their claim area. Hence, little practical damage is likely to result from the regime established by an accord, at least not in the foreseeable future. At the same time, they may stand to benefit should the territorial government be able to realize significant revenues from energy production in the western NWT. Moreover, because the regime which is negotiated for the NWT is likely to provide the model for the jurisdiction of Nunavut, should division of the NWT occur, and perhaps some precedents for the devolution of other resource responsibilities, such as mining, the Inuit have a particular interest in the shape of that regime. For their part, the Inuvialuit want to use accord negotiations to promote their goal of having their own regional government while also ensuring that the accord provides them with tangible benefits and does not conflict with their aboriginal claim settlement. Of all the northern aboriginal groups, the Council for Yukon Indians (CYI) has had the least involvement in the accord process. This pattern reflects both the lack of onshore hydrocarbon potential in the Yukon and the CYI's preoccupation with negotiating the agreement-in-principle for its claims settlement.

The interest of the final actor in the accord process, the energy industry, is straightforward. The industry has confronted several different regulatory regimes in the past decade. This history has made it difficult for the industry to calculate its interest in pursuing northern energy as the rules which determine its risk and potential benefits are not stable. It was motivated to drill during the era of the National Energy Program because very generous federal government incentives greatly reduced the cost of this activity. With drilling incentives reduced under the Frontier Energy Policy in favour of incentives for production, the energy industry needs other forms of encouragement to explore for energy. A stable regulatory regime would be one such form of encouragement. Indeed, the industry's position is that it cares less about the identity of the regulator than it does about the provision of a regulatory regime which is stable and predictable, which is administered in a consistent, competent and fair manner and which affords a reasonable expectation of profit.

Laying the Groundwork

That the quest for northern oil and gas accords has come as far as it has represents the triumph of political philosophy and will over bureaucratic caution and territoriality. The backdrop of this story is the gradual maturation of both territorial governments in the last decade. In 1980, the Yukon was granted responsible government. Since then its politics and government, based on the three party system found in Canadian politics at the national level, have closely resembled their provincial counterparts. The politics of the NWT at the territorial level do not feature party competition. However, the NWT has been developing the institutions of Cabinet government and, like the Yukon, a credible public service. The growing maturity of the processes of the territorial governments has made it seem plausible to expand their jurisdiction and thus to accord northerners more of the local self-determination which their fellow Canadians in the provinces enjoy. This democratic impulse as well as the desire of Ottawa to unburden itself of costly programs have given rise to the overall process of devolution, which has been a major northern policy thrust of the Progressive Conservatives since they gained office in 1984.

In the specific case of oil and gas, the wish to manage northern oil and gas resources was born out of the frustration which the GNWT experienced as a result of the National Energy Program. Before the NEP, the GNWT negotiated northern benefits agreements with energy companies and was satisfied with its ability to seek employment and contract opportunities for territorial workers and suppliers. The government had not formed any ambition for a broader role in making and administering energy policy. However, under the NEP, Ottawa centralized control over frontier energy. COGLA came to administer all aspects of government policy regarding frontier energy development, including northern benefits. COGLA and EMR viewed frontier energy as a matter of the national interest to such an extent that they were unwilling to consider the regional interest which the North had in northern resources. The result, from the perspective of the GNWT, was a pattern of federal government insensitivity to northern needs. The resulting frustration led the GNWT initially to conceive of its energy policy goal merely as one of finding a replacement for COGLA.

The election of the Conservatives in 1984 provided several necessary conditions for such a development. Most importantly, the Conservatives' approach to federalism emphasized "national reconciliation" a departure from the aggressive centralization of the preceding Liberal government[14]. In the realm of energy policy, this commitment expressed itself early in 1985 in the Atlantic Accord, by which the new federal government agreed to share equally with Newfoundland broad jurisdiction over offshore hydrocarbon development. The Atlantic Accord signalled an opportunity to the GNWT, but it did more. It suggested to the GNWT the possibility that, like Newfoundland, it could seek jurisdiction, or some share of it, over a broader range of matters than just benefits.

The federal government's Frontier Energy Policy, released in October of 1985, encouraged the GNWT to actively pursue this possibility. Specifically, the policy stated:

> "Shared management, based upon the principle of equality of governments, is a reality in Newfoundland....The Government of Canada has a clear commitment to shared management with other coastal provinces, and in the North. The structure and scope of shared management will be matters for bilateral discussions and may vary according to regional circumstances and priorities. The decisions set out here....set a broad and consistent policy framework within which equality in shared management can be fully realized."[15]

The emphasis which this passage places on the principle of equality between governments and its reference to the provinces and the territories without distinguishing between them in terms of their right to share power amounted to approval in principle for the devolution of jurisdiction over energy to the GNWT and YTG.

To realize the promise of this policy statement, the GNWT spent 1986 developing specific proposals to put to the Government of Canada. It retained a group of consultants, some of whom, such as Peter Lougheed and Vern Millard, had been involved in the development of Alberta's energy policy. These individuals were well-known to the energy industry, which felt as a result some assurance that the GNWT's planning was being guided by people who understood the industry and who were most unlikely to propose or support arrangements with which the industry could not live. In addition, the Albertans were veterans of the "energy wars" between their province and Ottawa in the late 1970s and early 1980s. Their experiences supported the views of the GNWT about the regional insensitivity of EMR and strengthened the resolve of the GNWT to try to wrest control from it.

In June of 1987, the GNWT submitted to DIAND a proposal which set out broad principles upon which a Northern Accord could be negotiated. In the same month, the federal cabinet approved *A Northern Political and Economic Framework.* This policy statement adopted DIAND's interpretation of the politics of northern energy in noting that "A Northern Accord which responds to the aspirations of territorial governments would provide the political stability necessary to develop northern oil and gas resources."[16] Early in 1988, DIAND submitted to Cabinet a proposed accord agreement in principle based on the GNWT proposal and also on a Yukon Government position paper on oil and gas.

Despite the positive signs, the following months proved frustrating for the northern governments and DIAND. In essence, the search for approval became mired in interdepartmental politics within the federal government. The Department of Finance expressed concern that the energy policy regime which would result from devolution would be sound and that the transition would be smooth. DIAND had no choice but to address these concerns in the enabling agreements. In contrast, the public servants in EMR objected in principle to devolution of their northern jurisdiction and responded to DIAND with a flow of questions and requests for clarifications which observers viewed as more obstructive than constructive.

This opposition could not be overcome at the public service level. The Yukon Government responded in a relatively passive fashion, reflecting the modest oil and gas prospects within the Yukon, hence its lack of lobbying clout concerning energy on the national stage. In contrast, the GNWT, with a great deal more at stake, mounted an energetic lobbying campaign. The GNWT set the stage by expressing its frustration over the provisions of the Meech Lake Accord in a firm but muted fashion. This restraint helped develop a rapport between the Prime Minister and the Government Leader of the NWT. This rapport in turn strengthened Mr. Mulroney's feeling that Ottawa had an obligation to do something for the North which would offset the constitutional cloud that Meech Lake had cast over the North. The GNWT also attempted to strengthen its case in two other ways. First, it worked to allay the energy industry's discomfort with the idea of devolution. In the end, much of the industry had been moved to neutrality on the question, while some companies did tell Ottawa that they viewed substantial northern involvement in energy policy as an essential precondition for a more energy related activities in the North. Second, the GNWT tried to persuade the aboriginal groups to support the concept of an energy accord. In April of 1988, the Tungavik Federation of Nunavut, the body which is responsible for negotiating the settlement of the Inuit land claim, signed a Memorandum of Understanding with the GNWT. In this document, the TFN supported the concept of devolution of "administration and control of oil and gas resources" in exchange for a promise from the GNWT that it would invite the TFN to sit on the GNWT team which would develop and negotiate with Ottawa the Territories' accord proposal.[17] The Inuit are not the biggest aboriginal players on the northern energy stage because the TFN settlement area has attracted relatively little interest on the part of the energy industry. However, the reaching of this agreement relating to energy as well as the existence of an earlier all-purpose devolution agreement with the Dene and Métis gave credence to the GNWT's assertion that it could deliver the northern consensus in favour of development which the industry and DIAND knew was both necessary and beyond Ottawa's reach.

Building on this base, the GNWT lobbied senior ministers, emphasizing the argument that only northern involvement would create the positive investment climate needed to promote northern energy exploration. At the same time, Bill McKnight, Minister of Indian Affairs and Northern Development, was energetically pursuing Cabinet approval of the Northern Accord proposal. Indeed, the fact that an enabling agreement was concluded owes a great deal to McKnight's determination to confront his Cabinet colleagues' objections, no matter how many times they were raised.

By the spring of 1988, he and the GNWT realized that their proposal had become mired in a morass of specific questions and objections. The GNWT was particularly sensitive to the ticking of the national electoral clock. The public opinion polls suggested the possibility of a minority Conservative government or perhaps a Conservative loss at the polls. The GNWT felt that either of these outcomes would limit the likelihood of devolution of energy policy. It was particularly disturbed by this prospect because it was becoming increasingly concerned about the NWT's economic future. Indeed the first policy statement of the new territorial government which was established after the territorial election late in 1987 identified stimulating economic growth as one of its basic policy goals, and northern control of energy as fundamental to the attainment of this goal.[18] The GNWT therefore felt that it had to get a commitment from Cabinet in favour of this devolution as quickly as possible so as to build some momentum for the uncertain future. Accordingly, the GNWT and DIAND withdrew their more detailed proposal to

Cabinet in place of a basic statement of principles. As this document had less specifics for departments to object to, the Minister was able to manoeuvre it past the Cabinet committees in which its predecessor had been stuck. With the support of the Prime Minister and of Joe Clark, a westerner sympathetic to hinterland interests regarding energy, it was approved by Cabinet late in the summer.

At this point, electoral politics telescoped the accord time frame, with dramatic results. During the summer, the Dene/Métis and the federal government reached an agreement in principle on a settlement for the Dene/Métis claim. It was decided that the Prime Minister would sign this agreement in principle in Yellowknife in order to enhance the Conservatives' image on the social policy front as they approached the coming election. While Cabinet had approved the terms of the enabling agreement, it was not ready for formal signing in that it had not been presented to the territorial governments for their consideration. Neither territorial government was aware of its precise contents because both had decided to let the minister of IAND take sole direction of the delicate final stages leading to Cabinet approval. Regardless, it was decided that the Prime Minister would sign the Northern Accord enabling agreement with the GNWT during his visit to Yellowknife in order to be able to present two success stories to the Canadian people. The territorial governments received the draft of their enabling agreements on September first. This gave the GNWT only a few days to address the document before the signing date of September 6. It was able to negotiate a few wording changes, but felt compelled to accept the bulk of the document as a reflection of the constraints which the federal departments of Finance, and EMR had imposed on DIAND. The alternative was to face the post-election future without any statement of federal government support for devolution of jurisdiction over energy.

The interaction between the GNWT and the Territories' aboriginal groups between September 1 and 6 is unclear. The GNWT asserts that it attempted to reach the aboriginal leadership before the signing of the agreement. However, meaningful contact was not accomplished. The aboriginal leaders were incensed that they had not been consulted, particularly in view of the promises of the GNWT to involve them in the devolution process. Not wishing to be excluded from a process which they felt could ultimately give them the benefits described above, they expressed their willingness to participate in the process of negotiation leading to an accord. However, they did set one condition, which reflected their overall strategy as well as their frustration with recent events. They asked the legislative assembly to "insist that the Government of the Northwest Territories agree to only sign a final Northern Energy Accord which is acceptable to (the aboriginal groups)."[19] However, the assembly did not endorse this request for a veto. Instead it passed a motion endorsing the enabling agreement, supporting the participation of representatives of the aboriginal groups on the NWT Accord negotiations team, and asserting that the negotiations team should attempt to reach a consensus on the aboriginal representatives' role in the process by which the NWT position for negotiating the Northern Accord with the federal government would be determined.[20]   By the end of 1988, the aboriginal groups had accepted this degree of assurance and agreed to take part on the negotiating team.

The Enabling Agreements[21]

The most important elements of the enabling agreement between Ottawa and the GNWT are:

1)   The agreement applies to all of Canada north of 60°, both onshore and offshore, except for the provinces, the Yukon, Hudson Bay and Hudson Strait. However, the federal government recognizes that the GNWT "has interests in" the two bodies of water.

2)   The agreement provides for a transfer of jurisdiction over management of onshore oil and gas resources to the GNWT, which accepts that the policies it adopts will conform to existing Canadian models. Initially, the *Canada Petroleum Resources Act* and the *Oil and Gas Production and Conservation Act* will comprise the legislative regime for managing oil and gas both onshore and offshore. This provision satisfies the desire of the

industry and the Department of Finance for a predictable and effective management regime. The GNWT will receive all of the revenues which accrue to government from the development of onshore resources.

3)   The agreement anticipates that Ottawa and the GNWT will share management power over and revenues from oil and gas resources offshore.

4)   The Government of the Yukon will share management power over and revenues from oil and gas development in the Beaufort Sea, "commensurate with their interest in these resources."

5)   The transfer of jurisdiction will be phased, and will occur more quickly onshore than offshore. The form of sharing jurisdiction offshore will not be decided until "there has been experience with significant offshore development."

6)   The agreement does not limit aboriginal rights or affect the rights and benefits provided by the Inuvialuit claim settlement.

The substance of the Canada-Yukon enabling agreement is identical to the NWT document, except where it is necessary to take into account differences of geography. For example, the Yukon agreement makes no reference to the Inuvialuit or to shared income or management in offshore regions other than the Beaufort, as the Yukon has no interest east of the Beaufort.

Issues Raised by the Enabling Agreements

The enabling agreements are significant in establishing Ottawa's commitment in principle to devolve jurisdiction over oil and gas. In addition, they have led to a substantial amount of federal-territorial consultation on day-to-day energy management questions as Ottawa has begun informally to implement the co-operative intent of the enabling agreements even before the accords are in place. However, the enabling agreements are only a way station on the long journey to achieving the accords. To reach this destination, the governments and aboriginal groups will have to resolve many issues. These fall into two broad categories. The first category, issues between the federal and territorial governments, involves fleshing out and implementing some of the terms of the agreement, as well as dealing with objections to other terms. The second broad category of issues is those on which the aboriginal groups and the government of the NWT differ.

A number of intergovernmental issues must be resolved in order to implement the terms of the enabling agreements. For example, the fiscal terms must be negotiated. The enabling agreements provide for revenue sharing offshore, but do not guarantee any minimum revenue from development. To encourage development, the Frontier Energy Policy stipulates a low initial royalty rate which climbs slowly. The initial royalty rate is one percent and climbs by an additional one percent every 18 months until the industry has recovered its expenses and a fair return on its investment. While this regime is "sensitive to the high costs and long lead times involved in frontier development,"[22] it may produce relatively small royalties. This might satisfy Ottawa if its main objective is adding to Canada's available oil and gas supplies. However it would deny the territorial governments and the aboriginal groups which have negotiated resource revenue sharing the income on which they have been counting. This concern has led the aboriginal groups of the NWT to insist that "Northerners should receive a net financial benefit from the onshore and offshore oil and gas resources...In any year of production, at least 10% of the revenues generated at the Canada/US border."[23]

The governments will also have to decide the basic formulas for sharing, one between Ottawa and the GNWT for the NWT offshore except the Beaufort, and a separate tripartite formula for the Beaufort. This latter formula may prove contentious in that the GNWT recognizes that a Yukon interest in the Beaufort does exist, but feels that it is significantly less than its own. If federal government agencies hope to obstruct the attainment of an accord, this may be an issue which they will find easy to exploit. Indeed, the failure of the two territorial governments to agree on their respective sharing of Beaufort resource revenues and management structures was one factor which prevented them from gaining the symbolic benefit of tabling a unified Accord negotiating position in the spring of 1990.

The enabling agreements provide that Ottawa will get a larger share of additional offshore income once revenues become particularly high. This is not quite a cap of territorial income, but it does make Ottawa the chief beneficiary of any very rich development which is put into production. The three governments will have to negotiate the threshold beyond which the federal government's share increases and the rate at which that share will grow. The fiscal issue is complicated by the fact that both territorial governments receive federal financial assistance under Formula Financing Agreements. The general purpose of these is the same as for Ottawa's equalization program for the provinces. The territories require a different type of arrangement, however, because equalization payments are calculated on the basis of government revenues. The territorial government revenues compare favourably with provincial revenues, hence they would be ineligible for equalization. However, territorial spending on a per capita basis is much higher than the provincial average and calls for a special basis for calculating equalization. The enabling agreements anticipate that this calculation will be altered to reduce the flow of money from Ottawa to the territorial governments once they begin to receive energy revenues. The issue to be negotiated here is the amount of the reduction. The enabling agreements provide that there will be a net benefit to the territorial governments, but the issue is how great that benefit will be. The territorial governments can be expected to argue that it should be quite substantial in that they may have to provide costly infrastructure to support energy development and also fund whatever costs of preventing or compensating for the social costs which may accompany energy development and not be covered by the developer itself. The federal government will likely argue the burden of the deficit it must bear and the billions of dollars which it has invested in the development of northern oil and gas, not to mention in subsidizing the territorial governments. Finally, the governments will have to negotiate the proportion of the costs each will pay for administering the oil and gas resources of the offshore.

A second major set of issues the three governments will have to negotiate concerns the administrative and legislative regime by which they will share the management of the offshore. The commitment to intergovernmental equality expressed in the Frontier Energy Policy suggests that the administrative process will not be as unequal as that contained in the the original federal government arrangement with Nova Scotia, which gave the province a primarily advisory role. However, the extent of power sharing in the relationship remains to be seen. Full intergovernmental equality would give each side a veto over decisions, a provision which the departments of Finance and EMR might succeed in arguing poses an unacceptable threat to the development of northern energy resources in the national interest.

The situation on land is somewhat simpler in that arrangements for sharing management responsibilities with Ottawa need not be negotiated; the territorial governments will exercise full authority. Initially, the existing legislative regime, as for the offshore, will apply. However, an issue which may arise after the Accords are negotiated is how constrained the territorial governments will be in redesigning their oil and gas management regimes. The enabling agreements stipulate that "...the eventual territorial onshore oil and gas legislative regime (and the offshore regime as well) would be modelled after existing regimes in Canada and compatible with the offshore regime." It will be most difficult to negotiate definitions of the terms "modelled after" and "compatible with" which will cover all of the possible regimes which the territorial governments might favour in the future. Should Ottawa disagree with a territorial government's plans to change its legislative regime, negotiations would undoubtedly ensue. These would reflect Ottawa's respect for the maturity and democratic base of the territorial government on the one hand, and on the other the ultimate fact that the territorial exercise of jurisdiction over oil and gas will rest on either legislation or an order-in-council of the federal government. This delicate situation is not likely to arise for a long time, in view of the territorial governments' ongoing acceptance of the existing regime, which they recognize to be most helpful in maintaining the oil industry confidence which is a prerequisite for development of these resources.

The phasing of the implementation of a Northern Accord presents a third set of issues to be negotiated. Onshore, devolution of jurisdiction is to take place "in agreed stages." This provision makes sense in that it gives the territorial governments time to gradually build up the administrative capacity to "take up" the new responsiblity. Also, it is likelier to provide for a stable transition period than would a comprehensive transfer at a single point in time. However, phasing creates the questions of the sequence in which specific aspects of jurisdiction or responsibilities are to be transferred, the time frame for the transfers and whether the time frame is guaranteed or open to unilateral deceleration by Ottawa should it dislike how a territorial government uses the powers which have already been devolved to it. Power sharing in the offshore, as has been noted, will follow "significant" offshore development. The obvious issue to negotiate here is the meaning of the term "significant." The territorial position will seek a definition which implies a relatively prompt transfer of jurisdiction. The federal government will seek a definition which puts devolution farther into the future, or which simply gives it the final say as to when a significant amont of offshore experience has been gained.

Renegotiating or Bypassing the Enabling Agreements

These three sets of issues — the fiscal regime, the sharing of power and the phasing of implementation — will command the bulk of the negotiators' attention as they attempt to translate the enabling agreements into a Northern Accord. However, the negotiators will be pursuing an additional agenda as well, which involves renegotiating the terms of the enabling agreement. The GNWT views its enabling agreement as flawed, but accepted it for lack of time to negotiate before the Prime Minister's visit[24]. Although the document is signed, the GNWT would like several of its provisions altered. For example, it wants to challenge the exclusion of Hudson Strait and the portion of Hudson Bay north of 60° from the area covered by the enabling agreement. As will be discussed below, the TFN wants territorial control over all the islands and water of Hudson Bay. However, the territorial government seems to prefer a cautious approach in the face of provincial claims to Hudson Bay[25]. It takes some comfort from the enabling agreement's recognition that it does possess interests in Hudson Bay and Hudson Strait, a recognition it did not enjoy previously. Still, it does want to press a claim for jurisdiction over waters north of 60°.

The GNWT also wants the Northern Accord to provide for a "development fund"[26]. This substantial sum of money would be available before oil and gas development begins and would be used to fund the social programs and economic infrastructure which must precede development if northerners are to suffer as little as possible and benefit as much as possible from development. Because the GNWT will have to prepare for development before it occurs, it will bear the costs of these activities well before it begins to receive resource revenues. The need to match income and expenditure argues for a special fund to cover the costs to government of preparing for energy development. It can also be argued that a special fund is justified in that its magnitude will be known when spending is being planned. In contrast, government revenue from royalties is less certain as it depends on a variety of cost and market factors which cannot be predicted in advance.

When they signed the enabling agreements, both territorial governments committed themselves to involving the aboriginal groups in the development of their Accord negotiating positions. Both promised to fund aboriginal participation in the Accord process. Indeed, particularly in the NWT, while aboriginal groups have not been granted a veto in advance of negotiations, aboriginal opposition to the terms of a draft Accord could sufficiently weaken DIAND's resolve to produce an Accord as to cause it to relent in the face of continuing opposition from other departments of the federal government. The territorial governments, and particularly the GNWT, know that they must defer to some extent to aboriginal concerns regarding the management of oil and gas.

As has been described above, the aboriginal groups' basic goal regarding an energy accord is to ensure that the regime which it puts in place to manage subsurface resources will be compatible with the provisions for managing the land and wildlife of the territories which they have negotiated through their claims. Only if this basic compatibility is assured and only if it is guaranteed that decisions regarding the subsurface cannot override the rights of wildlife harvesters and the protections of the surface land, water and renewable resources provided by the claims settlements can the aboriginal peoples feel that their way of life is secure. This basic goal leads the aboriginal groups to share some common goals regarding the Northern Accord process.

The first of these concerns the process itself. Particularly in the NWT, the aboriginal groups have pressed for a full role in developing the Territories' negotiating positions in order to avoid a recurrence of the imbroglio of September 1988 which left them feeling that the GNWT had broken its promise to involve them in the devolution process. They wanted to receive enough of the information on which the GNWT negotiating position would be based to be able to assess this information independently. They also wanted sufficient time to develop their positions to avoid the haste which precluded consultation over the enabling agreement. The GNWT responded positively to these wishes. Indeed, one factor which caused the GNWT to delay preparing its negotiating position was its desire to wait until the aboriginal groups were equipped to participate in this process.

In terms of substance, the aboriginal groups have focussed on the future balance of power between themselves and the territorial government regarding energy policy. They want to negotiate the strongest possible position for themselves on the management agencies which the Northern Accord will create. For example, an NWT Oil and Gas Board may be created to evaluate onshore oil and gas resources in terms of their volume and optimal rates of production and to regulate the pace of production. A Surface Rights and Compensation Board may come into being to weigh the respective rights of groups, primarily the aboriginal peoples, who have ownership of or interests in the surface of the land and of non-renewable resource developers who must travel across the surface of land in order to reach the areas where they have been granted exploration rights. This board would compensate the holders of surface rights for any disturbance which the land suffers as a result of energy exploration, development and transportation. A Benefits Agency may be created to negotiate with developers the obligations they will undertake as part of the price of doing business in the Territory. These benefits may involve their promising to hire northerners, contract with northern companies and provide other benefits such as infrastructure or social programs. The aboriginal groups want representation on such bodies which will determine, not only how much they benefit from oil and gas development, but more importantly, how much their traditional economy will be harmed by it. The aboriginal people also want a deviation from the standard provincial model in which a provincial department of energy decides how exploration and production rights will be distributed and the pattern of royalties to be levied against energy production. Because they will want to play an important role in such decisions, they will demand significant representation on a joint GNWT energy department-aboriginal board which will make the final decisions. Offshore, the aboriginal groups, or at least the Inuvialuit and the Inuit, will want to participate on the analogous boards which will include federal as well as territorial officials.

Onshore or offshore, the aboriginal groups want their representation on these agencies to be entrenched so that the government side cannot unilaterally undercut it. This appeared somewhat problematic in 1988, when the Dene/Métis and Inuit claims were far from their final settlement. In 1990, progress toward claims settlements suggests (although the uncertain prospects for ratification of the Dene/Métis settlement do not guarantee) that the management bodies which will be entrenched in these agreements will give the aboriginal groups the security they have been seeking. In addition to a guarantee of adequate funding to ensure that they can meaningfully participate in the work of the boards, they will seek adequate funding for the boards, themselves, so that they can undertake their own research and policy study, rather than having to rely on information provided by government which may be partial or incomplete.

In addition to these general concerns, the Inuit have an agenda which reflects their unique needs. First, they emphatically reject the clauses of the enabling agreements which exclude Hudson Bay and Hudson Strait from the Accord:

> "We view these clauses as an extraordinary and reprehensible concession on the part of your government. Inuit are of the opinion that Hudson Bay and Hudson Strait are within the Northwest Territories and are not part of the adjacent provinces. Have you now abandoned the Inuit of the Belcher Islands and Keewatin who depend upon natural resources in Hudson Bay? These clauses in your Agreement-in-Principle pave the way for Hudson Bay and Hudson Strait to be divided between Manitoba, Ontario and Quebec...[27]

Indeed, the TFN felt so strongly about this issue that it sought and received a motion from the Legislative Assembly urging the GNWT to work for provisions in the Northen Accord which will protect the rights of the NWT Inuit to all of Hudson Bay and Hudson Strait[28].

Second, the Inuit want the Accord to accommodate the future development of Nunavut, the largely Inuit territory whose creation by means of division of the existing NWT is a cornerstone of their vision of the future. They want the Accord to affirm that it will not prejudice the creation of Nunavut. Also, they hope it will contain a formula by which the future territory of Nunavut will share oil and gas revenues derived throughout the existing NWT.

Third, the TFN recognizes that the money that the industry spends will focus on where the oil and gas are located, primarily outside the TFN claim area. However, it wants to ensure that government activity related to oil and gas produces economic benefits throughout the NWT, not just in Yellowknife and in the areas where the oil and gas are being produced. For example, it wants assurances that the federal government's oil and gas related funding and staff positions which are transferred to the GNWT do not all cluster in Yellowknife. Also, it wants any development funding which the GNWT may be able to negotiate under the Accord to be distributed among all of the regions of the NWT according to a guaranteed formula.

Preparing for Accord Negotiations

During the 18 months following the signing of the enabling agreements, Ottawa waited while the territorial governments gradually gained momentum in the development of their negotiating positions. For its part, the Yukon Territorial Government (YTG) first worked to increase its technical capacity to manage oil and gas resources. In the winter of 1989-90, it began to define its negotiating position, which it hoped to present to the federal government in the summer of 1990. The CYI signed a Memorandum of Understanding (MOU) with the Yukon Territorial Government to ensure that it would be adequately informed of these developments. However, it did not pursue participation in and control over the intergovernmental negotiations regarding devolution of control over oil and gas, and in this way contrasts with the aboriginal goups of the NWT.

In the winter of 1988-89, the Government of the Northwest Territories began to meet frequently with the aboriginal groups of the Territories. At first, the meetings were bilateral, with the GNWT meeting each aboriginal group separately. The purposes of these meetings were to replace the antagonism surrounding the signing of the enabling agreements with a feeling of mutual confidence and respect, to communicate the objectives of the aboriginal groups concerning the Accord, and to begin to develop specific elements of the negotiating position the NWT would present to Ottawa. As these meetings achieved their goals, they gave way to multilateral meetings which produced both a negotiating position and a tentative MOU between the aboriginal groups and the GNWT expressing the former's support for the negotiating position on the basis of certain undertakings by the GNWT. The negotiating position was presented to the federal government in May of 1990.

One major element of the negotiating position is, as noted above, the acceptance of the existing federal legislation as the basis for the regimes which will operate onshore and offshore. The practice of issuing exploration permits under this legislation would be modified to better provide for benefits from the exploration activity to flow to northerners and in particular to nearby communities. In addition, the negotiating position proposes that jurisdiction over all offshore waters north of 60° and those portions of Hudson Bay which are used by the people of Saniqiluak and all islands be devolved to the GNWT.

The basic purpose of the MOU is to affirm the territorial government's commitment to accommodating the future oil and gas regime to the provisions of the aboriginal claims settlements, not the other way around. The MOU also states that a principal consideration which will guide oil and gas management by the NWT in the future will be the preservation and promotion of the social and cultural integrity of the aboriginal peoples of the territories. It also assures the aboriginal groups that the income from royalties promised in their claims settlements will be protected in the sense that the government will not attempt to receive its revenues from oil and gas in a some non-royalty form, such as taxes, which the aboriginal groups will not share under the terms of their settlements.

The process of developing the NWT negotiating position bore fruit for several reasons. The first of these was organizational. The territorial government appreciates that the chances of overcoming resistance in Ottawa to the Northern Accord will be much better if its position enjoys the support of the Territories' aboriginal groups. In part for this reason, a few months after the signing of the enabling agreement it put in place a new team of officials committed to full consultation with the aboriginal groups. The openness and efforts of this group made the aboriginal leaders more comfortable about pursuing the Accord. The success of their claims negotiations both assured the aboriginal groups about their future security and impressed upon them the limits of the benefits which their claims settlements would give them. Thus for example, the Inuit Agreement-in-Principle provides that the Inuit will be empowered to negotiate benefits agreements from non-renewable resource developments only if these take place on Inuit Settlement Lands.[29] Also, the settlements generally provide for management of the land surface, leading the aboriginal people to seek assurances that the Accord-based regimes for managing the subsurface will dovetail with the institutions they have gained through their claims settlements.

Both the aboriginal groups and the territorial governments have good reasons to work together to advance the Northern Accord. It is worth noting, however, that when the government's negotiating position was presented to Ottawa, the Memorandum of Understanding did not accompany it. The reason was that the aboriginal groups wanted the MOU to be affirmed as a binding document, a contract, which might be subject to arbitration if they felt that the territorial government was not living up to its terms, as they felt to have been the case in September of 1988. The territorial government resisted this suggestion on the grounds that the result would be an arrangement which would be too inflexible to be adapted to changing circumstances. The aboriginal groups have grown more confident in the territorial government's intentions vis-à-vis the Accord. This is evidenced by their willingness to let it negotiate directly with Ottawa without them being present. However, the delay in signing the MOU suggests that they continue to be concerned about the GNWT's ultimate goals and the degree of its commitment to their interests, particularly where these come in conflict with GNWT constitutional ambitions.

The Northern Accords as a Case Study of Devolution

It is not possible to predict the future of the Northern Accords or, indeed, whether they will come into being. In this regard, it should be remembered that the enabling agreements themselves owed more to the Prime Minister's electoral strategy than to a strong commitment to energy devolution on the part of the various actors and agencies which define federal policy. Much will depend on the performance of the minister or ministers of Indian Affairs and Northern Development who will oversee the process of negotiating the Accords. Many observers credit Bill McKnight's determination as a major factor in the attainment of enabling agreements which, during the summer of 1988, seemed out of reach. In part this determination reflected his Saskatchewan background, which led him to believe that locally developed policies are more responsive to regional needs than are policies developed thousands of miles away. It remains to be seen whether his successors will bring the same intensity of conviction to the struggle against departments of the federal government which will try to dilute or block the Northern Accord.

Timing has played and will play an important role in shaping the final terms of the Northern Accords. Late in the 1980s, the Accord and the aboriginal claims processes were proceeding simultaneously. It was not certain which would be concluded first and thus, perhaps, define the context to which the other would have to conform. In mid-1990, it appears that the claims have won the race, although it is not certain that the Dene and Métis will ratify their proposed settlement. The parties preparing to negotiate the Accord are assuming that the settlements will be ratified and therefore that the Accord will have to recognize the joint management boards established by the settlements and the interests which settlements will convey to aboriginal groups, particularly as they will be constitutionally entrenched under S 35 of the *Constitution Act, 1982.*

Finally, the outcome will depend on the interaction of the agendas of the players who comprise each of the teams. It has been shown that the federal government is internally divided on whether a Northern Accord should be created and, if it is, what the terms ought to be. Similarly, the territorial teams suffer from mixed motives. The territorial governments want to maximize their power over oil and gas, although this desire is much stronger for the NWT than for the Yukon. The aboriginal groups see potential opportunities in Accord discussions, but will not stay on board if they feel that the discussions will lead to legislative regimes or decision-making bodies which harm their fundamental interests. Also, the Yukon and the Northwest Territories will have to sort out their differences over resource revenue sharing and their respective weights in the management of Beaufort Sea oil and gas. In the end, whether an Accord will eventuate, how long it will take and its terms will depend on the interaction among these many interests.

If the Northern Accords are successfully negotiated, they will influence the constitutional development of the Territories and the real independence of the Territories in very important ways, which raise a set of questions which can be applied to most instances of devolution.

The first of these is the extent to which a Northern Accord will itself diminish the colonialism of the oil and gas regime under which the territories currently labour. To what extent will the Territories be able to fashion energy development policies which are more sensitive to the regional interest than the present regime is? The NWT has already signalled its desire for a regime which enables it to negotiate northern benefits more fully than does the present system while resembling it in other respects. Ottawa's response remains to be seen.

The fiscal arrangements which the territorial governments negotiate with Ottawa may reinforce this colonialism. The territorial governments, and particularly the GNWT, want development funding, favourable royalty regimes and royalty sharing arrangements for the offshore and a reasonable formula for decreasing formula financing once they begin to receive energy revenues. In view of its deficit and the sums it has already invested in northern hydrocarbon development and the territorial governments, Ottawa will resist these demands. It will probably offer trade-offs among them in order to reach agreement within a fixed bottom line. For example, it might offer an increased share of royalties in exchange for less up front development funding. The territorial governments will need to calculate their interests very shrewdly before they respond. Development spending imposes costs which are inescapable, even if the development which they anticipate proves less lucrative than had been expected. The prudent policy would be to seek federal funding which would be equally certain, as well as promptly available. If, however, the territorial governments choose to depend more on income based on production than on secure grants, they will be running a risk. Indeed, to make the risk pay off and to recoup the money they have invested on infrastructure, they may come to feel compelled to promote or accept energy activities which they would not otherwise wish to support. If such a scenario comes to pass, the territorial governments will have gambled, not so much their income, as their independence.

Over and above the constraints of the patterns of intergovernmental power sharing and fiscal arrangements, the territorial governments will be constrained by the dependence on the energy industry which Larry Pratt and John Richards attributed to Alberta and Saskatchewan's early years as energy producers. They noted that these provinces were compelled to put in place energy management regimes which were familiar and attractive to the oil industry in order to induce it to seek and produce their energy resources.[30] Northern energy resources are high cost resources. The industry will only seek them if it sees a profit in the undertaking. This means that the territorial governments may have little room for imposing costly benefits packages or substantial royalties without driving off the industry. Thus, the harsh realities of economics may prevent the territorial governments from realizing the dreams of social and economic development which led them, and particularly the GNWT, to long for a Northern Accord. In the end, the marketplace may impose the most confining dependence of all on the North.

While economics may dictate a dependent future, the Northern Accord may undercut the constitutional colonialism the North faces. By itself, any devolution of jurisdiction brings the territorial governments closer to possessing the full range of powers enjoyed by the provinces, hence it represents a constitutional advance. However, the significance of a Northern Accord could go well beyond this. To the extent that it may direct a substantial flow of money to the territorial governments — and it should be emphasized that this revenue is not assured in view of the high cost of northern exploration and production — they will be able to refute the argument that they lack the fiscal strength which is a prerequisite for provincial status. In addition, if the territorial governments can successfully over a number of years manage the surface and subsurface resources of their lands, they will be in a stronger position to argue, once land claims have been settled, that the land of the North which has not been transferred to aboriginal ownership should be transferred to them. The legally simplest way of accomplishing the transfer of the full array of rights which the federal Crown holds over the land would be to create crowns in the right of the Yukon and the NWT[31]. Once this is accomplished, the Territories will have gained another of the fundamental attributes of provincial status. Such a development would reduce the apparent distance between territorial and provincial status and make it that much easier for the territorial governments to assert their case for being made provinces.

A second set of issues concerns the balance between the communities and regions of the NWT on the one hand, and the GNWT focussed in Yellowknife on the other. As noted above, the Inuit want the Accord to spread the economic benefits of oil and gas development among all the the regions of the NWT and they want a significant role for their regions in the determination and implementation of oil and gas policy. However, the enabling agreement makes no reference to regional consultation or benefits whatever. GNWT policy emphasizes community rather than regional governments.[32] Given that the communities tend to lack adequate resources to deal effectively with oil and gas-related policy issues, and that the interests of the communities within a region may conflict, the absence of strong regional governments makes it likely that the GNWT will dominate any consideration of the regional impacts of energy development, unless one of the aboriginal groups is able to enter the fray. While the Accord might have provided an opportunity to strengthen regional government, it appears that that opportunity will be lost.

A third and perhaps most important set of issues is the impact of a Northern Accord on the relations and political balance between the governments and the aboriginal groups of the two Territories, particularly the NWT. While the GNWT has supported aboriginal goals in many instances, the aboriginal groups tend to feel that it will subordinate their interests to its own. They see the GNWT as more interested in establishing itself as a fullfledged public government than in building a North which accommodates their unique land- and water-based cultures. They doubt that the GNWT is prepared to share with them adequate jurisdiction over the land and water to preserve the material basis of their cultures. They also doubt, should the GNWT monopolize this jurisdiction, that it will exercise it in a fashion adequately responsive to their needs, despite the aboriginal majority in the Legislative Assembly.

For this reason they are seeking guaranteed participation on public agencies having management responsibilities relating to oil and gas, to complement their participation on public boards managing surface resources which they have gained through their claims settlements. The outcome of this pursuit will be crucial in defining the role of the GNWT and its relationship to aboriginal residents of the Territories. To the extent that the GNWT manages oil and gas on its own or with weak advisory bodies, it will enjoy the power to define the "public interest", which will thus appear to reflect the unity of the NWT. However, if significant — that is, adequately staffed and funded — joint management boards with powerful representation of aboriginal interests are created, policy becomes the result of negotiation, which emphasizes the separate interests of the aboriginal people and suggests that the GNWT is not capable of fully representing these special interests. In other words, above and beyond the actual decisions which will be reached, the way in which the NWT develops and implements its oil and gas policy raises larger questions of the legitimacy of the GNWT and whether it is truly a public government. To the extent that the aboriginal groups can create oil and gas agencies which suggest that it is not, they will reinforce the plausibility of their call for the development of aboriginal self-governments in the NWT. The politics of this process will be complex. The GNWT will want to avoid the intergovernmental duplication and conflict which substantial aboriginal self-government would bring. This will lead it to make concessions to maintain its legitimacy among the aboriginal people. Already it has committed itself in both the Inuit and the Dene/Métis claims settlements to pursue negotiations about reforming public government in the Territories.[33] However, the GNWT will be careful to ensure that the concessions it makes are not so extensive as to validate the claims they are intended to allay, or as to weaken it unnecessarily.

The fact that the NWT is not yet a province with a fully elaborated Westminster model of government gives the aboriginal groups the ability to pursue this possible path of constitutional development, an opportunity enjoyed by no other aboriginal groups in Canada.[34] Even in the Yukon, the form of government is well established. However, the absence of party politics, the weaker tradition of responsible government,[35] the issue of division of the NWT and the fact that aboriginal people comprise 50 percent of the population combine to make a new form of government — one which deviates from the parliamentary model — at least a possibility. This possibility gives the aboriginal groups of the NWT a political agenda. Their goal is to shape a pattern of government in the NWT which will protect their basic interests. They sense that they will only gain a novel form of public government if they can compel the non-aboriginal population of the Territory to accept it. Non-aboriginals tend to feel comfortable with the parliamentary system which emphasizes majority rule and individual rights, values in which they believe. They view it as the natural direction of evolution for the Territories in that it is found everywhere else in Canada. As the GNWT comes to gain more of the features of the parliamentary system — an elected government leader and an executive composed exclusively of elected MLAs — they feel more confident of this outcome. Devolution in general and a Northern Accord in particular, given its importance, will add to this confidence. They will imply that Ottawa accepts the current direction of evolution of the GNWT, hence that they need make no basic concessions to the aboriginal peoples of the Territory in order to gain eventually more powers.

A Northern Accord will enhance the territorial government at the expense of the aboriginal groups in another way. Devolution implies the expansion of the territorial state. As power moves northward, more "person-years" are added to the territorial government's staff complement. If these positions are filled by non-aboriginals from outside the NWT, they will alter — albeit modestly — the ethnic balance in the territorial population. To the extent that they are filled by aboriginal people, these individuals may well identify with the territorial government and see their interests as intertwined with its goals more than with those of the aboriginal organizations. In general, as the territorial government does more, people, whether they like it or not, will see the government as powerful and the aboriginal groups as proportionately less so, hence, perhaps, less credible.

Such an evolution may affect the aboriginal groups' agendas in two ways. First, to the extent that they are seeking some form of aboriginal self-government, the size and complexity of the GNWT's activities as a result of devolution may prove daunting to their members, who must be persuaded that aboriginal self-government is not just desirable in principle, but actually viable in practice. Second, for the Inuit leaders, devolution poses the threat that their people will become so dependent on the jobs, contracts and services provided by the GNWT, even if they have complaints about them, that they will be reluctant to risk the uncertainties that division of the NWT involves. In this way, devolution may enable the GNWT to co-opt the Inuit.

Given these possibilities, the aboriginal peoples will want equivalent benefits in return for their support of the Northern Accord. The Northern Accord process will be the greatest challenge which devolution has presented the aboriginal peoples of the NWT. The Northern Accord is one of the most powerful levers which they may still use against the GNWT in that there are few other advances over which they may exercise significant control and which the GNWT wants as much as it wants an energy accord.

Conclusion

World oil and gas prices may promote the attainment of the Northern Accords because the rents to be divided in the near future are likely to be modest. There is not much to fight over. However, the conflicting interests represented in both the territorial and the national positions will make the negotiations complex, as will the linkages to basic issues of northern politics and the future fiscal implications of northern resources. In the end, Northern Accords may be as elusive to contemporary politicians as a northern passage to the Orient proved to be to explorers of an earlier era.

NOTES

1   *Statutes of Canada, 1986,* (Ottawa: Queen's Printer, 1987), chapter 45.

2   R.S., c. O-4, s. 1.

3   This decline can be traced by comparing DIAND, *North of 60: Oil and Gas Statistical Report No. 3 1920-1981,* (Ottawa: 1984) and COGLA Annual Reports for recent years.

4   "Schedule, Constitutional Amendment 1987", *1987 Constitutional Accord,* S9 and Gurston Dacks, "The View from Meech Lake: The Constitutional Future of the Governments of the Yukon and the Northwest Territories in Rebecca Aird, ed., *Running the North: The Getting and Spending of Public Finances by Canada's Territorial Governments,* (Ottawa: Canadian Arctic Resources Committee, 1988), pp. 69-110.

5   Government of the Northwest Territories, *Direction for the 1990s,* (Yellowknife: GNWT, 1988) p. 2.

6   Gurston Dacks *A Choice of Futures,* (Toronto: Methuen, 1981) pages 13-9; Northwest Territories, Legislative Assembly, Special Committee on the Northern Economy. *The SCONE Report: Building Our Economic Future,* (Yellowknife, Legislative Assembly of the N.W.T., 1990).

7   Gordon Robertson, *Northern Provinces: A Mistaken Goal ,* (Montreal: The Institute for Research on Public Policy, 1985), pp. 25-35.

8   See, for example, Dene/Métis Negotiations Secretariat, Comprehensive Claims Branch (DIAND), Aboriginal Rights and Constitutional Development (GNWT), *Comprehensive Land Claim Agreement between Canada and the Dene Nation and Métis Association of the Northwest Territories,* (mimeo, April 9, 1990), Sections 28-30 and Indian and Northern Affairs Canada, *Tungavik Federation of Nunavut Land Claim Agreement-in-Principle,* (mimeo, February 2, 1990).

9   Dene/Métis Negotiations Secretariat, Comprehensive Claims Branch (DIAND), Aboriginal Rights and Constitutional Development (GNWT), *Comprehensive Land Claim Agreement between Canada and the Dene Nation and Metis Association of the Northwest Territories,* (mimeo, April 9, 1990), Section 22.

10   Department of Indian Affairs and Northern Development. *Western Arctic Claim: The Inuvialuit Final Agreement*, (Ottawa: DIAND, 1984), pp. 15-16.

11   Minister of Indian Affairs and Northern Development, *Comprehensive Land Claims Policy* (Ottawa: Supply and Services Canada, 1987), p. 18.

12   Indian and Northern Affairs Canada, *op. cit.*, Article 30; Dene Nation, Métis Association of the N.W.T. and Government of the Northwest Territories (mimeo, April 24, 1986), also personal interview with Bill Erasmus, December 16, 1988.

13   IRC, Dene Nation, Métis Association, TFN, "News Release", September 27, 1988, p. 2.

14   David Milne, *Tug of War: Ottawa and the Provinces Under Trudeau and Mulroney* (Toronto: Lorimer, 1986), pp. 27-28, 201.

15   Government of Canada, *Canada's Energy Frontiers: A Framework for Investment and Jobs* (Ottawa: Supply and Services Canada, 1985), p. 2.

16   Government of Canada, *A Northern Political and Economic Framework*, (Ottawa: Supply and Services Canada, 1988), p. 8.

17   Memorandum of Understanding on the Negotiation and Implementation of a Northern Accord, (Yellowknife: April 11, 1988).

18   Government of the Northwest Territories, *Direction for the 1990s* (Yellowknife: Government of the NWT, 1988), p. 2.

19   Presidents of the TFN, Dene Nation and Métis Association and Chief Councillor of the Inuvialuit Regional Corporation to the Legislative Assembly of the NWT, October 25, 1988.

20   Motion 29-88 (2) in Legislative Assembly of the Northwest Territories, *Hansard*, 11th Assembly, Third Session, November 2, 1988, p. 727.

21   The documents signed in September of 1988 are entitled "Agreement in Principle". However, the GNWT insists that this is a misnomer in that this term implies a much more detailed agreement than was actually signed and that part of the displeasure of the aboriginal groups arose from their presumption, based on the use of the incorrect term, that much more had been decided behind their backs than was really the case. The GNWT insists that the correct term is "enabling agreement". As

this usage seems more common and in order to avoid confusion with the Dene/Métis claims agreement in principle, this paper will use the term, "enabling agreement".

22   Government of Canada, *Canada's Energy Frontiers*, p. 13.

23   Inuvialuit Regional Corporation, Dene Nation, Métis Association, TFN, "Press Release", September 27, 1988, p. 1.

24   Interview with Dennis Patterson, Leader of the Government of the NWT, October 26, 1988.

25   Nigel Bankes, "The Status of Hudson Bay" in *Northern Perspectives*, Vol. 15, No. 3 (October, 1987), pp. 15-16.

26   "Notes for Remarks by the Honourable Dennis Patterson, Government Leader, Government of the Northwest Territories on the Northern Accord", September 6, 1988, mimeo, p. 5.

27   Letter from Donat Milortuk, President of the TFN, to Dennis Patterson, Government Leader of the Government of the NWT, September 9, 1988.

28   Legislative Assembly of the Northwest Territories, *Hansard*, 11th Assembly, 3rd Session, Wednesday, November 2, 1988, pp. 732-34.

29   Article 28. Large water power generating or water exploitation projects throughout the Settlement Area, not just on Inuit lands, will be the subject of Benefits Agreements.

30   Larry Pratt and John Richards, *Prairie Capitalism*, (Toronto: McClelland and Stewart, 1979), pp. 71-73.

31   Gurston Dacks, "Life after Meech Lake", pp. 73, 92-93.

32   Government of the Northwest Territories, *Direction for the 1990s* (Yellowknife: GNWT, 1988), p. 8; and Katherine Graham, "Devolution and Local Government" in this volume.

33   Indian and Northern Affairs Canada, op. cit., Article 4 and Dene/Métis Negotiation Secretariat, op. cit., Section 7.

34   This theme is discussed at greater length in Gurston Dacks, "Devolution and Political Development in the Canadian North", this volume.

35   Graham Eglington, "Matters of Confidence in the Legislative Assembly of the Northwest Territories" in Special Committee on Rules, Procedures and Privileges, Tenth Legislative Assembly of the Northwest Territories, *Third Report*, (Yellowknife: 1986).

8   Implementing the Policy to Devolve: Learning by Doing

Katherine A. Graham

It is important to step back from the individual case studies of devolution recounted in this volume to consider whether any general patterns emerge in the negotiation of devolution agreements. In essence, this represents an examination of the implementation of the federal government's policy to devolve additional responsibilities to the two Territories and the territorial governments' corresponding policy of embracing devolution, when it seems appropriate.

This thematic examination of devolution negotiations through the prism of implementation is worthwhile for at least two reasons.[1] First, it will help to inform future negotiations. Devolution of responsibilities from the federal government to the NWT and Yukon has tended to occur in waves. In recent years, the development of the Government of the Northwest Territories (GNWT) provides the most striking example of this pattern. The shift of the territorial capital to Yellowknife in the late 1960s, plus the creation of an independent legislative assembly and civil service, represents an earlier wave of devolution which is significant in and of itself, but which also provided the foundation for many of the cases of devolution in the 1980s which are recounted here. By drawing out the patterns and trends in negotiating devolution in this more recent period, we can inform ourselves for the future when, presumably, additional devolution will occur.

It is also important to assess overall patterns in devolution negotiations because those negotiations themselves may shape the future. A major impetus for devolution is the notion that the assumption of new responsibilities by a territorial government will somehow contribute to the development of more responsive government in the North and to the positive advancement of the people of the Territories. The potential for positive change in the post-transfer period is examined by Frances Abele elsewhere in this volume. However, this thematic examination of the negotiation process leading up to the transfer also informs our understanding of what might occur in the post-transfer period. By assessing such things as political and bureaucratic commitment in different cases of negotiating devolution, the timing of negotiations in the context of other important events in the evolution of the Territories and the role of non-government interests or stakeholders in the negotiation process, we can consider the extent to which the negotiation process itself casts an influence over implementation of change in the post-transfer period.

This chapter examines four basic questions about the negotiations to implement devolution. First, it will consider to what extent the overall policy environment within which the devolution policy was implemented was important in determining various stakeholders' views of devolution and in shaping their actions. Devolution was but one policy in a complex constellation. Initiatives and debates in such areas as aboriginal claims, the role of the federal state, the overall political and constitutional development of the two Territories (including the development of local and regional government) and economic development, just to name a few, appeared to exert an important influence on devolution negotiations. Two dimensions of this influence will be probed: the extent to which the broader policy environment informed and influenced different stakeholders' conceptions of what devolution meant, in terms of shifting responsibility and authority between the federal government and the territorial governments; and the extent to which the broader policy environment influenced the interplay of different actors as negotiations proceeded.

The second focus of this chapter is to probe the extent to which particular characteristics of the negotiation process itself influenced the implementation of devolution policy. In this context, it will examine the effort to reach broad federal-territorial government agreements (framework agreements) concerning the transfer process. It will also assess the role of central agencies at the territorial and federal levels in shaping the process, as well as the roles played by politicians and bureaucrats. Finally, it will examine efforts within the GNWT to systematize negotiations, in the context of some of the debates in the literature on implementation and development administration about blueprint versus more adaptive or iterative approaches to implementation.[2]

The third stream of inquiry concerns the extent to which specific substantive issues — budgets, personnel, facilities, etc. — emerged as prominent in the discussion of devolving particular functions. Two basic questions which will be addressed concern how these substantive issues were dealt with and the extent to which the resolution of these issues constrains or enlarges the potential for positive change in the post-transfer period.

Finally, the chapter will conclude with an assessment of the most important patterns (if any) that emerge from the various cases and the lessons that can be learned.

The evidentiary base for this analysis is primarily provided by the specific case studies of the devolution of health services, forest and fire management and other powers found in this volume. However, reference will also be made to two other instances of devolution: the transfer of control of the Northern Canada Power Commission (NCPC) to the two territorial governments[3] and the devolution of responsibility for the Science Institute of the Northwest Territories and federal science laboratories in the NWT to the Government of the Northwest Territories.

Looking at all of the cases that will be considered, we cannot identify any examples of absolute failure to negotiate some form of devolution agreement. However, examining the cases from the standpoint of the two territorial governments, we can point to variations in the ease and efficacy of negotiations. It is these variations that are important to probe.[4]

Devolution and the Policy Environment

In both Territories, the devolution negotiations were undertaken in a complex policy environment. Although devolution was a high priority item, especially in the eyes of the GNWT, it shared the stage with aboriginal claims, federal government downsizing and fiscal restraint (which would have an effect on spending in areas important to the two territorial governments), and the search for a sustainable economic development strategy for the two Territories. These are just a few elements in the constellation of policy issues faced by the Government of the Northwest Territories and the Yukon Territorial Government (YTG) in the 1980s.

The situation was perhaps clearest in the Yukon. The YTG acknowledged that devolution would have an important role to play in the evolution of that Territory. However, the dominant priority was to resolve the outstanding CYI claim. As a result, devolution took a back seat and was not as actively pursued as in the NWT case.

There appear to be three main reasons for the pursuit of devolution in the Yukon. The first was in instances where gaining control of a particular function was thought to be important to all Yukoners. Ownership of NCPC was sought for this reason. The second context in which devolution was pursued was in cases where the opportunity presented itself to obtain responsibility for rather minor programs which were, nonetheless, important to a small segment of Yukoners. Negotiations to devolve mine safety and land titles to the YTG are two cases in point. Finally, there is the case of devolution of responsibility for the inland fishery to the Yukon. In this instance, the prospect of federal-territorial devolution was of some concern to the CYI, as the Council was worried that devolution would prejudice the claim. However, devolution went ahead because the particular Yukon minister responsible for the devolution negotiations (David Porter) had a great deal of personal credibility with the CYI executive and membership. With his assurances, federal-territorial negotiations were permitted to proceed. Under another minister, this may not have occurred. For its part, the federal government seems to have been sympathetic to the priority accorded the claim settlement in the Yukon. Indeed, settlement of the CYI claim may have been the federal government's own priority in the Yukon.

In contrast, there was a tension in the NWT between the GNWT and federal government's quest to pursue devolution and other interests. In the case of the Northern Accord, extra-territorial interests had to be assuaged. The oil and gas industry was concerned that an increased role for the GNWT in the management of oil and gas development would lead to uncertainty in regulatory and management regimes and, perhaps, to policies which were harmful to industry interests. The GNWT had to engage in an extensive consultation process with the industry to gain its support for the idea of an accord. This was done with the help of some notable industry insiders, and Peter Lougheed, the former premier of Alberta.

However, the most significant tension was between the GNWT devolution initiative and the interests of those aboriginal organizations in the NWT with outstanding claims. They wanted to see their claims settled before devolution. The affected groups were the Dene and Métis in the west and the Inuit of the central and eastern arctic, represented by the Tungavik Federation of Nunavut (TFN).

The stance taken by officials of the GNWT was that devolution did not have any direct bearing on such issues as claims and resolution of the question of whether or not the NWT should be divided into two territories. For their part, the aboriginal organizations worried that pursuit of devolution would close off various options for governance of the NWT in the post-claims era. This concern led to an effort by the Dene/Métis to conclude a Memorandum of Understanding with the GNWT which committed the territorial government not to pursue devolution in areas prejudicial to their claim. The TFN's concern was manifested in its broad objection to GNWT devolution initiatives. The two exceptions were in the area of health services and the quest for an oil and gas accord. The TFN supported devolution of health because of the Inuit Tapirisat of Canada's positive experience with the devolution of health services in the Baffin in the early 1980s.[5] It did not oppose the idea of an oil and gas accord because such an accord would not have any immediate impact on Inuit interests in the central and eastern Arctic. If oil and gas development were to occur there in the longer term,

TFN officials thought that an oil and gas accord could pave the way for financial benefits for their people.

As various devolution negotiations evolved in the NWT, the actions of the GNWT were not always seen by the Dene/Métis as consistent with the Memorandum of Understanding not to tread on the subject matter of claims negotiations. For example, the Dene/Métis became exercised when the GNWT sought owner- ship of forests as federal-territorial negotiations concerning the devolution of responsibility for fire management proceeded. There were similar tensions evident in the discussions associ- ated with the devolution of responsibility for wildlife and inland fisheries.

One obvious result of the tension between devolution and other issues was that the quest for devolution by GNWT politi- cians and bureaucrats was accompanied by some degree of suspicion by at least one major stakeholder — aboriginal organizations with outstanding claims. One consequence of this is that the political stakes in the post-devolution period have been raised. In areas where devolution has occurred, the GNWT is being closely watched by aboriginal organizations and other stakeholders to ensure that subsequent territorial government initiatives are consistent with local, regional and aboriginal interests in different parts of the Territories. The vociferous objections to the 1989 GNWT Transfer Policy, which appeared to consolidate territorial government control over personnel and other key resources, even in areas such as health where regional boards were established, suggests that GNWT initiatives are indeed being closely monitored. The participation of the Denendeh Conservation Board (DCB) in the development of a new fire management policy for the NWT is another example of the keen desire of other stakeholders to exert the maximum influence possible in the post-transfer period and to ensure that their concerns about the prejudicial influence of devolution on other areas, such as claims, are met.

The tension between the GNWT and other stakeholders at the time of devolution negotiations also suggests that the future role of the GNWT as the lead authority in areas that have been devolved is by no means guaranteed. One aspect of this may be the GNWT's own willingness to devolve authority further in light of concerns of other stakeholders. Some signs of this are evident in the GNWT's involvement of wildlife management boards, Hunters and Trappers Associations, the DCB and regional health boards in a management or advisory capacity in areas where it has received responsibility from the federal government. The chapters in this volume on the devolution of health care in the Baffin and on devolution and local government suggest that there is some scepticism about whether the GNWT will devolve real powers to health boards or local and regional governments. However, we have to wait before passing judgment on where the devolution process will end.

Another aspect may be the persistent efforts of other stakeholders to achieve power through other forums. For example, the wildlife and forest/fire management cases allude to the efforts of aboriginal organizations to achieve authority over land and natural resources. The study of the impact of devolution on local government suggests that communities in the western part of the NWT with predominantly Dene populations may attempt to negotiate self-government agreements with the federal government to achieve the power and autonomy at the local level that they want.

These initiatives by other stakeholders are bolstered by the fact that devolution has been accomplished by administrative change, rather than by legislative change. The *Northwest Territories Act* has not been amended during the course of this wave of devolution to suggest that the Government of the Northwest Territories has any new powers. The GNWT has negotiated devolution agreements which give it new responsibilities, but not any formal authority in the legal sense. This may serve the interests of other stakeholders in the NWT and also those of the other major stakeholder — the federal government.

At the federal level, there appear to have been two major reasons for pursuing devolution. Perhaps the most prevalent of the two was to reduce the size of the federal state by transferring resources and responsibilities to the territorial governments. This objective was certainly important as the Conservative government began its downsizing initiative after the 1984 election. The other federal objective was to transfer responsibility for decision making about the territorial north closer to the people who were directly affected. In short, devolution was seen in some quarters within the federal government as a vehicle for the empowerment of northerners and their governments.

The degree of support for devolution as a vehicle for empowerment varied widely within the federal government. Case study evidence suggests that the Minister of Health and Welfare and his senior officials were very supportive of the transfer of health services. At least at the bureaucratic level, the departments of Fisheries and Oceans, Environment and Energy, Mines and Resources were reluctant to loosen or cut existing strings of control. The Department of Indian Affairs and Northern Development (DIAND) seems to have fallen somewhere in the middle.

In some cases, such as wildlife, initial reluctance on the part of federal officials to embrace the devolution initiative subsided as negotiations proceeded. However, as the whole process of devolution evolved during the 1980s, there began to be some concern in the federal ranks about where the whole process would end up, in terms of the federal government having sufficient policy and program levers to influence northern development. For some departments, most notably EMR in the case of the northern oil and gas accords, the pressures of other demands, for example for energy resources and environmental probity, were seen as more important than territorial aspirations for an enhanced role.

Overall then, we can conclude that the broad policy environment was important in the implementation of devolution during the negotiation stage. Where other elements of the policy constellation were seen as superseding devolution, various stakeholders pulled back. This is exemplified by the approach taken by the Yukon Territorial Government to devolution and by the reluctance of EMR to participate in the negotiation of oil and gas accords because of that department's view that central control of northern energy was consistent with the national interest. The preoccupation of one important stakeholder in the

NWT, aboriginal organizations with claims, dampened the ability of the GNWT to pursue devolution to its fullest and casts some doubt about the permanence of arrangements for governance in the NWT in the immediate post-transfer era. The pressure emanating from this source during the negotiation period may be very positive in the sense that it heightens the need for the GNWT to demonstrate its commitment to use its devolved responsibities to improve the responsiveness of policies and programs to the needs of people in the NWT. In that sense, the policy decision by either territorial government to pursue devolution can be seen as potentially the beginning of an extended chain of decisions which will change the way people in the North are governed in a manner that is responsive to their needs as time goes on. In this context, the policy to grasp at the brass ring of devolution can be viewed, not as a single policy decision, but as the beginning of an iterative process of policy redesign. There is considerable evidence in the literature to suggest that this process is the essence of implementation.[6]

The Negotiation Process Itself and Implementing Devolution

One of the central debates in the literature on policy and program implementation concerns the relative merits of "blueprint" versus "process" approaches to implementation.[7] Advocates of blueprint or programmed implementation see detailed policy design as the engine which drives execution. In contrast, the process approach conceives of policy as necessarily being in a continuous state of evolution. Part of that evolution is the continuous adaptation of the programs and organizations that emerge at the beginning of a particular initiative. Forces creating the need for such modifications include: changes in the level of interest and commitment by key actors, changes in the availability of different kinds of resources and the emergence of different policies, programs and organizations to deal with the issue at hand. From the "process" perspective, implementation of the policy decision to pursue devolution by either territorial government should be marked by experimentation and adaptation, rather than by ironclad plans of implementation, which may prove inappropriate but may still retain a life of their own.

The previous section of this chapter suggests the extent to which the complex and changing policy environment contributed to the sporadic and sometimes rocky implementation of devolution. There were also particular characteristics of the negotiation process itself which suggest that an adaptive or process approach to implementation was the only feasible option.

The above is not intended to suggest that the negotiation process was characterized by unorganized ad hocery. On the contrary, there were several initiatives to systematize the process, although several dimensions of the negotiating process itself served to limit constructive efforts to systematize.

There were three main efforts to systematize the devolution negotiations. The first, and perhaps most fundamental, involved an effort to conclude a "master agreement" between the federal government and each territorial government on the order of negotiating the devolution of specific functions.

In the Yukon, there were two overarching agreements between the YTG and the federal government regarding devolution. The first involved an exchange of letters, at the official and ministerial level, in 1987 which reflected a consensus between the Yukon and federal governments about the priority list of functions for discussion. These included forestry and health services.[8] One significant difference between the parties does emerge from these letters. It relates to the financial principles each government intended to pursue in the negotiations. The federal government indicated it would transfer the existing financial base of each program devolved to the YTG. In contrast, the Yukon letters indicate that the territorial government would seek sufficient financial resources through the negotiations to meet program needs, as identified by the YTG. The second agreement was a Memorandum of Understanding (MOU) concluded in 1988. From the YTG perspective, conclusion of this second agreement was aimed at tying devolution more closely to the broader issue of the future constitutional development of the territory.[9] However, federal interest in pursuing devolution in this broader context has not been sustained. Negotiations in the Yukon continue on a function-by-function basis.

The effort to conclude a formal MOU failed in the NWT case. The GNWT wanted a detailed master agreement that contained a specific schedule of negotiations and stipulated a range of commitments to be made in each negotiating round. For its part, the federal government did not want to be tied down in this manner, partly because it was concerned that a detailed commitment to negotiate devolution might prejudice claims negotiations. As a result, negotiations to devolve responsibility for health care, airports, etc. occurred on a case-by-case basis.

The failure to reach a Memorandum of Understanding on the order of negotiations between the GNWT and the federal government meant that the initiation of negotiations for the devolution of any specific function often stemmed from the interest of particular individuals. Sometimes, these were federal representatives. For example, the head of the Science Insitute of the Northwest Territories was instrumental in initiating the negotiations on the Science Institute and labs. In other cases, the first federal response to a proposal that a particular function be devolved set the priority for an agreement to be negotiated. For example, the then Minister of Health and Welfare was very supportive of the idea of devolving health services to the GNWT and so negotiations related to that function became a high priority. In the forest and fire management case, the apparent support for devolution by the then Associate Deputy Minister of DIAND responsible for the Northern Program likely spurred on the negotiating efforts of the Minister and Deputy Minister of Renewable Resources in the GNWT. This pattern of emphasising negotiations in those areas where there was greatest federal interest contributed to the conclusion of agreements to devolve specific functions. These negotiations were easier because of federal interest. However, the absence of an agreed upon game plan for the order of devolution negotiations also gave the federal government the advantage of being able to pick and choose when it would put the negotiating process on a fast track. Despite the avowed federal philosophy that the initiative for devolution should come from the territorial level, the federal government exerted considerable control over the process. This is not surprising, given that the federal government held all the jurisdictional power and the financial resources.

The second effort to systematize the negotiation process involved the establishment of a Devolution Office by each territorial government. In the GNWT case, the Devolution Office was given the specific responsibility to act as the central staff resource to the NWT Assembly, Cabinet and GNWT departments as negotiations for transfers proceeded. It was established in 1986, following the negotiations on the devolution of fire and forest management. These negotiations, while ultimately fruitful, were accompanied by some last minute surprises related to those aspects of the transfer involving personnel and the need to deal with the interests of the Dene and Métis. One aspect of the office's mandate was to help the GNWT avoid such difficulties in future negotiations. The Yukon Territorial Government established a similar office. However, as will be seen, its approach to carrying out its mandate was more low-key. This was partly a reflection of the relatively low priority accorded the wholesale pursuit of devolution by the YTG during the period studied.[10] The same phenomenon can be observed in the GNWT context. By late 1989, the sense in the NWT was that the current round of devolution was coming to an end. As a result, key personnel in the GNWT Devolution Office were given new postings and the operation was downsized. Its work was subsequently absorbed into the work of another office dealing with broader political development issues in the NWT. Presumably, if the process of devolution reintensifies, the GNWT will consider resuscitating a distinct Devolution Office.

There are at least two good reasons for establishing a central agency to help implement devolution. The first is to provide each territorial government with a cumulative memory of previous experience negotiating devolution agreements. When something as intensive as the various negotiations on devolution is occurring, a central office at the territorial level can help negotiators from departments that will be receiving the specific responsibilities under discussion by acting as an experienced coach concerning the negotiation process *per se*. Appropriately staffed, such an office can also help by giving neophytes from line departments an understanding of the complex dynamics which frequently accompany dealing with the federal government. A territorial administrator in the wildlife area may feel quite experienced dealing with locally based federal counterparts. However, the dynamics of the relations between Ottawa headquarters and the territorial offices of federal departments may be unfamiliar. Evidence suggests that Ottawa and regional offices were sometimes prone to disagree during the negotiation process. Similarly, it may be difficult for someone from a specialized field to deal with the interest of central agencies in the federal government, such as Treasury Board and the departments of Finance and Justice, during devolution negotiations. A broad knowledge of the negotiating environment is, then, one important contribution of a devolution office.

The second major contribution of such an office is to make departmental negotiators aware of central issues that are likely to emerge during the negotiations. In the NWT case, before the devolution office was established, GNWT was caught off guard when issues related to the personnel aspects of the transfer became problematic in the forest and fire management and NCPC negotiations. While no one can be completely prescient, the broad experience of staff from a central office focussing on devolution appeared to help both territorial governments avoid unpleasant surprises.

These two efforts to systematize the negotiation process were evident in both territorial governments. The third initiative to bring order to the negotiating process occurred in the NWT. While the effort to conclude a master MOU with the federal government to program the course of all devolution negotiations foundered, the GNWT did produce its own Devolution Policy and related directives.[11] To support these, the Devolution Office prepared a detailed manual for GNWT use on the organization, process and techniques to be used when negotiating specific transfers. The second volume of this manual is a negotiator's guide.[12] In addition to outlining stages of the negotiation process, it defines the responsibilities of line departments, such as

Health or Renewable Resources, which might be taking the lead in transfer negotiations. It concludes with a series of questions and answers, designed to stimulate the thought processes of territorial negotiators and a transfer checklist to help make certain that all bases are covered before negotiations are ended. This document is as close to a negotiator's blueprint as one could get, although it is a guide rather than a mandatory procedures manual.

The case study evidence suggests that there were inherent limits to the influence these efforts at systematization could have on the negotiating process.

Perhaps the most fundamental source of variability in the negotiating process stemmed from the differences in the substance of what was being negotiated in each case. To be sure, a common thread in all of the devolution negotiations was that they were concerned with the transfer of resources — personnel, budgets, equipment and facilities — from one government to another. But the influence of the specific nature of the functions under discussion — health, wildlife, forest and fire management, and so on — on the negotiating process should not be minimized.

This history of politics and administration of the particular area under discussion is important. For example, in the health and wildlife cases, northerners had experienced a long history of knowing that these services were critical to their well-being. But this history was accompanied by a sense of alienation from the approach taken by the federal government to providing those services. As a result, the political stakes associated with obtaining responsibility for providing such services were higher than in the case of a relatively low impact and uncontentious service, such as that provided by the Science Institute of the NWT. There is at least some evidence to suggest that the territorial governments were more willing to compromise in order to break negotiating logjams in the negotiations related to services which were seen as high priority. For example, the GNWT agreed to an enriched benefit package for northern health care workers who would be transferred in order to meet the objections of those workers, despite the later problems that this would cause with health care workers hired directly by the GNWT. The Science Institute/lab negotiations were much lower profile and affected a much more limited constituency. (Indeed, one might argue that the main interested parties in these negotiations were southern based researchers.) With relatively little at stake, these negotiations became the most difficult and protracted.

The second influence of the substance of what was being negotiated on the negotiating process stemmed from the importance of the subject matter under negotiation to outstanding aboriginal claims. In cases such as wildlife and forest management, the potential impact on the interests of native claimants of a transfer of responsibility from the federal government to either territorial government made the negotiation process more complex. This additional complexity had two dimensions. First, aboriginal organizations representing claimants wanted to be involved in the devolution negotiations, thereby increasing the number of parties at the table. Second, the precise nature of native interests with respect to the transfer had to be determined and dealt with before devolution could proceed. As indicated earlier, some unique (and one would hope positive) arrangements for the involvement of native interests in the management of responsibilities for wildlife and forests in the post-transfer period have resulted.

The second variable which limited predictablity in the negotiations was the nature of involvement of territorial and federal politicians.

At the territorial level, the experience in the NWT is most instructive. Individual negotiations were accompanied by different levels of political interest by the NWT Cabinet and its individual ministers. For example, ministers (especially the Government Leader) played important roles in the negotiation of the Memorandum of Understanding concerning an oil and gas accord and the Minister of Renewable Resources was a key player in the decision to seek the devolution of responsibility for forest and fire management. In contrast, there was very little political involvement in the negotiation of the transfer of the Science Institute and labs.

One of the main challenges for territorial negotiators seems to have been to obtain the sustained interest of individual ministers and Cabinet in each negotiation so that their good offices could be used in the negotiating process at what they considered appropriate times. Difficulties that were experienced in this regard were likely due, at least in part, to the quickly changing political environment in the NWT.

Ministers and MLAs have to deal with the political needs and interests of their respective constituencies. As is already evident, a very important constituency in the context of devolution was that of the territory's aboriginal peoples, the majority of whom have outstanding aboriginal claims. The role of aboriginal organizations varied across the cases. These differences were accompanied by variations in the pattern of involvement of territorial ministers in the negotiations. When negotiations were perceived by one or more aboriginal organizations as prejudicial to their claim, there was considerable ministerial involvement. This was the case in forest and fire management, the negotiations related to the Northern Accord on oil and gas, and some aspects of wildlife. When these organizations supported a territorial takeover, as was the case in health services, territorial ministers appear to have been less active in the negotiations. When there was downright disinterest on the part of aboriginal organizations in the subject of negotiations (as was the case with the Science Institute and labs), there was minimal ministerial involvement. This suggests that territorial ministers viewed the devolution negotiations themselves as part of their total political agenda. They were to be managed in the face of other political pressures. The negotiations were not seen as self-contained or inherently subject to technocratic management.

At the federal level, ministerial interest in the negotiations seems to have been more directly related to each minister's personal agenda and level of support for the policy of devolution. Perhaps the most glaring example of this is the involvement of the Prime Minister's Office in insuring that the Memorandums of Understanding on the oil and gas accords with the two Territories were completed before the 1988 federal election.

However, Jake Epp, as Minister of Health and Welfare also played an important role in the negotiations to devolve health care by giving his support to the principle of devolution and ensuring that the team of officials from his department participating in the negotiations was staffed by people who were well-disposed to the idea.

Federal ministers have also become involved in negotiations when they viewed the direction being taken as potentially damaging to their interests. For example, the Minister of Fisheries and Oceans protracted negotiations on the devolution of fisheries in the early 1980s by vetoing the idea that joint management boards involving aboriginal organizations might be given substantial control over management of the fishery in the post-devolution period.

The overall pattern that emerges when we look at the role of federal and territorial politicians in the negotiation process is not really surprising. They became involved when they thought they had to. However, the specific impetus for ministerial involvement does seem to have varied between the two groups. Territorial ministers tended to become involved to move the devolution initiative through the complex political agenda in the Territories. Federal ministers seem to have become involved either as aggressive proponents or opponents of devolution. In both cases, ministerial involvement influenced the pace and climate of the negotiating process, as well as the substance of the negotiations themselves.

A third variable influencing the negotiation process was the difference in the level of support for devolution found in the federal bureaucracy. Elsewhere in this volume Gurston Dacks discusses the differences of opinion among officials from the federal departments of Indian Affairs and Northern Development and Energy, Mines and Resources about the wisdom of negotiating an oil and gas accord with the territorial governments which would enhance their role in the development of northern energy resources and give them a designated share in the benefits of energy development. DIAND favoured the accords while officials in EMR saw themselves as the guardians of the national interest.

These interdepartmental differences were important in most of the cases. Sometimes they were between line departments with specific responsibilities subject to devolution. In addition to doing battle with officials from EMR, DIAND also had to overcome the reluctance of the Departments of Environment and Fisheries and Oceans about devolving functions within their respective jurisdictions.

Sometimes, there were differences in perception between line departments negotiating devolution agreements and the central agencies of the federal government, such as Treasury Board, the Department of Finance and the Department of Justice. These differences tended to relate to the question of whether the federal interest had been served by the specific terms of an agreement. For example, federal central agencies became concerned about the financial implications for the federal government of giving the Territories a share in oil and gas revenues. Treasury Board also minutely examined provisions in the agreement to devolve the science labs that committed the federal government to improve the condition of the labs to ensure that this would be a one-time-only cost.

Very often, it was the territorial government negotiators who had to discern these differences of opinion and negotiate with the various federal parties to satisfy their divergent needs and interests. This suggests that it may not always be accurate to think of one set of devolution negotiations. Rather, the process may be more akin to a territorial government negotiating with various federal departments and agencies to achieve a devolution agreement. The fluidity with which various federal departments and agencies became involved in specific sets of negotiations doubtless made the negotiating process unpredictable.

There appears to have been another cleavage within the federal ranks: namely between senior departmental officials based in the Territories and those based in Ottawa. Evidence suggests that senior officials in DIAND and other departments with program responsibilities under negotiation who were based in the two Territories tended to be more supportive of the idea of devolution than their Ottawa colleagues. As a result, territorial negotiators frequently thought that they had agreement on specific negotiating points at the regional office level, only to find that they had to renegotiate with officials from Ottawa. This protracted the negotiations in several cases.

There are a number of understandable reasons for this pattern. Senior federal officials located in the Territories are themselves residents and, like other northerners, see the sense in having federal responsibilities transferred to a government that is more likely to be responsive to the needs of northerners. In terms of their professional futures, federal officials resident in the Territories appeared to be quite sanguine about their career prospects with a territorial government or elsewhere. The effect of devolution on the careers of officials resident in Ottawa was less clear. Also, Ottawa-based officials likely appeared more cautious about agreements because they tended to deal more directly with conservative central agencies and with ministerial concerns. In short, the differences in the professional environment of federal public servants in the Territories and in Ottawa resulted in a double layer negotiating process which took some confounding turns as discussions moved from one layer to another.

All of these factors limited the ability of any party to systematize the process by which the policy of devolution was implemented. There were too many points at which new interests with divergent views could insert themselves into the negotiations. It was difficult for those involved in specific sets of negotiations to forecast when and why these different interests would come into play. From the perspective of the territorial governments, particularly the GNWT, there was some organizational learning as experience with various sets of negotiations accumulated. This was largely due to the existence of the Devolution Office.

One of the most important lessons learned was that it was impossible to pre-program the negotiating process. Another lesson learned was the importance of involving early on staff from territorial departments with specific expertise in areas such as personnel and finance which were critical to the negotiations, to deal with potential problems as the specifics of what will be devolved are discussed.

The Substantive Issues

An awareness of the substantive issues that emerged during the negotiations is important to inform our understanding of the implementation of devolution. A review of the substantive issues which emerged as problematic during the various devolution negotiations reveals a pattern which may not be surprising, but is striking. Personnel issues were consistently the most difficult. It is worthwhile to explore the dimensions of these personnel issues because the way in which some were dealt with would affect implementation in the post-transfer period.

Personnel issues which emerged during the negotiations can be crudely divided into two types: those that deal with terms of employment and those that deal with professional status and hegemony.

The forest and fire management negotiations in the NWT were accompanied by the most intense difficulties concerning terms of employment. Specifically, federal fire control personnel in the NWT were concerned that they would lose their jobs upon transfer and that the federal work force adjustment policy was not designed to give them adequate assistance to obtain other employment in the federal public service. There were also concerns that personnel transferring to the NWT public service would have lower job classifications and that their salaries would be "red circled" — frozen — until their territorial counterparts caught up to them. The negotiations also were accompanied by a decision to change the terms of employment for people hired on a seasonal basis to fight fires in the "transitional year," 1986. People hired for such positions had traditionally been classified as "seasonal indeterminant," meaning that they could expect employment in future years. Those hired in 1986 were hired for "term" positions, which meant that they had no automatic prospect to be rehired. Unfortunately, this change in status was not adequately explained to the affected employees, many of whom were native. Overall, communications on personnel-related issues were poorly handled in the forest and fire management case.

Issues related to terms of employment also figured prominently in the health services transfer in the NWT. Again, there were concerns among affected federal health care workers that they should have fair opportunities for re-deployment in the federal public service if they decided not to move to the territorial level. Those who did move immediately when this agreement was concluded received an employee benefit package which the GNWT has not seen fit to extend to new employees. This has created the problem of two classes of citizen in the new territorial health service.

Other problems related to terms of employment also proved difficult. For example, in the NCPC case difficulties emerged when the federal Department of Public Works, which acts as landlord for federal employees in the North who occupy government housing, appeared reluctant to transfer the houses in which NCPC empoyees resided. Affected employees objected strenuously to those houses initially offered as substitutes on the grounds that they were of inferior quality. In the NWT case, Edmonton-based employees of NCPC were concerned about unemployment if they did not transfer to the newly designated headquarters in Hay River.

The number of personnel transferred in all of these cases was significant and so it is perhaps not surprising that such issues were thorny. However, issues related to professional interest and hegemony have emerged as equally problematic. The earliest transfer studied — the transfer of responsibility for wildlife services — foreshadowed later events. In that case, federal biologists were concerned that devolution from the federal to the territorial level would result in the ascendancy of harvesters, rather than professional biologists, as the managers of wildlife species.

The concerns evident in the wildlife case were magnified in the NWT health services transfer. The study of the impact of devolution of health care service in the Baffin indicates that health care professionals in the region were the most dominant source of resistance to the transfer. They were concerned that their primary line of accountability would shift from supervision by other members of the health care profession to the community at large. When the territory-wide health care transfer was completed in the NWT, nurses and other health care professionals were upset to find that they were to be considered as employees of the GNWT Department of Personnel, rather than the Department of Health.

Finally, health care workers were concerned about their status as union members. Under the federal regime, they were members of the Professional Institute of the Public Service (PIPS). With the transfer, they were to become members of the umbrella union for territorial government employees, the Union of Northern Workers. A group of nurses felt sufficiently aggrieved by this loss of specialized union membership that they took the matter to court. They lost and so the issue was officially dead. However, it is safe to say that the intensity of the concerns about professional hegemony that were evident during the negotiation period may contribute to difficulties in implementing innovation in the post-transfer period, at least over the short term.

There are other substantive issues which consistently emerged as difficult in the negotiations. Again not surprisingly, these most often related to the amount of budget allocation to be transferred to the Territories to support their new responsibilities and the identification and condition of physical assets (buildings, equipment, etc.) to be taken over by the territorial government involved. Territorial negotiators were concerned that the federal government would try to strip programs of budgetary and other resources so that they would have to transfer less.

These issues were important. However, the case evidence suggests that they are different from personnel-related issues in that they are somewhat more amenable to final resolution at the negotiating table. Personnel issues throw a longer shadow over implementation in the post-transfer period.

Patterns and Conclusions

Four major conclusions emerge from this review. First, it is very evident that the overall policy environment exerted a significant influence on the implementation of devolution in the two Territories. This can be seen in the difference in priority accorded the pursuit of devolution in the Yukon and the NWT. In the NWT case, the decision to pursue devolution led to the implementation process being more complex. Implementation of devolution in the NWT was buffeted by initiatives and interests arising from different policy arenas, such as claims, aboriginal self-government and the development of local and regional government in the Territory.

The second conclusion is that the negotiations phase of implementation had to be seen as an adaptive learning process. There was a variety of factors at work at the territorial and at the federal level which limited the ability of the parties to systematize devolution negotiations.

This having been said, it appears essential for those governments on the receiving end, the Government of the Northwest Territories and the Yukon Territorial Government, to take conscious steps to ensure that organizational learning does occur as experience with negotiating devolution agreements builds. The key way to achieve this seems to be through the establishment of a devolution office or a similar organization with a central role in the negotiating process.

This is not to suggest that a devolution office or other central agency assigned this role should be the front line negotiator. Substantive concerns in individual areas, such as health care or fisheries, are very important in the negotiations. It seems important that senior territorial government officials with knowledge of the function under negotiation play a lead role to ensure that substantive concerns are dealt with and that the integrity of the program being transferred is maintained up to the moment of transfer. This is one way that officials who will be responsible for policy and program changes in the post-transfer period can get an early understanding of what exists and what changes might be desirable and feasible once the territorial government receives control. Likewise, there is also a role in the negotiations for staff specialists in areas such as personnel, finance and facilities management to ensure that issues in these areas are adequately dealt with.

On balance, then, it seems best to think of a negotiating team at the territorial level, with the lead role being most commonly taken by the department or group that will be responsible for the post-transfer implementation of the service or program. This seems to be the most common pattern that evolved in the two Territories, although there were some variations. The role of a devolution office seems best suited to be that of coach and keeper of the institutional memory of devolution negotiations.

Because we have no examples of failed negotiations (although there were long hiatuses in some cases), our third conclusion is that the substantive issues under discussion are generally capable of resolution. However, it is equally important to realize that the specific approach taken to dealing with substantive issues related to personnel, finance and so on will have implications for the territorial governments' room to manoeuvre in the post-transfer period. The approach taken may have objective implications, in the sense that this facility may or may not be transferred, etc. However, equally important is the climate of expectation that is created among the northern residents who are affected by the programs to be transferred, and the climate of enthusiasm or resistance to change created among the staff who are affected by decisions made during the negotiation phase.

The final conclusion emerges more obliquely from the preceding text. It is remarkable how much has been accomplished in such a short period. Unlike previous waves of devolution to the two territorial governments, the cases studied in this research effort involved the negotiation of responsibility by a territorial government from the federal government, on a case-by-case basis. Earlier waves of devolution, although much sought after by residents of the two Territories, were largely implemented by federal fiat. The fact that officials from both the territorial governments and the federal level could successfully conclude negotiations on transfer agreements for such a wide range of functions in such a relatively short period attests to their stamina, as well as their capacity to adapt and innovate in the implementation process.

NOTES

1   It is also worthwhile to study devolution from the perspective of implementation in light of the range of debates that have occurred in the so-called implementation literature and in the literature on development administration. A sampling of relevant implementation literature includes: Jeffrey L. Pressman and Aaron Wildavsky, *Implementation*, (Berkeley: University of California Press, 1984), Robert Montjoy and Laurence O'Toole, "Toward a Theory of Policy Implementation: An Organizational Perspective," *Public Administration Review*, vol.39, no. 5, 1979; D. Van Meter and C. Van Horn, "The Policy Implementation Process: A Conceptual Framework," *Administration and Society*, vol. 6, no. 4, 1975 and M. Rein and F. Rabinovitz, "Implementation: A Theoretical Perspective," Working Paper #43, Joint Centre For Urban Studies of MIT and Harvard, 1977. A good sample of implementation issues raised in the development administration literature can be found in D. Rondinelli, *Development Projects as Policy Experiments: An Adaptive Approach to Development Administration*, (Toronto: Methuen, 1983) and Merilee Grindle (ed.) *Politics and Policy Implementation in the Third World*, (Princeton: Princeton University Press, 1980).

2   See, for example, Pressman and Wildavsky and Rondinelli.

3   One may view the NCPC transfer as fundamentally different from the others in the sense that it involved the sale of the relevant assets of NCPC to each territorial government. The territorial governments did not pay for any of the other functions they assumed. However, the characteristics of the negotiating process in the NCPC case were sufficiently similar to the others to warrant its inclusion.

4   This is not to deny the importance of looking at the negotiations from the perspective of other stakeholders, such as the federal government, aboriginal organizations, communities in the Territories and affected employees. However, the perspective taken here is to try to inform future devolution negotiations by looking at what occurred primarily from the perspective of the recipient of the responsibilities that were being devolved, namely the two territorial governments.

5   See Geoffrey Weller, "Health Care Devolution to Canada's Territorial North," in this volume.

6   Pressman and Wildavsky, op. cit., pp. 163-180.

7   See for example, P. Berman, "Thinking about Programmed and Adaptive Implementation: Matching Strategies to Situations," H. Ingram and D. Mann (eds.) *Why Policies Succeed or Fail*, (Beverly Hills: Sage, 1980); D. Calista, "Linking Policy Intention and Implementation: The Role of Organization in the Integration of Human Services," *Administration and Society*, vol. 18, no. 2, 1986 and R. Ripley and G. Franklin, *Bureaucracy and Policy Implementation*, (Homewood, Ill: Dorsey Press, 1983).

8   However, discussions were also occurring in other areas. For example, from 1984 onward, there were periodic discussions between the federal government and the YTG about the devolution of responsibility for small community airports, which ultimately occurred in 1989.

9   See Government of Canada, Yukon News Release, *Canada and Yukon Governments Agree on Program Transfer Process*, September 22, 1988.

10   The same phenomenon can be observed in the GNWT context. By late 1989, the sense in the NWT was that the current round of devolution was coming to an end. As a result, key personnel in the NWT Devolution Office were given new postings and the operation was downsized.

11   The Government of the Northwest Territories, *Policy: Devolution*, Yellowknife, October 23, 1987.

12   Devolution Office, Government of the Northwest Territories, *Planning for Devolution: Principles, Process and Guidelines*, vol. 2, Yellowknife, 1987.

9 The Democratic Potential in Administrative Expansion: Assessing the Impact of the Transfer of Governing Responsibilities from the Federal Government to the Governments of the Yukon and Northwest Territories

Frances Abele

Two general goals shape this chapter. The first is to arrive at a preliminary assessment of the northern impact of the current wave of devolution. The second is to work from this assessment to propose a particular analytical framework for thinking about devolution. The framework is meant to encourage creativity and experimentation towards a mode of northern administration that is efficient *and* appropriate to the special circumstances and aspirations of the Territories. Although it is not my purpose to demonstrate this here, the framework I will propose could also contribute to all forms of institution-building that will occupy northerners for the next several years, whatever the source of the new institutions.[1]

The current wave of devolution began with the 1984 election of the Progressive Conservative government and the appointment of David Crombie as the first Tory Minister of Indian Affairs and Northern Development.[2] The cycle of devolution initiated under Crombie is probably completed for the time being in the NWT but it is still very much "in progress" in the Yukon. During 1986-89, 593 person-years and $81.3 million were transferred to the NWT government, for programs in health services, forestry and fire suppression, and for scientific laboratory facilities in several northern locations. To date, only four person-years and $1.25 million have been devolved to the Yukon, with responsibility for regulation of the inland fishery and mine safety. Transfer of health services and forestry and fire suppression to the Yukon are still under negotiation.[3]

To speak of waves of devolution is to emphasize the continuity of the process: both the Yukon Territorial Government (YTG) and the Government of the Northwest Territories (GNWT) were entirely created by the transfer of governing responsibilities from federal to territorial hands.[4] For most of their histories, though, the two Territories received additional powers on different schedules, the Yukon transfers beginning at the end of the nineteenth century while those to the NWT did not begin until 1967. One distinctive feature of the current wave is the federal intention to transfer major responsibilities to each Territory roughly concurrently, as part of a general federal policy to reduce direct northern administration responsibilities. The federal aspiration was welcomed by each territorial government, but as usual each government responded differently. The Yukon entered devolution negotiations willingly but cautiously, reserving most staff attention for settlement of the outstanding Council for Yukon Indians land claim. The GNWT at first denied any relationship at all between devolution and the outstanding Inuit and Dene-Métis claims; after the connection was recognized, the GNWT proceeded as quickly as possible with devolution negotiations under the auspices of a memorandum of agreement with aboriginal organizations.

The current wave of devolution has attracted probably the highest level of public attention — and certainly has been marked by the most political sensitivity and controversy — since the creation of the northern territorial governments. (It is also the first to be studied contemporaneously by academics.) No doubt the political visibility of the 1980s devolution initiatives is mainly a consequence of the greater organization and politicization of the northern citizenry as a whole, and particularly of the effectiveness of indigenous peoples in making their collective voices heard. Thus any general characterization of the devolution process is likely to be controversial: those most affected by the process see it variously as a massive power grab by territorial government officials; another case of federal "offloading" of responsibilities to other, inadequately funded levels of government; or as merely a technical and administrative change with minimal political significance. There is no doubt a degree of truth in each of these characterizations, but I chose none of them as a starting point for this analysis. Instead, what I want to propose is a more complex and adventurous reading of the process, intended not to replace but to supplement the other interpretations. The discussion moves through four parts.

"What's at Stake?", below, introduces the analytical project, which is to enhance the potential for the creation in the territorial north of civil services that both blend and reflect *all* of the cultures of the North. In an atmosphere of creative experimentation, I believe much more appropriate and cost-effective administrative practices could be developed.[5] The next section is a preliminary assessment of the impact of the 1980s wave of devolution which suggests that reform of administrative practices is both possible and necessary. In the third part of the paper, I propose a way of maximizing the possibilities for helpful innovation by viewing devolution as a policy experiment, thus establishing the basis for the rash (some might say impertinent) suggestions offered in the fourth and final section. These are all intended to promote harmonization of northern administrative practices with northerners' stated political and constitutional goals — and especially their goal to build a northern goverment in which aboriginal peoples take their rightful place.

What's At Stake in Devolution?

For a number of years, northerners have been engaged in a strikingly democratic and multifarious public process. They have sought to redesign the terms of various of their collective relationships to other Canadians and to the federal and territorial states, in three main areas of activity.

First, there has been the renegotiation of native political rights. Comprehensive claims agreements, all now nearly concluded, will provide the northern First Nations with the institutions, fiscal means, rights and negotiated access to certain areas of public decision making to exercise a significantly greater degree of self-determination. Second, native and non-native citizens of the Northwest Territories (NWT) have concurrently been developing new political spaces within which to live — literally, by agreeing in principle to divide the NWT, and politically, by writing constitutions appropriate to the new jurisdictions division would create.[6] And finally, over the last 20 years each territorial government has accepted increasing levels of responsibility from the federal government, as executive, legislative and administrative powers have been devolved.[7]

All three of these processes — claims negotiation, constitutional development, and devolution — will create new public organizations in the North. Given northerners' long-standing political, cultural and constitutional ambitions, it is important to pay attention to the **nature** of the organizations that will be formed. As Pressman and Wildavsky have observed:

> Organizations are more than instruments: they are themselves bundles of desires, for organizations encapsulate ways of life as well as modes of achievement. How, indeed, could people be persuaded to commit themselves to organized life (omitting, of course, the dominated) unless the organizations themselves contain the ties that bind — their values legitimating their desired practices.[8]

Naturally, the "bundles of desires" devolved to the territorial north have been quintessentially foreign or exogenous desires. The territorial states in the first instance reflected the desires of non-native Canadians working within a British parliamentary practice that had been modified for a large, federal country in which there were two colonizing nationalities. Furthermore, in Canada as elsewhere, administrative practice has increasingly incorporated fiscal and personnel control systems characteristic of every modern state. Important features of these systems are impersonality, systemic rather than human rationality, and transcendence of human individuality, temporally as well as spatially.[9] The British inheritance, the Canadian modifications, and modern bureaucratic practices have all been transferred to the Territories along with the personnel and fiscal wherewithal to run programs.

If public organizations "encapsulate ways of life," they at once reflect and re-create core social values. In northern Canada, it is particularly important to reconsider organizational operating principles and systems, because of the predominance of public service employment in the territorial economies and because there is the potential for native people to be, in Pressman and Wildavsky's language, "the dominated" — that is, to remain a population for whom government practices are largely involuntary and contradictory to their social and political values.[10] Such an outcome would by no means exclude all individuals of the "dominated" group from civil service employment. It would merely ensure that those who adapted to work in governing organizations would have to leave their cultural identity at home, and it would contradict the premises that underlie the careful labours of northerners in the areas of constitutional development, political development and land claims.

In liberal democracies, the problem of exclusion is often understood as one of inadequate cultural or ethnic **representation**. In the territorial north as in the Canadian public service generally, the relative exclusion of natives (among others) has been dealt with through formal and informal affirmative action programs of various types. Such policies sometimes do increase the decision-making or administrative roles played by individuals from the "disadvantaged" or "target" groups. Similarly, the election of more representative numbers of native northerners to the legislatures of each Territory has ensured that government policies reflect more accurately the interests of natives.[11]

Neither of these changes really addresses the issue I am raising here, about administrative practices, though they may be helpful or enabling measures. Beyond a representative civil service, we may imagine one, two or three that are fully bicultural. They would produce not just different policies, but different means for the development of policy; not simply more appropriate programs, but programs administered along different — and more indigenous — lines. There is of course a mutually reinforcing relationship between the institutions of policy development and policy outcomes (since the institutions determine whose voice is heard, and whose is loudest), and also between the character of programs and their means of delivery. Beyond this, it must be said that it is difficult to imagine in advance just what the "northern difference" would be like. There is already something of a different flavour to northern administration, easily perceptible in regional and "field" offices of the civil service, not so apparent in Yellowknife or Whitehorse, and unmistakable in hamlet and band council offices. The first step is to recognize that the different impressions created in these offices are likely indications of important and valuable innovations, yet to be made transparent.

All manner of northern bureaucracies may be assessed for their potential to complement the larger political projects that northerners have been pursuing in constitutional development discussions and at the claims table. Devolution, though, creates a special opportunity for northerners to fill an important gap in their overall developmental project. It is the pace and nature of devolution that makes it unusually suitable for experimentation. Claims negotiations and ordered public discussion of constitutions are both future-oriented processes that take place at a fairly high level of generality. Participants in these processes must constantly try to envision the detailed and concrete expression of the arrangements they are prefiguring, but there is little chance for real testing. No one knows how it will all work until the agreement at the level of principle is reached, and implementation begins. Some things are obvious, such as the need for certain kinds of trained personnel, but the shape of institutions, and detailed institutional practices, must necessarily remain somewhat indeterminate until negotiations are concluded. Until that point, no one can be specific about the reach, resources and powers of the new organizations. Furthermore, whatever we may surmise about the nature of the post-claims and post-division public institutions is bound to be eclipsed by practice: the new institutions can be expected to evolve quickly, the more so because there will be an *interaction*, administratively and legally, between the outcome of claims negotiations and the conclusion of constitutional development.

Devolution, on the other hand, is a much less future-oriented and less apocalyptic project. Within the parameters that have now been negotiated, it takes place gradually, functional area by functional area. The pace is relatively slow and steady. There is no historic moment when the implementation of changes begin. Rather, implementation is integral to the process itself, occurring in stages as the negotiations for each specific function are completed. Devolution, already integral to the overall process of political development, provides an opportunity for residents of the Northwest Territories to experiment with different institutional forms, and so to lay the groundwork for effective and more economical implementation of claims agreements and constitutional development decisions.

What has been the impact of devolution so far?

Its major impact, of course, has been the creation of each territorial government. Both governments were formed rather rapidly, the YTG in the early 1900s and the GNWT in 1967-70, and then were augmented piecemeal and periodically. The governments formed in this way initially resembled proto-provincial governments. Allowing for differences due to historical period, they closely resemble the governments of Alberta and Saskatchewan formed in 1905, being province-like but cash-poor administrations lacking control over natural resources.[12]

The recent wave of devolution will increase the size of the territorial governments while adding significant responsibilities for the delivery of certain services. The legislative mandate of the territorial government has not expanded nearly so greatly; rather changes to the jurisdictional scope of territorial government have been constrained by still-unresolved and more primary issues in native claims, specifically those which bear on territorial aspirations for province-like control of land, water and resources. In the NWT forestry transfer, for example, the authority to administer forestry regulations passed from the federal to the territorial level, but the Minister of Northern Affairs retained legal responsibility for and ownership of the forests. In this case, the prospect that devolution of a proprietory interest in NWT forests could have disrupted claims negotiations, then at a delicate stage, led to the division of ownership and management responsibilities. The YTG accepted this separation at the outset of negotiations, in line with that government's commitment to avoid disruption of the Council for Yukon Indians claim.

The Northern Oil and Gas Accords between Ottawa and each Territory are yet to be signed. The Accords would provide for shared management authority between the federal and territorial governments.[13] The inland fishery has been devolved to the Yukon but is yet to be transferred to the NWT. Both cases will entail federal retention of legislative authority, following the practice elsewhere in Canada. The federal minister authorizes inland fishery regulations on the advice of provincial authorities, who also have responsibility for enforcement.[14]

To summarize: the territorial governments have (in the NWT) and will (in the Yukon) become larger, with more or less adequate means to fulfil their new program responsibilities, but with no *extra* resources and no change in their constitutional status. In this circumstance, is there any reason to expect that the two territorial bureaucracies will be motivated to innovate along the lines discussed earlier? Certainly the pressures for adopting "normal (federal) operating procedures" are present, but several different instances of devolution suggest that the outcome is not predetermined. Let us first look at an interesting and promising case, the devolution of responsibility for wildlife regulation to the NWT in 1968 (although I believe an equally good case could be made for the evolution of local government).[15]

Peter Clancy's research on territorial innovations in the area of wildlife management illustrates the effectiveness of local pressure over a considerable period of time, and the potential for alliances between territorial program delivery staff and their "clients."[16] For a few years after devolution to the GNWT, the Wildlife Service operated along then-traditional lines, with emphasis on non-native use of wildlife resources and small business development. Eventually, however, public controversy and extreme political pressure led to a complete reorganization and reorientation of this government office. The reorientation, which involved political conflict and controversy over nearly a decade, brought active government support for the organization of (primarily but not exclusively native) hunters and trappers into community-based associations (HTAs, or Hunters and Trappers Associations), government officials' determined cultivation of a good relationship with this constituency, and public participation in a complete revision of the regulatory regime for wildlife management. Clancy emphasizes that there remain many outstanding organizational and policy issues, particularly as the claims process introduces new structures through which decisions about renewable resource use will be made, and he is reluctant to put too much weight on the transfer of wildlife jurisdiction to the territorial government as the explanation for the transformation of the Wildlife Service. It seems a clear implication of his study, however, that devolution of the Wildlife Service to the territorial government constituted a first step towards transforming this body into a more democratic and responsive institution, because it placed the relevant officials within reach of both territorial legislators and aboriginal organizations.

In the Wildlife Service case, it is important to note that not only were policies affected, but bureaucratic practices and structures were also reformed. This created, in turn, new opportunities for formerly excluded recipients of services to make their influence felt. The establishment of Hunters and Trappers Associations, for example, was integral to the reform of wildlife regulation; in addition, these organizations continue to be an influential voice for land-based producers, and not only with respect to "their" territorial government department. For example, the original impetus for the transfer of fire control responsibilities to the NWT came from well-organized and activist HTAs south of Great Slave Lake who were concerned that adequate procedures be in place to protect their hunting and trapping areas.

The case of the devolution of fire control responsibilities forms one of two contrasting instances of attempts to modify bureaucratic structures to meet northern particularities. Responsibility for fire control and forest management was transferred to the GNWT in the absence of a plan for how these services might be reorganized to better meet local needs, even though local concerns about the adequacy of the service were a major impetus for the territorial government to seek the transfer. Three years after the transfer, no new plan has been approved or implemented. Since the GNWT had no new policies to replace the federal ones, officials have continued to follow past federal practice while politicians, officials and members of the community struggle to develop new — and presumably more appropriate — policies. Federal fire control practices, in particular, had been heavily criticized by the residents of northern communities most affected by these, but to date it is not clear to what extent the new territorial policy will reflect residents' concerns. The transfer of responsibility for forest management and fire control began in response to extreme public pressure, proceeded through a great deal of conflict and controversy, and so far has not resolved any of the original thorny issues. In particular, neither policy nor practice has been reformed in a locally supported direction. It seems unlikely, though, that the story will end here. If the case of the Wildlife Service is any indication, the story will not end until acceptable community relations have been established.

Then there is the contrasting case of the transfer of health services to the NWT. This transfer entailed a major reorganization of the delivery of health services, towards more community participation and control of local services.[17] The reorganization of health services was planned before resources and powers were devolved. Since the transfer, northerners have been engaged in establishing the new institutions and finding ways to reorient staff and develop new lines of communication. This process has not been without serious conflicts, reflecting the reluctance of GNWT politicians and/or bureaucrats to allow the maximum amount of devolution to the communities. However much more political struggle remains (and there may be a considerable amount), there is no question that citizens of the NWT now have a much more decentralized health care delivery system. It is interesting to note that in this case the decentralization to the local level appears to be as much a result of the commitment of federal officials who were relinquishing the program as it was a consequence of local pressure on the "receiving" level of government.[18]

In summary, it seems that there are clear indications that northern governing institutions need not follow a southern blueprint, and indeed that the form of the institutions may become an object of struggle within the territory. One axis of struggle is already most apparent in the NWT: this is the one between department staff based in Yellowknife, and staff and community members living in "the regions." This dynamic may be expected to prevail through all exercises in administrative innovation in the NWT. There is insufficient evidence to date to determine whether this factor will be equally important in the Yukon, though it is clear that the "playing field" is rapidly being transformed in the community-by-community self-government negotiations now under way as an aspect of the land claims settlement. This circumstance alone would appear to guarantee that the Yukon experience will be somewhat different.

Understanding Devolution as a Policy Experiment

One way of making sense of the political vicissitudes just discussed is to label the process "experimental" and to give the convulsions of the northern political process the dignity of recognition as a chosen — or at least inevitable — path. There is a solid basis for doing so, found in one of at least two important schools of thought concerning policy and program implementation. This perspective emphasizes the importance of adaptive, experimental approaches to the implementation of new policies and programs. The other approach is synoptic, envisioning centralized control of the implementation process through predetermined plans and "simplification" (reduction of the number of actors who have a purchase on the process). The debate between these two contrasting approaches is present in both the literature on implementation in advanced capitalist countries and the literature of development administration.[19]

For present purposes, the experimental approach is more promising, since I have chosen to stress the relationship between the implementation of devolution and other processes of political development underway in the territorial north, and to seek in the devolution process ways in which it might complement northerners' broader political goals.[20] Considering the weighty matters at stake it is hard to imagine how the hotly contested politics of northern life could have been (or could ever be) entirely excluded from devolution negotiations. Devolution does increase the scope of the territorial governments, sometimes requires the reorganization of service delivery, and occasionally impinges on legitimately contested terrain. Therefore, it is essential that native organization, unions, communities and other organizations with memberships' interests to protect, have sufficient purchase to do so. Yet there is one unfortunate aspect of even regularized conflict over the details of devolution of a program or responsibility.[21] Once the political contest is entered, institutional development takes place in an extraordinarily inhospitable setting where no one feels like taking a risk, and where errors can lead to poltical disaster. An experimental approach to policy implementation can "improve the neighbourhood" to promote creativity and risk taking, though it can be no substitute for measures designed to ensure that all stakeholders have adequate information and adequate purchase on key decisions.

A useful experimental approach has been developed by Dennis Rondinelli, based on an analysis of the administrative aspects of international development projects all over the world. Rondinelli prefers an approach to planning for policy and program implementation that is "based more on social learning than on scientific management:"

> [T]he key to social learning is not analytical method, but organizational process; and the central methodological concern is not with the isolation of variables or the control of bureaucratic deviations from centrally-designed blueprints, but effectively engaging the necessary participation of system members in contributing to the collective knowledge of the system.[22]

In line with this objective, Rondinelli has derived a number of practical suggestions — including an overall way to organize development implementation planning — but here I want to concentrate on one particular insight and one practical recommendation in his work.

The insight that interests me addresses the issue of administrative capacity, and I think casts the conflict-ridden political process through which the territorial governments have been trying to come to grips with various contentious policy issues — for example, wildlife management — in a promising light. Rondinelli notes that "the ability of planners and managers to implement projects and programs as policy experiments depends on building administrative capacity at all levels in developing nations, both by involving a wider range of organizations and by decentralizing authority and responsibility." This is, of course, precisely the conclusion eventually reached by territorial officials responsible for wildlife management in the NWT during the 1970s (no doubt without the aid of texts on development administration), and it has given them the means and the room to experiment with various approaches. In the process, policy authority over management of this vital resource has been shared with the users. One can understand the evolution of wildlife management regimes in the NWT as a rather fraught policy experiment, still underway after many years, but bearing fruit. It may be that fire control and forest management policy are on their way to such a lengthy and difficult genesis, though officials might shorten the process by learning from the experience with wildlife regulation.

Rondinelli has a practical recommendation for maximizing the opportunities for such institutional learning by experience (and legitimizing this process). He proposes reliance upon staged and orderly policy or program implementation experiments, undertaken in the expectation that as much can be learned from failures as from successes, provided that appropriate arrangements are made. He identifies five types of implementation project, each appropriate for a different situation.[23] **Experimental projects** are necessary in cases where "little is known about problems or the most effective means of setting objectives." They are meant to be tried in a protected and contained environment, "sheltered from routine administrative responsibilities and from political pressures to replicate them too soon or to abandon them too early." **Pilot projects** are used to test the results of experimental projects under a greater variety of conditions. They are appropriate when objectives are relatively well-defined, and should be designed with careful attention to "choosing appropriate locations, structuring activities to fit local needs and conditions, collecting baseline data, and, especially, monitoring and evaluating the project to determine conditions that influence success or failure." After this process has been completed, **demonstration projects** "can be used to exhibit the effectiveness and to increase the acceptability of new methods, techniques or forms of social interaction on a broader scale." Finally, **replication, diffusion or production projects** may evolve from these earlier phases. Here, attention shifts to wider organizational questions, and integrating the innovation practices into the prevailing social and economic systems.

The health transfer entailed a major reorganization of the delivery of health services, towards more community participation and control of local services.[24] The reorganization of health services was planned before resources and powers were devolved; since the transfer northerners have been engaged in establishing the new institutions and finding ways to reorient staff and develop new lines of communication. The magnitude of these tasks suggests that it might be very helpful indeed to consider the newly established arrangements as an experiment on the level of a pilot project in Rondinelli's sequence, with careful provisions for evaluation and the expectation that adjustments will be necessary as experience is gained.

Responsibility for fire control and forestry was devolved to the GNWT in the absence of a plan for how these services might be reorganized; as a result, officials are following past federal practice for the first three years after the transfer, while new policies are being developed. Since fire control, particularly, involves a basic service with which there has been much public dissatisfaction, and since no new fire control policy has yet been put in place, another opportunity to experiment exists. In this case, there is probably still time to begin with a modest pilot project, perhaps local control of firefighting in one or two fire districts.

While Rondinelli's experimental categories were developed with reference to Third World development projects funded by external agencies based in other nations, the overall concept has obvious relevance to administrative innovation in the North. It may not be necessary for each innovation to pass through each of the phases he identifies, but the emphasis on controlled risk taking and learning from experience (rather than punishing "errors") may have considerable utility. Overall, both territorial governments would seem to be ideal settings for an experimental approach. There is local pressure for change, outside the civil service a distinctive "local culture," and sufficient personnel and fiscal resources to support experimentation.

Some Further Suggestions

Most northerners would agree that it will not be sufficient for them to replicate the forms of government and administration found in southern Canada. Although there might be disagreement about specific modalities, there is support for innovations to ensure that native self-determination is expressed in NWT government institutions, as long as the rights and interests of all other northerners are also reflected in these institutions. Furthermore, geography, population distribution and climate impose special imperatives that have already led to administrative innovation (in for example, the establishment of cross-cutting regional directorates). Many ideas for constitutional changes have been explored,[25] but at this stage, there has been little concrete discussion of what native self-determination expressed through revised administrative practices would look like. I want to conclude with some comments about possible areas for strategic experimentation. These suggestions are offered neither as "sure-fire" techniques that should be adopted, nor as artificially derived standards against which to judge the performance of the officials who have been involved in the devolution process. Instead, the suggestions could be starting points for experimental or pilot projects that might advance knowledge about practical obstacles to developing administrative structures that complement northerners' broad political goals.

There is potential for experimentation at two different levels. First, changes may be made to the institutions through which policy is developed. Clearly, important changes will attend the establishment of the system of management boards for regulation in the areas of land and water management, wildlife management (and perhaps some other fields). The powers of these boards will be specified initially in constitutionally protected claims agreements, but precise delineation of their resources and scope awaits legislation. There already exist, of course, management boards for caribou and land use planning boards established under different auspices. In addition, the Denendeh Conservation Board was established as a product of claims negotiations with the intention that its first years should be experimental. What seems to be missing from the plans made to date is a provision for systematic review of the effectiveness of the DCB, with the objective of overcoming obstacles to effectiveness once they have been identified.

At the level of program delivery, a number of experiments can be envisioned. Above the level of local government, the language of work in the territorial bureaucracy is English. An experimental project might alter job descriptions in one unit, requiring fluency in Inuktitut or a Dene language for all employees. This step would likely transform the ethnic distribution in the unit, since relatively few non-native northerners could qualify, and it might also transform the labour process itself. The language of work would be the language most people used to speak with their families (particularly elders) and the way of thinking "at work" would be much less distant from the way of thinking in the household. Eventually, such a change could lead to more regionally appropriate regimes of accountability and decision making.[26]

Similar effects might be produced by revising entry level qualifications for positions in one unit, to relax the requirement for professional certification in favour of some currently under-valued or ignored employee competencies required for effective service delivery in the North. This change would have to be carefully monitored, but it might be that under these circumstances public service workers would find simpler, cheaper and more effective ways to meet program goals. Finally, units could be reorganized so that reporting relationships were formally "flattened" (within the unit) or redrawn "outward," to local committees of service recipients. "Outward" reporting lines have been envisioned by some to bring regional directorates into a reporting relationship with the regional councils now established across the NWT. While this measure has been resisted for various reasons, it might be possible to experiment with "outward" reporting lines more conservatively, involving more specialized services in certain areas for a limited number of issues. With careful monitoring, a good deal could be learned about what is and is not in fact practical.

All of the measures mentioned above would be controversial, risky and perhaps politically impossible if they were contemplated for the civil service as a whole, but as carefully controlled and monitored experiments, they might provide an important source of new information about what is, in fact, possible. They offer the prospect that northerners might continue their long collective labour towards a new form of government, taking advantage of the power of administrative regularity to support rather than inhibit more democratic constitutional and political development.

Acknowledgments

I am grateful to Katherine Graham, Peter Kulchyski, and Jack Stagg for constructive critical comments made on a much earlier draft of this paper, to Gurston Dacks for being a firm but very kind editor and colleague, to Alex Kerr and Jon Pierce for early research assistance, and most of all to my husband George Kinloch for generous practical and intellectual support.

NOTES

1   For a compatible and much more extensive discussion of similar issues for post-claims aboriginal organizations, see Don Cozzetto, *Governance in Nunavut*, Ph.D. Thesis, Centre for Public Administration and Public Policy, Virginia Polytechnic Institute and State University, Blackburg, Virginia, 1990.

2   For one perspective on Crombie's motivations and impact, see Frances Abele, "Conservative Northern Development Policy: A New Broom in an Old Bottleneck?" in Michael Prince, ed. *Tracking the Tories: How Ottawa Spends 1986-7*, (Toronto: Methuen, 1986); and Frances Abele and Katherine Graham, "Plus Que Ca Change: The North and Native Peoples, "*How Ottawa Spends 1988-89*, (Ottawa: Carleton University Press), 1988.

3   All figures are from a letter to Gurston Dacks, Co-ordinator, Consortium for Devolution Research from Jack Stagg, Director General, Constitutional Development and Strategic Planning, Department of Indian Affairs and Northern Development, July 10, 1989. The figures exclude the former federal Crown corporation, the Northern Canada Power Commission, whose assets were sold (not devolved) to the Yukon and Northwest Territories governments in 1987 and 1988.

4   Cf. Peter Clancy, "Politics by Remote Control" in this volume. The Yukon has delivered most province-like programs since the early twentieth century, receiving only relatively minor responsibilities since then: workers' compensation (1971), sports fishing (1972), territorial elections (1978), income tax and highway maintenance (1980), inland fisheries (1988), and mine safety (1989). The NWT, on the other hand, received a large and difficult-to-manage basket of responsibilities in 1969-70: education, social assistance, municipal services, local government, public works, development of small industries. This was followed by workers' compensation (1971), administration of justice, excluding the Attorney General (1973), low rental housing (1974), sports fishing (1976), income tax and territorial elections (1978), mining safety (1981), Frobisher Bay hospital (1982), road construction (1984), nursing stations and health services in the Baffin Region (1986), forestry management and fire suppression (1987), and the northern science centres (1988).

5   The basis for such a task is argued in Francis Abele, *Gathering Strength*, (Calgary: Arctic Institute of North America Komatik Series), 1989.

6   Constitutional discussions took place through the Constitutional Alliance, a body comprised of representatives of the Legislative Assembly and the native organizations. After the plebiscite, these deliberations took place through the Nunavut Constitutional Forum and the Western Constitutional Forum. By the end of the 1980s, these bodies were no longer active, while the process of constitution writing and boundary selection is still incomplete. Cf. Western Constitutional Forum, *Partners for the Future.* (Yellowknife, 1986; Nunavut Constitutional Forum), *Building Nunavut,* (Ottawa, 1985); Gurston Dacks, "The Politics of 'Partnership' in the Western Northwest Territories" in K. Coates, ed. *For the Purposes of Dominion: Essays in Honour of Morris Zaslow;* (North York: Captus University Publications, 1989) Dacks, "Politics on the Last Frontier: Consociationalism in the Northwest Territories," *Canadian Journal of Political Science* v. 19 n. 2 (June 1986); Michael Asch, *Home and Native Land,* (Toronto: Methuen, 1984), ch. 7.

7   In discussing devolution I follow the distinctions and definitions developed by Peter Clancy, "Politics by Remote Control" in this volume. For a more subtle and complete discussion of the relationship of devolution to the other political projects of northerners, see Gurston Dacks, "Devolution and Political Development in the Canadian North" in this volume.

8   Jeffery L. Pressman and Aaron Wildavsky, *Implementation,* (3rd ed. Berkeley: University of California Press, 1984), p. 252.

9   For a powerful characterization of the generic modern state (hardly captured in the single sentence above), see Douglas Torgerson, "Limits of the Administrative Mind: The Problem of Defining Environmental Problems" in R. Paehlke and D. Torgerson, eds. *Managing Leviathan: Environmental Politics and the Administrative State,* (Peterborough: Broadview, 1990).

10   The "administrative mind" explored by Torgerson is of course an involuntary imposition on us all, though it is surely *more* foreign to northern native culture than to that of urban Canada. The extent to which this one difference makes any moral or political difference is an interesting question, which I must here leave unexamined.

11   In the Yukon, where party politics organize the legislative process, all parties have courted native candidates. The governing party (the New Democrats) has to date been most successful in maintaining good relations with native organizations. The change

in the Northwest Territories has meant that native people have been in the majority in the Legislative Assembly since 1979, a circumstance that has kept native issues firmly on the public agenda.

12   Cf. Clancy, "Politics by Remote Control" op. cit.

13   Gurston Dacks, "The Quest for Northern Oil and Gas Accords" in this volume.

14   Peter Clancy, "Political Devolution and Wildlife Management" in this volume.

15   Katherine Graham, "Devolution and Local Government: One Step Forward and Two Steps Back" in this volume.

16   Peter Clancy, "Political Devolution and Wildlife Management" in this volume.

17   John D. O'Neil , "The Impact of Devolution on Health Services in the Baffin Region, NWT: A Case Study;" Geoffrey Weller, "The Devolution of Health Care to Canada's North, " both in this volume.

18   Ibid.

19   I shall draw most heavily on the work of D. Rondinelli, particularly *Development Projects as Policy Experiments: An Adaptive Approach to Development Administration*, (Methuen, 1983) and "Government Decentralization in Comparative Perspective: Theory and Practice in Developing Countries" in *International Review of Administrative Sciences* 47:2 (1981) pp. 135-6. Similar views, developed with respect to First World implementation issues, are found in M. Rein and F. Rabinowitz, "Implementation: A Theoretical Perspective," Working Paper #43, Joint Centre for Urban Studies of MIT and Harvard, 1977; D. Majone and A. Wildavsky, "Implementation as Evolution" in *Implementation*, (University of California Press, 1979); Paul Berman, "The Study of Macro and Micro Implementation" *Public Policy* 26:2 (1978).

20   Here I deliberately set aside the ways in which devolution threatened and could have obstructed progress in claims negotiations.

21   "Regularization" of areas of conflict is provided by the Memorandums of Understanding signed by each territorial government and respective native organizations, and, less formally, it has occurred in the Yukon through the development of relatively

trustful working relations between territorial staff and staff of the Council for Yukon Indians.

22   Dennis Rondinelli, *Development Projects as Policy Experiments*, p. 129.

23   Rondinelli, pp. 19-21.

24   John D. O'Neil and Geoffrey Weller,.op. cit.

25   For example, G. Robertson, *Northern Provinces: A Mistaken Goal*, (Montreal: Institute for Research on Public Policy, 1985); G. Dacks, "The View from Meech Lake: The Constitutional Future of the Governments of the Yukon and Northwest Territories" in R. Aird, ed. *Running the North: The Getting and Spending of Public Finances by Canada's Northern Governments*, (Ottawa: Canadian Arctic Resources Committee, 1988).

26   That a change in the language of work would produce some changes in operating procedures — though not radical changes — will be evident to anyone who has been fortunate to observe hamlet councils at work in Inuktitut.

10 Devolution, Regionalism and Division of the Northwest Territories

Geoffrey R. Weller

Introduction

Canada is a politically incomplete nation. Some 45 percent of its land area is not organized into provinces and remains federal territory. The path of political development in the largest part of this area, the Northwest Territories (NWT), has been complicated. Three processes have been going on at once, creating a great deal of confusion. Firstly, there has been an accelerated process of devolution of authority from the federal government to the Government of the Northwest Territories (GNWT). Secondly, there have been voices within the NWT, especially those of organizations representing indigenous populations, wishing to enhance regional structures of all kinds. At the same time, these moves have been strenuously resisted by the GNWT. Thirdly, the option of dividing the Northwest Territories into two has been advocated and worked for by a number of groups.

While the federal government in recent decades has transferred many of its powers to the existing Yukon Territorial Government (YTG) and the GNWT (the process of devolution), there is no clear indication of just when and under precisely what conditions the two Territories might become provinces. The process of devolution is a kind of lurching towards provincehood affected by the vagaries of territorial and national party politics. However, just as the target came into sight a severe complication was threatened by the Meech Lake Accord which would have increased the provinces' control over the process of determining when and if provincehood might be granted. However, the death of the Meech Lake Accord on June 23, 1990 removed this complication.

The degree of power given to regional organizations in the Northwest Territories has fluctuated over the years. When greater influence has been accorded the regions, it has been claimed that this enhanced the degree of local government and brought government closer to the people. It was usually advocated on two grounds. The first was that the NWT was so large that a high degree of regionalism was needed simply to effect rational administration. The second was that it would allow for greater input by the various racial groupings that could be identified by region within the Northwest Territories, that is, it would allow for a degree of ethnic self–determination. This, however, has been complicated by the land claims negotiations and the desire of the various indigenous peoples to have a degree of self–determination within that context. Thus it is not clear what the strength of regional organizations is likely to be and it is not clear what type of regional structures will eventually evolve.

The development of the concept of the division of the NWT has complicated both the process of devolution and regionalism. The concept is that the eastern Arctic would be separated from the Northwest Territories and be called Nunavut. The proponents of this idea argue that both would initially be territories but would eventually become two provinces. This concept of division was endorsed by nearly all the major players involved in the constitutional development of the North. However, the process was stalled as the result of a dispute over the boundary between the two territories and it is unclear just what future developments will occur. However it is clear that the prospects for division have been revived in the light of the signing of the Agreement–in–Principle over land claims with the Tungavik Federation of Nunavut and the death of the Meech Lake Accord.

This paper will analyse each of these processes in turn and also try to discern the patterns of interaction between them. It will then conclude, firstly, by arguing for the need for planned political development toward a clear common goal in the North rather than a continuation of the battling among various forces that is likely to be debilitating for all involved and, secondly, by arguing for the need to take a decisive step on the issue of division.

Devolution

Devolution is the process of transferring rights, powers or responsibilities from a higher level of government to a lower one. Such devolution or transfer has been going on for some time in relation to the Northwest Territories. The list of transfers prior to the mid-1980s is quite long but tends to go relatively unrecognized.[1] In 1967 Yellowknife was named the capital and in the following years responsibility for education, social assistance, municipal services, local government, public works, the development of small industries, workers' compensation, the administration of justice, sports fishing, income tax, territorial elections, mining safety, and other areas was transferred.

The speed of the process of devolution increased in the early and mid-1980s. One of the reasons for this was probably the changing and weakening constitutional position of the NWT and the diminishing likelihood of it ever becoming a province. Prior to 1982 and the *Constitution Act,* Parliament could admit new provinces without the approval of the provincial legislatures. With the passage of the *Constitution Act,* 1982 the admission of a new province required a constitutional amendment. Such an amendment needed approval of two thirds of the provinces which between them represented at least one half of the population of all the provinces to be successful. The Meech Lake Accord made the prospect of the attainment of provincehood appear even more remote as the Accord required the approval of all of the existing provinces and of the federal government for a new province to be established.

Given this weakening constitutional status in the period prior to the death of Meech Lake the federal authorities no doubt felt that northern residents had to be given some hope that they would be able to affect their own destinies so the devolution process was accelerated. The GNWT was also no doubt acting reactively in this area when in 1984 the Government Leader announced that one of the priorities of the GNWT would be to further pursue the acquisition of province-like powers and, indeed, to begin negotiating the transfer of all remaining provincial-type powers held by the Government of Canada. In 1985 the GNWT identified some 30 programs over which it wished to assume control in the near future.[2] With the election of the federal Progressive Conservatives in 1984 the GNWT thought it a window of opportunity to make real headway. Consequently the GNWT put on a big push to effect transfer beginning in 1985. As it turned out a number of the smaller transfers desired were not effected, but this was largely because it was discovered that resources would have to be concentrated on a few big transfers such as health and forestry.

The Government of the Northwest Territories has been motivated to push for the devolution of authority by several factors including administrative rationality, administrative expansionism and political expansionism. In terms of administrative rationality it is argued that devolution is a way in which a single administrative regime would replace the split administrative regime between the GNWT and the federal government. The GNWT believes that a single regime would administer financial and other matters more efficiently, would eliminate extraneous influences imposed on the North by generalized federal government policies such as hiring freezes, and would allow for the introduction of programs that would be specifically suited to the needs of the NWT and not all of Canada. It is generally thought that a single administrative regime would speed up the government's response times to problems.

The GNWT has also been motivated to support devolution because it quite clearly produces a larger and more expert civil service. In recent years, the process of devolution has indeed resulted in a very significant expansion of the public service in the NWT. The health transfer of 1988 alone added about 500 people to a total establishment of some 3,800.[3] Growth may be desired simply for job creation purposes, but there are other benefits to having a larger civil service. Not only is it likely to be more expert but career paths become longer and more satisfying.

The GNWT has also been motivated to support devolution because it is likely to extend the legitimacy, power and influence of established political structures and better equip politicians to resist what some see as the destructive calls for division and the uncertain and disruptive process of land claims settlements. If the established political structures and the people occupying them can be seen to have the capacity and the will to deliver a wide variety of services, then calls for change would be less insistent and established positions would be entrenched. In short, rapid devolution was wanted by the GNWT because it was likely to prevent division and reduce the influence of whatever political structures might result from the land claims process.

The federal government has been motivated to support devolution for a variety of reasons. Firstly, successive federal governments have been sympathetic to the process of transferring more province–like powers to the GNWT because it was thought to be administratively sensible to avoid divided authority. Secondly, and most recently, in an era of downsizing the transferring of responsibilities would allow government departments to meet person-year reduction targets more easily. Thirdly, it could be argued that if the federal government wished to minimize the likelihood of division — and indeed this has been argued — then a more powerful GNWT would likely produce that result. Fourthly, and whatever the real attitude towards division, the federal government has stated that "the transfer of all remaining provincial–type programs to governments directly elected by northerners is the primary means to encourage accountable and responsible decision making and the development of effective political institutions in the North."[4] Gurston Dacks has argued that the recent pursuit of devolution by the Progressive Conservative government is also the result of a feeling that there was a need to make amends for the poor treatment the territories would have received under the Meech Lake Accord. That is, it was hoped that the anger of northerners could be mitigated by speeding up the transfer of province–like powers.[5]

Even aboriginal organizations in the NWT have been motivated to support the idea of the transfer of authority over some areas to the GNWT despite the fact that they generally dislike the policy and see it as a ploy to defeat division or adversely affect their land claims objectives. They have supported the idea largely because they think, in some instances, it will result in a regime and policies that will be more responsive, both organizationally and programmatically, to the needs of native peoples.[6] They also tend to agree with the GNWT that split authority between the GNWT and the federal government is not likely to be the most efficient approach. To ensure the desired service outcome, native groups have insisted that they be consulted or even involved in the transfer negotiations and process.[7] In fact, many of the transfers that have taken place could not have been accomplished without the acquiescence of native groups, not only because it would have been impractical but because the federal government recently made this a condition of its support for transfers.

By supporting a number of aspects of devolution, aboriginal groups may indeed have undercut their position. They correctly perceived that the process in and of itself would do nothing to protect group rights such as language. Moreover, they may well be correct in arguing that devolution was intended by the federal government to distract them and others from pursuing division and land claims issues. Even if not intentional it is clear it has had that effect, especially in relation to division. In addition, they are probably correct in arguing that devolution, at least in part, is an attempt on the part of what they call a "transitional" government to become the permanent government of the Northwest Territories. While a transfer such as health is likely to benefit aboriginal peoples by providing an improved level and more responsive type of health care, it benefits the GNWT and the civil servants by vastly expanding their role and numbers and, hence, their political legitimacy.

Regionalism

A certain degree of regionalism in the Northwest Territories is inevitable. The NWT's land area is huge and its people, or more accurately peoples, very diverse. However, regionalism can have many forms ranging from simply decentralized central authority to relatively powerful multipurpose regional elected governments. The regionalism initially found in the Northwest Territories in the 1970's was decentralized central authority. This gradually developed towards multipurpose regional authorities that were also identified with specific racial groups as well as geographic areas. More recently, and especially since the accelerated push for devolution, there have been moves by the GNWT to reverse this tendency and return to the situation that pertained in the seventies when regionalism meant decentralized central government.

Regionalism was developed in the Northwest Territories partly as a consequence of administrative convenience. It developed most notably in the 1970s and regional authorities tended to compete with local governments. Gradually over the decade the GNWT and federal government departments and agencies established regional offices and advisory bodies for administrative purposes. Often the regions created by the two levels of government were not coterminous. Sanikiluaq on the Belcher Islands, for instance, was in the GNWT Baffin Region but the Medical Services Branch Keewatin Zone.[8] Thus at least one advantage of devolution has been to eliminate much of this kind of problem. This tendency to administrative regionalism or decentralization was enhanced by the fact that communication links were essentially north to south by region rather than east to west across the whole Northwest Territories. In fact, the communication links were north to south by region to points outside the NWT as in the case of health evacuation and referral patterns and seaborne resupply.

Regionalism also occurred in the Northwest Territories in response to the development of regional aboriginal organizations. Various Inuit groups, for example, developed regional organizations such as the Baffin Inuit Association, the Keewatin Inuit Association, the Kitikmeot Inuit Association (central Arctic) and the Committee for Original People's Entitlement (western Arctic). This, of course, prompted regional responses from the two senior levels of government and prompted some of the Inuit groups to suggest the formation of regional municipalities such as the Committee for Original People's suggestion of a Western Arctic Regional Municipality. The first regional council established was the Baffin Regional Council formed in April 1977 and incorporated by legislation in 1980. This was followed in 1983 by the *Regional and Tribal Councils Act*. This led the GNWT to rethink its entire local government policy which then led to the creation of a new *Charter Communities Act* in 1987. It should be noted here that there is a greater logic or coherence to regionalism in the eastern Arctic than in the West, which is more localized or community-based. Thus it is not surprising that the Baffin developed the first Regional Council.

The Northwest Territories eventually developed a regional layer of government. Five regions were created, the Baffin, Keewatin, Inuvik, Fort Smith and Kitikmeot regions. Each region had a superintendent who co-ordinated the actions of all the departments with field operations. The regional superintendent functioned independently of Yellowknife on a day–to–day basis and some departments delegated responsibilities to the regions. While resulting in some overlap regionalization was important for the development of a sense of regional autonomy and local control.[9] These developments were the result of the adoption of the devolution policy of 1980 by the GNWT. This policy and subsequent actions may well have been intended to stave off demands for the division of the Northwest Territories.

However, the application of the policy has still not cleared up a great many problems. Devolution in this context does not necessarily imply self–government for it has been the case that regional units of government have largely been regional units of the central authority in Yellowknife. Furthermore, the role of the regional organizations remained unclear, as did the exact relationship between the local governments within a region and the regional authority. In any event the GNWT appears to have backed away from strong administrative regional administration as illustrated by the Regional Administrator no longer having responsibility for line departments within the region. In effect the GNWT had implemented decentralization rather than devolution anyway.

More recently, additional regionalism has come to the Northwest Territories as a result of devolution — that is, devolution from the federal government to the GNWT. For example, the GNWT placed a regional school board in the Baffin after it gained control of education. More recently with the devolution of authority over health, the GNWT established regional health boards. Under the Territorial Hospital Insurance Services Act there are five regional health boards which are broadly representative of the communities in their regions. The members of the regional health boards are appointed by the Minister of Health from nominations by the municipal councils or band councils and the nominees are generally members — or chairpersons — of local Community Health Committees.[10] This type of regionalism, billed as giving the local communities a say in service delivery, was one of the major reasons why the native groups agreed to the devolution of areas such as health.

The native groups were not at all pleased by the GNWT's announcement in February 1988 of a Transfer Policy.[11] It was felt that it was a betrayal by the GNWT of those very promises that led the native groups to agree to some of the transfers, especially the large ones such as health. The aspect of the Transfer Policy that upset the aboriginal groups was that which called for the transfer of individuals in the areas of personnel, public works and the like to be to their equivalent GNWT department and not to a regional authority. Thus someone working in the health field in personnel for the federal government would not be transferred to the appropriate Regional Health Council but to the Personnel Department of the GNWT. While the native groups were upset, the GNWT argued that the location of such a person in a line department was more efficient for the GNWT and it was also likely to be helpful to the Regional Boards, especially the small ones.

The announcement of the Transfer Policy did not come as a great surprise to those who suspected the GNWT was about to reduce its support for regional councils and perhaps eliminate them altogether. Katherine Graham points out that a committee to review regional councils submitted its report in 1988 and recommended strengthening the powers of regional and tribal councils.[12] The report was rejected completely because among other things it "failed to consider the evolution of ministerial authority in the Northwest Territories."[13] As Katherine Graham also points out some groups such as the Baffin Regional Council now fear a withdrawal of GNWT funding and the reassertion of the role of GNWT regional offices, that is a return to the 1970s system.[14] This fear is reinforced by the experience in health of the GNWT devolving to a special Regional Health Board and not the Baffin Regional Council and by the imposition of the Transfer Policy. Clearly the GNWT did not want to enhance the power of a regional council by giving it more responsibility and, thereby legitimacy. It seems reasonably clear that the GNWT is seeking to ensure that the power devolved to it by the federal government is not devolved further down the line to groups that might end up being rival governmental units. If all the various powers devolved to the GNWT were further devolved to regional authorities clearly there would be little need for a government in Yellowknife. There are others, primarily from the aboriginal groups who, by contrast, want to see regional councils play a strong role in the future forms of northern government. One of these is Roger Gruben, the President of the Inuvialuit Regional Corporation, who argued in the Legislative Assembly recently that regional bodies could bring greater "efficiency" and "fairness" to the delivery of some programs. His argument for constitutionally responsible regional bodies met a lukewarm response from Government Leader Dennis Patterson, who reiterated the GNWT's long-held view that regional governments were emanations of and the servants of the individual communities which were the "prime public authority."[15]

The GNWT was also clearly worried concerning the effect of the land claims negotiations on local and regional government structures. The Dene/Métis have negotiated an Agreement–in–Principle with the federal government as has the Tungavik Federation of Nunavut (TFN). Discussions took place with both groups concerning local government matters and concerning local and regional boards for purposes such as wildlife management. Both the TFN and the Dene/Métis, before reaching a final agreement, may try to entrench their desire for self–government within the context of the land claims. The uncertainty surrounding the eventual outcome of the land claims process may thus be one of the reasons why the GNWT moved more rapidly to establish its legitimacy by indicating it can deliver a wide range of services to individuals as a result of devolution.

Division

The concept of division is now intimately linked with the creation of a homeland for the Inuit. The concept did appear once before in a purely administrative form when Knut Lang moved in the Legislative Assembly that the Northwest Territories be divided.[16] The resolution was adopted and the Diefenbaker government introduced bills in Ottawa to create the Territory of Mackenzie and the Territory of Nunassiaq. However, when the Diefenbaker government was defeated in 1963 these bills died on the order paper. The succeeding Liberal government under Mr. Pearson did not agree with division and set up the Carrothers Commission in 1963 to investigate the situation in the NWT. The Carrothers Commission did not favour division but it did advocate greater self–government.[17] This resulted in the move of the seat of government to Yellowknife and the gradual devolution of authority already discussed. The concept of division did not reappear for over a decade and then when it did reappear it took a radically different form. Initially, this new form was remarkably successful but its prospects very rapidly dimmed.

The Inuit Tapirisat of Canada presented its proposal for the creation of Nunavut in 1979.[18] The proposal called for the creation of a new territory with the name of Nunavut to be created out of that part of the Northwest Territories above and to the east of the tree line. The area would begin as a federal territory but would over 15 years develop into a province with powers that would be the same as all the others. The objective was to create a jurisdiction within which Inuit culture and tradition could be preserved. It was deliberately designed to avoid an Alaskan or James Bay type land claims settlement. It was also deliberately designed to overcome a dependent and colonial relationship by obtaining the right to manage natural resources and obtain taxation power and royalties with which to replace federal government subsidies.

Although there was initially suspicion of and opposition to the proposal it rapidly gained support. In large part this was because the 1979 NWT election changed the complexion of the Legislative Assembly. The election resulted in the dominance over the Legislature by Inuit, Dene, Métis and a group of more supportive whites. These elements in the Legislature actually began to promote the idea of division. A committee of the Assembly reported that most residents of the Northwest Territories saw the GNWT as a government created without their consent and wanted to see two jurisdictions in the area. In 1980 the Legislature voted for division in principle and agreed to hold a plebiscite on the issue.

In 1982 the Constitutional Alliance was formed. This was made up of some members of the Legislative Assembly and the leadership of the Dene, Métis, Inuit and Inuvialuit. The aim of the Constitutional Alliance was to work for a "yes" vote in the plebiscite by facilitating wide public participation. Shortly thereafter the Legislative Assembly voted unanimously to support the Constitutional Alliance as a working group. The plebiscite, held in April 1982, resulted in a vote clearly in favour of division, although the support for division was much stronger in the East than in the West.[19] In May 1982 the Legislative Assembly voted 19 to 0 to adopt a policy of division of the NWT. That same month, Commissioner Parker moved from opposition to support of division and then in November the Minister of Indian Affairs and Northern Development, John Munro, indicated that the federal government endorsed in principle the concept of division.

In July of 1982 the Constitutional Alliance met to decide how to proceed after the plebiscite. It decided to form two subcommittees, the Nunavut Constitutional Forum (NCF) and the Western Constitutional Forum (WCF). Each forum was to develop proposals for the structure of government of both of the proposed new territories. The Constitutional Alliance itself would decide upon a specific boundary between the two proposed territories and negotiate this boundary with Ottawa. The NCF was the first subcommittee to report with its 1983 document entitled *Building Nunavut*.[20] Despite a great deal of conflict the Alliance reached an initial boundary agreement on January 14, 1985. The stage for division then seemed finally set when on February 6, 1985 the Minister of Northern Affairs, David Crombie, made a major policy statement to the Northwest Territories

Assembly stating that it was the common resolve of all involved to convert the Northwest Territories into two territories by 1987.[21]

For a moment it looked as if Canada would take a major leap forward in its constitutional development. It also looked as if the arguments for division had overcome those against. The arguments for division were that the NWT was too big to govern from one place; that the GNWT was insensitive to the needs of the Arctic portion of the NWT; that the creation of Nunavut would create an Inuit homeland; that a Nunavut government would create government by the Inuit for the Inuit, and that it would largely eliminate an essentially colonial situation in both the East and the West.[22] The arguments against division were that it was an attempt to create an ethnic government in the East; that it would reduce the strength of the entire North in arguments with the South, that the populations were too small; that there was no adequate tax base, and that it would be too expensive to have two governments for such a small number of people.[23]

The prospects for division, initially so bright, rapidly began to diminish almost as soon as the Agreement had been signed. In late February 1985 the Nunavut Constitutional Forum announced that it was backing out of the agreement. The NCF could not accept, it seemed, the exclusion of the Inuvialuit area from Nunavut. While two years were then lost, along with a great deal of momentum, the WCF and the NCF finally signed an agreement in Iquluit on a revised boundary. However, in March of 1987 this agreement also collapsed. This was ostensibly because of a dispute over uninhabited land near the provincial borders. No agreement has ever been signed and the federal government has taken the stance that it should not intervene to produce an agreement.

The lack of an agreement meant that a narrow window of opportunity was lost and ample time was given to those who opposed division to work against it. In addition, it meant that the newly elected members of the Legislative Assembly had time to develop a liking for the trappings of power and influence and to develop an attitude that they could meet the needs of all the people of the NWT from Yellowknife. The result was largely predictable in that a big push was mounted to effect devolution. Clearly this would mean the GNWT would become regarded not only as a legitimate government but also as one that could deliver things for people in all localities, that is, it could shift from being seen as a colonial government to a government that could represent and deliver things for individual northerners. The result was also predictable in that it resulted in a move away from the creation of multipurpose regional governments by the GNWT. This was largely because they would be seen as the level of government with a close contact with individuals and Yellowknife would have been regarded as being "remote" and, no doubt, "insensitive."

For a time the concept of division appeared almost as if it were dead. The Western Constitutional Forum shut its doors in 1988 when it ran out of funds. The Constitutional Alliance itself largely ceased talking about division, and its federal funds were cut off. The inaction was such that the Tungavik Federation of Nunavut demanded arbitration in the boundary dispute with the Dene/Métis. The Dene/Métis rejected this idea. In another attempt to get discussions going again, Jack Anawak, the MP for Nunatsiaq, formed a new Nunavut Committee on Constitutional Issues.[24] This seemed to go nowhere and in April 1989, during joint leadership meetings of the Dene, the suggestion arose that a peace treaty should be signed between the Dene Nation and Tungavik Federation of Nunavut. The Dene leaders argued that this would help get rid of old antagonisms between the two groups left over from past conflicts and, thereby, might enable a negotiated settlement to be reached over the boundary between them.[25] No such treaty was signed.

In the absence of division it appeared likely that in the eastern Arctic there would be a push for strong regionalism. This was because the Inuit wanted a degree of self–government as a coherent group. In the West, as previously noted, there was and is a much greater localism around the land claims areas. In this the aboriginal groups in the East are much more like the status Indians south of 60° than the Inuit. Thus, even in the absence of division, it would be difficult to treat the East and the West in the same way, thereby indicating that there was a certain logic for division.

Conclusions

It is clear that an opportunity for a very innovative approach to constitutional development, namely division, that would have held real possibilities for racial or ethnic protection and self-government was nearly lost. The course of constitutional development was clearly towards the entrenchment of a single territorial government in Yellowknife. The inability of the Dene/Métis and the Inuit to agree on a boundary line not only gave the opponents of division a chance to push devolution but it meant that a majority aboriginal Legislative Assembly was given the time to be, in essence, co-opted into the belief that it should be the sole government in the Territory. No doubt that belief strengthened as the size of the civil service they controlled and the range of responsibilities they dealt with became greater, as a consequence of the process of devolution. The combination of an aboriginal majority and added responsibilities quite naturally meant that the GNWT rapidly increased its legitimacy throughout the Northwest Territories. It is difficult to avoid the conclusion that the rush to devolution and the move away from regionalism after 1982 were deliberately intended to diminish the likelihood of division and to camouflage the fact that the Constitution Act and Meech Lake actually set back the process of constitutional development rather than advanced it. This conflict between varying concepts and goals has been debilitating for all involved and a more thoughtful and decisive approach is needed.

Fortunately the opportunity to adopt one has been provided by two developments. Firstly, the death of the Meech Lake Accord and the role played by northern and native peoples in its death means that the whole constitutional question will have to be reopened at some time in the future. When it is reopened it is highly likely that more attention will be paid to northern and native concerns. Secondly, the signing of the Agreement-in-Principle on land claims by the Tungavik Federation of Nunavut

331

in May 1990 following the settlement already signed by the Dene–Métis means that the issue of division has been revived. The very logic of the TFN claim depends upon there being an Inuit-dominated government. There are now no real obstacles in the way of taking decisive action in this regard. It is time for the federal government to establish a Nunavut government with the clear intention of eventually creating two new provinces.

NOTES

1   See Carol Baker, *Presentation to the Devolution Workshop*, Ottawa: Carleton University, June 4, 1988 p. 2.

2   Interview, Lee Horne, Manager, Devolution Office of the GNWT, February 13, 1989.

3   See Geoffrey R. Weller, "The Devolution of Health Care to Canada's North" in this volume.

4   Canada, *Policy Statement on the North*, (Ottawa: DIAND, June 1987), p. 1.

5   Gurston Dacks, "The Quest for Northern Oil and Gas Accords," in this volume.

6   In fact the initial support for the transfer of health services came from the Inuit Tapirisat of Canada in a 1980 resolution.

7   The Dene and the Métis insisted on a signed agreement. See *Memorandum of Understanding on Devolution of Power and Authority to GNWT from Canada with the Involvement of the Dene and Métis*, April 24, 1986.

8   See Peter Ruderman and Geoffrey R. Weller, *Report of a Study of Inuit Health and Health Services in the Keewatin Zone of the Northwest Territories*, (Ottawa: Medical Services Branch, Department of National Health and Welfare, 1981).

9   See M. Whittington (ed), *The North*, (Toronto: University of Toronto Press, 1985), p. 74.

10 See Geoffrey R. Weller, op. cit.

11 Government of the Northwest Territories, *GNWT Transfer Policy*, (Yellowknife: GNWT, February 24, 1988).

12 Katherine A. Graham, "Devolution and Local Government" in this volume.

13 GNWT, *Government Response to the Report of the Regional and Tribal Councils Review Co-ordinating Committee*, Legislative Assembly of the Northwest Territories. Tabled document No 57–88(2). Tabled November 14, 1988.

14 Katherine A. Graham, op. cit.

15 See *News/North*, April 10, 1989.

16 See Geoffrey R. Weller, "Self–Government for Canada's Inuit: The Nunavut Proposal," *The American Review of Canadian Studies*, Vol. XVIII, No. 3, Autumn 1988, p. 345.

17   A.W.R. Carrothers, *Report to the Minister of Northern Affairs and National Resources*, Ottawa: Information Canada, 1966.

18   Inuit Tapirisat of Canada, *Political Development in Nunavut*, Ottawa: Inuit Tapirisat of Canada, 1979.

19   See Government of the Northwest Territories, *Report of the Chief Plebiscite Officer on Division of the Northwest Territories, 1982*, Yellowknife: GNWT, 1982.

20   Nunavut Constitutional Forum, *Building Nunavut*, (Yellowknife: Nunavut Constitutional Forum, 1983).

21   See the *Toronto Globe and Mail*, February 7, 1985.

22   The arguments for division are detailed in Geoffrey R. Weller, "Self–Government for Canada's Inuit: The Nunavut Proposal," op. cit. pp. 350–352.

23   The arguments against division can be found in Gordon Robertson, *Northern Provinces: A Mistaken Goal*, (Montreal: Institute for Research on Public Policy, 1985); and Gurston Dacks, "The Case Against Dividing the Northwest Territories," *Canadian Public Policy* Vol. 10, No. II, (March 1986) pp. 202–223.

24   See *News/North*, February 13, 1989.

25   See *News/North*, April 10, 1989.

11 Devolution and Political Development in the Canadian North

Gurston Dacks

Introduction

In Canada's North, constitutional and political development are engaged in an intricate dance, each guiding the pace and direction of the other in ways which are complex and fluid. In part, these complexities reflect the fact that the constitutional development suite involves the intricate orchestration of a variety of simultaneous motifs in the North. These include the pursuit of regional government, territorial division and changes to the form of public government in the Northwest Territories, and, in both territories, aboriginal claims, aboriginal self-government and the approach to provincial status. The dance is also complicated because northern politics brings together different traditions of political practice and widely divergent goals; the partners in the dance do not always understand each other or want to move in the same direction. At the same time, increasingly, they do share common purposes. They recognize a need to seek common goals and thus must choreograph their movements as an interplay between competition and co-operation.

The subject of this chapter is how devolution influences the dynamics of the dance. Devolution will be the focus of this paper because it has been one of the most prominent themes of northern policy since the Conservatives gained office in Ottawa. While now overtaken by progress on aboriginal claims, it appeared in the 1980s to be accomplishing more tangible results than any of the other policies, hence provided a context in which the other processes unfolded, a great opportunity for some northern policy actors and a serious threat for others.

Constitutional and Political Development

Constitutional development is a process of increasing jurisdictional span, autonomy and structural refinement of public government. Political development is the ability of the members of a society to make binding, legitimate decisions concerning their affairs. Critical to the attainment of a high level of political development is a consensus on the boundaries of the polity and on the nature of the politically relevant entities in society whose interests must be represented in the institutions of government if it is to be legitimate. In the larger Canadian context, a consensus exists that the individual is the primary entity. The principles of universal suffrage and relatively uniform constituency sizes, at least within each province, aim at the representation of individual interests. At the same time, Canadian practice recognizes the relevance of ethnicity and regionalism through the federal system and provincial representation in the Senate and the Cabinet. However, even the pan-Canadian system is challenged by debates about the representational needs and the basic rights of particular groups in Canada's social structure. Most dramatically, the debate about the Meech Lake Accord centred on the question of how to reflect the special circumstances of Quebec in Confederation. Calls for a triple-E Senate from western and Atlantic Canada suggest that national institutions do not adequately reflect the special needs of Canada's hinterland. The constitutional status of Canada's aboriginal peoples remains a sadly unresolved question.

In these and similar issues constitutional and political development are linked; even legally powerful and elaborate institutions need to rest on an adequate political foundation in order to function effectively and to be accepted as legitimate. Processes must be in place which enable significant groups in society to communicate their desires to government. These groups must feel confident that the social consensus on basic issues will assure their concerns a fair hearing. Until these groups feel this confidence, entrenching institutions will be a risky enterprise. They may function, reach decisions promptly and administer policy efficiently. However, they may not act responsively or gain the trust of important social groupings.

Constitutional development which is not accompanied by appropriate political development may become a trap for these groups, as present federal government structures appear to some hinterland, aboriginal and other Canadians to be.

The Role of Collectivity in the North

In the North, this interaction between political and constitutional development turns on the significance of social collectivity in its society and politics. As the literature on consociationalism demonstrates, the political role of social collectivities challenges a great many countries. Canada, for example, continues to struggle with the questions of how to fit Quebec into Confederation and how to balance collective rights — the distinct society — and individual freedoms. The northern analogue to these questions is how to accommodate aboriginal peoples within the political and governmental frameworks of the North. While this issue also appears in southern Canada, it exerts less presssure on southern governments for several reasons. Aboriginal people constitute only a small fraction of the southern population, very much more in the North. These numbers give aboriginal northerners substantial strength at the ballot box and also mean that they have the potential to create relatively powerful forms of self-government in the future, should they wish to do so. Moreover, the institutions of the Territories, and particularly the NWT, are not yet fully formed, hence the aboriginal people have an opportunity to share in the shaping of them which the established forms of government in the provinces deny to their aboriginal peoples.

Accommodating aboriginal peoples means accommodating aboriginal collectivities. While generalizations always admit of exceptions, aboriginal people traditionally see themselves as social collectivities — in effect, as distinct societies. Their relationship to their aboriginal roots remains rich and vital; it is usually a fundamental source of their identity, more so than ethnic background tends to be for many other Canadians. The security and future of their aboriginal group are basic elements of their political agenda. This traditional valuing of the collectivity has been reinforced by two modern-day political processes. The first of these is the land claims process. This process caused aboriginal people to develop strong representative organizations which serve as voices for their aboriginal collectivities. The claims themselves are collective claims whose settlements will convey collective rights and benefits. For the foreseeable future, the pursuit of these rights and the management of settlement benefits will engage aboriginal peoples in collective activities. These will encourage them to conceive of their interests as collective and their relationships with non-aboriginal people and institutions as at least in part collective in character. The second, and related, process has been the attempt to constitutionalize the meaning of aboriginal rights through the first ministers' process. This process sensitized native people to the issue of their collective self-determination. Its failure to date has reinforced the determination of northern aboriginal people to seek regional constitutions which avoid the national failure of aboriginal peoples to achieve a satisfactory collective relationship with the Canadian state.

In contrast, non-aboriginal northerners tend to hold the individualistic values of North American liberal-democracy. Tending not to see themselves a part of a social collectivity, a sub-group in northern society, they feel no need for the institutions of public government in the North to reflect any ethnic collectivity of which they might be a part. They recognize aboriginal rights but feel that they should be expressed through the settlement of claims and possibly through aboriginal self-government. In this way, they reject as a violation of the principle of equality public government structures which aboriginal leaders see as logical extensions of their aboriginal rights, essential to securing the benefits of their claims settlements and acknowledging their distinctness as societies within northern society.

The constitutional uniqueness — and complexity — of the North flows from the immediacy of the question of how to express the interests and protect the rights of aboriginal collectivities within northern public governments which must conform to the individualist bias of the *Charter of Rights and Freedoms*. If not for this issue, the direction of constitutional development in the

North, responsible government through the Westminster model reflecting non-aboriginal political culture, would be completely predictable. Indeed, it is almost guaranteed to come to pass in the Yukon, and may also do so in the NWT. Whether it will depends on the answers to several questions. First, how much cross-pressure do aboriginal people feel between their collective interests and their self-interest as individuals? Second, how important are factors — including the responsiveness of the present GNWT — which undercut the mobilization of effective pressure for constitutional innovation to reflect the aboriginal collectivities in northern society? Third, what is the likelihood that other forms of government will develop to express collective interests in the North, thus reducing or eliminating the need to modify the Westminster model to provide for this representation within the public government?

The experience of the devolution process provides a number of insights into these questions. However, before devolution can be considered, some context and important contrasts between the two Territories must be identified.

The Yukon

Responsible government is already institutionalized in the Yukon. Canada's three national parties contest elections and participate in the Legislative Assembly in ways which mirror behaviour in the legislatures of southern Canada. Because aboriginal people account for about one quarter of the territorial population, they have no prospect of using the ballot box to pursue a restructuring of the institutions of public government in the Territory. Moreover, because they live in a widely dispersed pattern in the Yukon, it would not be possible to identify a portion of the Territory which could be allotted to them as their own — an application of the logic of federalism to their need for collective representation and self-determination.

In any case, they have not sought to change the nature of the Government of the Yukon for at least three reasons, in addition to the minimal likelihood of success. First, the Yukon Indians tend to view their 14 communities as their prime political units. Indeed, the Agreement in Principle for the settlement of their aboriginal claim anticipates the creation of 14 locally based aboriginal self-governments, with no reference to any Territory-wide institution.[1] The local focus of Yukon Indian political culture disinclines them to seek Territory-wide constitutional change. Second, the presence of disciplined political parties provides a link between government and the aboriginal people and enables the latter to exercise a degree of accountability over the former, enhancing governmental responsiveness. Third, the present New Democratic government of the Yukon, in power since 1984, has taken as its first constitutional priority the settlement of the aboriginal claim of the Council for Yukon Indians. This has led it to give a lower priority to devolution. As a result, devolution has not proven to be a source of changes that complicate claims negotiations or threaten understandings once they have been negotiated.

All of these factors underpin a clear social expectation that the form of government of the Yukon has already been decided. Collective interests are not given institutional expression in this structure, but this has not led to aboriginal calls for a new form of public government. Rather there is a clear consensus that these interests will have to be expressed through other institutions, if they are to receive institutional expression at all.

The Northwest Territories

The NWT presents a very different picture. Its form of government is significantly less institutionalized than is the Government of the Yukon. While it largely resembles the Government of the Yukon in having a Cabinet composed entirely of elected members of the Assembly and responsible to the Assembly, it cannot be said to be fully a system of responsible government.[2] The reason for this is the absence of party affiliation in what is termed a "consensus" form of government. This absence impedes the operation of Cabinet solidarity and denies the accountability which party politics gives to the parliamentary system as one of its greatest strengths. This feature displeases many, primarily non-aboriginal northerners, who value the accountability which responsible government entails. However, aboriginal people in particular resist the development of party politics because they feel that it would entrench a system which would subordinate the expression of their collective interests to the dictates of party discipline. However, in taking this position, they deny themselves the instrument of party discipline and accountability which has proven effective in improving relations between Indians and government in the Yukon.

Demographics make this resistance by the aboriginal people of the NWT more than plausible. According to the 1986 census, they account for about 50 percent of the territorial population. This does not guarantee them domination of territorial politics through the ballot box. However, it makes them a very significant force, particularly in the future in view of their high birth rate and the possible adoption of a two-year residence requirement for voting, a requirement which would disenfranchise quite a few non-natives but, of course, no aboriginal people. In addition, the Inuit of the NWT account for over 80 percent of the population north of the treeline. This and their conviction that the GNWT does not and cannot govern them responsively[3] has led them to promote a federal solution to their representation needs. Division of the NWT into a western territory and an eastern territory to be called Nunavut would give them a jurisdiction which they could be assured would support their collective interests yet do so through the same type of institutions of government which are found elsewhere in Canada.[4] Nunavut has not come into existence because it has proven impossible to resolve the issue of where to draw the boundary.[5] However, this state of affairs should not be taken as evidence that the Inuit believe that the present Government of the Northwest Territories satisfactorily protects and promotes their collective interests. To the contrary, the Tungavik Federation of Nunavut, the body which represents the Inuit of the NWT, emphasizes that division of the territories is a complement to their claims settlement which is not only essential, but inevitable.[6] The Inuit Agreement-In-Principle reaffirms the commitment of the territorial and federal governments to support division in principle and promises that a process for creating

341

Nunavut will be initiated promptly after the signing of the final claim settlement.[7]

Similarly, while the Dene and Métis of the western NWT continue to take part in the Government of the NWT, their pursuit of aboriginal self-government strongly suggests that they find its present format not fully satisfactory as a vehicle for expressing their collective needs. For example, in 1988, the Dene and Métis argued that,

> ...for aboriginal peoples, the existing GNWT is still an interim government, because it has yet to represent them directly or directly incorporate their values or priorities....Aboriginal self-government has not been achieved in the Northwest Territories by the participation of aboriginal people in the public government.[8]

The Dene and Métis achieved a comprehensive land claim agreement in 1990. However, because of the constraints of the federal government's aboriginal claims policy, this not-yet-ratified agreement will not afford the Dene and Métis the full range of protection of their rights and interests which many, particularly Dene, feel they must have to secure their culture and lifestyle in the future. They therefore feel compelled either to change the structure of the GNWT to make it more responsive or escape its jurisdiction to some degree through the mechanism of aboriginal self-government.

It would appear that the GNWT is less institutionalized and accepted than governments elsewhere in Canada. In particular, the criticism it encounters from aboriginal organizations suggests that they may be closer to aboriginal people than it is. What is probably closest to the truth is that the government and the aboriginal groups are locked in a struggle for the support of aboriginal northerners.

For its part, the GNWT argues that "...many of the goals of aboriginal self-government are already in place or potentially in place within the present (GNWT) system."[9] It often points to the aboriginal majority among the members of the Legislative

Assembly and the ample representation of aboriginal peoples in the Cabinet to legitimize itself in reply to criticisms that it is a "white government."

However, the GNWT cannot be an institutional voice for the collective interests of the aboriginal peoples in the way that their own groups can. The GNWT is not structured directly to represent the collective interests of the aboriginal groups of the Territories as contrasted with the interests of aboriginal persons as individuals. It must govern in the interest of all northerners, not just aboriginal people. This responsibility, the outlook of the primarily non-aboriginal bureaucracy and the need in some cases to conform to southern models to gain the co-operation of Ottawa[10] can lead ministers, even ministers who are themselves aboriginal, away from the agendas of the aboriginal groups. The absence of party politics prevents aboriginal people from electing a government committed to their collective goals and holding it accountable for its fidelity to those goals once in office. In their constituencies, the absence of party politics may combine with the local community orientation of many voters to make the success of ministers and ordinary members as advocates of local interests a more important determinant of their electoral fate than is their promotion of aboriginal interests. All of these structural factors can work together to lead the GNWT to develop policies inconsistent with aboriginal goals, and to pursue its institutional interest vigorously at the expense of the interests of the aboriginal groups when and to the extent that they have come into conflict.

At the same time, the government does represent aboriginal people as individuals and serve their individual interests quite effectively. It provides housing and electricity. It is the biggest employer in the Territories, employing many aboriginal people.

Moreover, the government can appeal to the aboriginal interests of aboriginal voters. As noted above, it can claim legitimacy on the basis of the number of aboriginal people in the assembly and the executive. As would be expected of such a group of politicians serving such a large aboriginal constituency, the Government of the Northwest Territories does often respond to a significant degree to the collective needs of the aboriginal peoples of the Territories. For example, it has supported the settlement of aboriginal claims and the positions which the aboriginal groups advocated during the national constitutional process which attempted to define the concept of aboriginal rights.[11] It also helped fund the court challenge to uranium development which the Inuit community of Baker Lake launched on the basis of aboriginal rights.[12]

In addition, the GNWT has co-operated with attempts to restructure it to achieve collective representation within it. It participated in the Constitutional Alliance of the Northwest Territories from its inception in 1982 until 1990, when it ceased to exist. This advisory body, composed of MLAs and representatives of aboriginal groups, was responsible for preparing a plan for dividing the Territories, including recommending a form of government for the western NWT which, in the words of Bob MacQuarrie, then an MLA and member of the Alliance, would establish "an appropriate balance between individual and collective rights."[13] Most recently, the GNWT has committed itself in claims settlements to pursue processes of constitutional development which, if they reach fruition, could diminish its power significantly.[14]

The responsiveness of the GNWT to the principle of aboriginal collectivity can be debated. What is less debatable is that the aboriginal groups have failed to press effectively for changes in the structures of government which would institutionalize the representation of their collective interests. They have presented some rather extensive proposals, such as the Dene/Métis statement, *Public Government for the People of the North*[15] and the Nunavut proposal of the Inuit. However, these have not accomplished any change to date in the operation of the government. As will be argued below, devolution makes such change less likely in the future.

The aboriginal groups have failed in pursuing their constitutional agenda for a range of reasons. The first is that the support they enjoy from their people is less than absolute. For one thing, aboriginal people may experience a degree of cross-pressure over the pursuit of their collective interests. Instances can arise in which aboriginal people must weigh their interests as members of ethnic collectivities against their interests as wage earners or residents of particular regions. For example, their collective interests have led the Dene Nation and the Métis Association to seek a delay in the construction of a natural gas pipeline in the Mackenzie Valley until their aboriginal claim is settled.[16] However, the desire of individual Dene and Métis to work on the construction phase of the pipeline leads many of them to support the stance of the territorial government in favour of construction. In addition, the government can appeal quite persuasively for aboriginal support on the representational and policy grounds suggested above. Finally, there is no aboriginal tradition of pursuing politics over as large an area as each of the aboriginal groups covers. Aboriginal people feel a strong identification with their extended family and their linguistic group, but their loyalty to the umbrella organizations which brings these groups together at the territorial level is a relatively recent phenomenon. This means that the leaders of the aboriginal organizations cannot count on unequivocal support and may have to face difficult internal politics as they attempt to manage the relations among the diverse components of their organizations. Thus, for example, the leaders of the Dene Nation found in 1987 that they could not ratify the agreement on a boundary for dividing the NWT which they had negotiated because of pressure from a small minority of Dene people.

This case illustrates a second general problem — that aboriginal political culture, while admirably suited to meeting the needs for which it traditionally evolved, imposes some severe liabilities on aboriginal leaders attempting to work effectively in non-aboriginal political settings. Because of the dispersion of authority in aboriginal communities, it is more difficult for leaders of the aboriginal groups to commit themselves than it is for the government to do so. In addition, aboriginal political culture calls for extensive consultation between leaders and their people. For example, before approving their claims Agreement in Principle, the Dene and Métis held assemblies attended by large numbers of their people lasting five days. The need for this type of consultation forces aboriginal leaders to work in a different time frame than politicians working in a non-aboriginal setting who can make executive decisions with quite limited consultation, if they wish. Moreover, aboriginal leaders find that they must manage the gap between aborginal and non-aboriginal political culture. They must operate in two different modes, dealing with elders and communities on one hand and the policy processes of public government on the other. They respect the former, but must deal with the overwhelming power of the latter. This is not only extremely stressful for them, but also limits their ability to steer a proposition all the way through governmental policy processes. When the needs they may encounter to deal with issues internal to the aboriginal community distract them from their policy goals or force a revision of plans, relations with government suffer.

A third problem of a more practical nature has kept the issue of representing collectivities from coming to a head. Aboriginal groups' resources are usually quite modest, yet they are called upon to respond to a variety of external developments ranging from devolution itself to pipeline proposals to issues of northern sovereignty and strategic policy, not to mention doing what is necessary to maintain the flow of federal government money to fund their activities. Even more labour-intensive is their preoccupation with negotiating the settlement of their all-important aboriginal claims. Faced with challenges such as these, the aboriginal groups simply lack the personnel they need to devote to issues of governmental structure. This is particularly the case because no occasion, such as a decision to proceed with dividing the Territories, has presented itself to make this issue immediate and pressing.

A fourth problem is that the various aboriginal groups have pursued different strategies of constitutional development. The Inuit have pursued Nunavut and ignored discussions about reforming the structure of the GNWT because it will not govern them after division. Through much of the 1980s, the Dene and Métis focussed on reforming the public government; more recently they have begun to explore options for separate institutions of self-government. For their part, the Inuvialuit, the Inuit people of the western Arctic, have sought a strong regional government as a vehicle for their self-determination. The pursuit of these different goals has divided the strength of the aboriginal people of the territory and prevented their representatives in the Assembly from forming a voting bloc, although the members from the eastern Arctic have sometimes voted as a group.

These various infirmities on the part of the aboriginal groups of the Territories pose a basic problem of political development. The determination with which they have pursued their aboriginal claims demonstrates indisputably that the aboriginal people feel a strong collective identity and share important collective interests. However, they have to date proven unable to bring sufficient pressure to bear on the political system to ensure that the public government of the Territories is structured in a fashion which would faciliate the expression of this identity and these interests. The result is a continuation of incoherence in territorial politics, a continuing absence of consensus on the political role of social collectivities and how to represent the aboriginal collectivities in public government. The resulting inability to achieve a broadly based approach to planning constitutional change has allowed other forces, such as devolution, to determine the direction of constitutional change. This is a basic feature of the dance as it is done in the NWT: constitutional development proceeds, but political development not only does not lead it, but fails to keep pace with it.

In this uncertain climate, and driven by the universal desire of governments to be as fully empowered as possible to serve their people, the GNWT has sought to increase its strength. Devolution has been one of the basic elements of its strategy. Indeed, the high priority it has attached to devolution stands in contrast to the subordination of devolution to claims in the priorities of the Government of the Yukon.

Devolution

The devolution of authority over provincial-type jurisdictions from the federal government to the governments of the two

Territories was a priority of the first two Conservative ministers of Indian Affairs and Northern Development, David Crombie and Bill McKnight. From 1984 to 1988, management of forests, forest fire suppression and electrical generation were transferred to both territorial governments. The Government of the NWT also assumed jurisdiction over hospitals and health services, a responsiblity whose transfer the Yukon and federal governments began to negotiate in the spring of 1989. The completion of these devolutions will bring the span of authority of the territorial governments very close to that of the provinces. They and not the federal government will provide their people with the vast bulk of services which Canadians south of 60° receive from their provincial governments. The major powers the Territories will lack are few, but very important: oil, gas and minerals, land management and ownership and the prosecutions function. The pace at which the Territories acquire these powers and the conditions which are attached to their transfer bear important implications for the overall processes of constitutional and political development in the North.

Some of these processes touch directly on the issue of how representation of northern aboriginal collective interests can be accomplished. These include the structure of public government, the claims themselves and possible forms of aboriginal self-government. Other changes would indirectly represent aboriginal interests by creating or strengthening institutions whose constituencies would be predominantly aboriginal. These include division of the NWT and the pressure for powerful regional governments, which is strongest in the regions of the Territories where the Inuit comprise the bulk of the population. Geoffrey Weller's second chapter in this volume discusses these possible developments. A final constitutional process which devolution affects, but which only very indirectly relates to the issue of collective representation is the attainment of, or at least the approach to, provincial status by the Territories. This paper will now turn its attention to the linkages between devolution and these processes in both the Yukon and the Northwest Territories.

Devolution and the Form of Public Government

Devolution will add to the powers of the government of the Yukon, but it will not alter the government's basic structure or its approach to representation. In the Yukon, the process of molding the institutions of public government is largely complete; a parliamentary system of responsible government based on party competition has operated there for more than a decade. No one expects it to change in the foreseeable future, nor is any sentiment being expressed that it do so. Indeed, the only remaining step for it to take is for its basis to be changed from ministerial directive, which can be unilaterally altered or withdrawn by Ottawa (a highly unlikely prospect) to constitutional entrenchment. While devolution may raise a variety of questions in the Yukon, its impact on the underlying structure of government is not one of these questions.

In contrast, devolution does affect constitutional development in the Northwest Territories by adding to the credibility of the present direction of evolution. Each additional power the government receives symbolizes the acquiescence of the federal government to the development in the NWT of the institutions of representation and responsible government found everywhere else in Canada among the federal and provincial governments. This symbolism builds the confidence of northerners who support this evolution and who see it as natural and preordained. It is not that devolution has shaped the government of the Northwest Territories. Rather, each instance of devolution represents the closing off of an opportunity to force a joining of the issue about the shape of government, leading, perhaps, to an altered direction of constitutional development.

In a practical sense, devolution is institution-building. Devolution gives the government more money, more person-years and more services to provide. In this way, it enables the government to expand its clientele, whether they be employees who depend on the GNWT for their jobs or recipients of GNWT-provided services. As the government becomes larger and more powerful, the contrast grows between it and the smallness and the inability of the aboriginal groups to deliver equivalent benefits. As time passes, it becomes less and less credible that aboriginal institutions might be developed which would be as effective as is the government of the NWT. It becomes harder for the aboriginal groups to scrutinize the activities of the government to ensure that the interests of their people are being served. Their opposition to devolution in the absence of accommodation of their collective interests in public government institutions becomes less and less credible each time it is ignored. Increasingly, the aboriginal groups look less like governments in waiting or the voices of sovereign peoples and more and more like mere interest groups.

The Northwest Territories has been interesting for political scientists because it has been the only jurisdiction in Canada which has held out some promise of deviating from the model of public government found elsewhere. The operation of the Assembly in a non-partisan, "consensus-government" fashion and the consideration of a form of consociational government for the western NWT after division[17] have suggested that room exists for some form of institutional innovation which would lead to the more effective representation of aboriginal collective concerns than the parliamentary system has tended to provide throughout Canadian history. Devolution has reduced the odds of this type of development by enabling the GNWT, in instances which will be discussed below, to seek and to acquire powers without having to confront the issue of how it represents the collective interests within its society.

Devolution and Aboriginal Claims

The purpose of the aboriginal claims in the North is to protect the material basis of the traditional economies of the aboriginal peoples and in this way to ensure their economic well-being and the sense of identity and spirituality which is based on their relationship to the land and water. In the words of Michael Whittington, "...the land (and one might add for the Inuit, 'the arctic waters') holds a central place in the social, economic and spiritual lives of the native peoples, and as such it is the disposition of that land that is the dominant concern of the Dene, Métis and Inuit alike."[18] In particular, the aboriginal people are concerned that government may approve large-scale non-renewable resource development projects such as pipelines or uranium mines, which may make it impossible or at least much more difficult for them to hunt, fish and trap. The settlements of aboriginal claims have given or will give the aboriginal peoples substantial control over the land. The settlements confirm aboriginal ownership of large areas of land. On some of this land, the aboriginal people own the subsurface as well as the surface rights. This enables them to prevent non-renewable resource development by the simple expedient of not developing their property. In the other portions of aboriginal lands, where companies do hold subsurface rights, the aboriginal groups will be able to negotiate fair compensation for granting the companies access to their lands.[19] However, they have not been in a position to control the pace at which government makes exploration and development rights available to developers nor such policies as royalty rates, incentive grants, tax arrangements and worker and environmental safety requirements, which will determine the impact of non-renewable resource exploitation on their use of the land.

The devolution process will interact with the claims settlements to answer the absolutely fundamental question of the extent to which the aboriginal peoples will be able to escape their historic inability to protect the lands and waters on which they depend. The devolution of jurisdiction over oil and gas will empower ministers of the territorial governments to develop and implement northern energy management regimes. It remains to be seen how emphatically the transfer will instruct them to treat aboriginal interests as a principle consideration in their policy making.[20] Equally unclear is how effectively the settlements have safeguarded aboriginal interests. The settlements will create planning, land and water use and impact assessment bodies. While these will be public government bodies, they will be compelled to treat aboriginal needs very seriously because of the numbers of aboriginal people who will sit on them and because they owe their existence to claims settlements, not to the devolution process. It would appear therefore that, while devolution dominated claims in the late 1980s, the claims process gained the upper hand at the start of the 1990s. This judgment may prove premature in that, in the final analysis, government ministers can reject what will be recommendations — not binding decisions — of these bodies. Ministers will be discouraged from doing so by having to state their reasons publicly, but, whenever push comes to shove, they will have the authority to proceed on their own judgment, not that of the boards. Furthermore, they may be able to point to the technical resources of their public services to legitimize their decisions as better supported than the views of boards which may not rest on a comparable base. In the end, the vision which will dominate the northern land and seascapes of the future will reflect two factors. The first is the degree to which the territorial governments and the resource planning and management boards share common values and co-operate. The second, to the extent that they work at cross purposes, is the balance of technical resources and political legitimacy between them.

A final note must be added to complete the story of the relationship between devolution and claims. While in the 1980s they appeared to be parallel and at times competing processes, the approaching settlement of the claims at the start of the 1990s has caused them to converge. In one sense, the settlement of claims has enabled at least the GNWT to assert more aggressively the need to devolve jurisdiction over land and water to it. The argument is not merely that this transfer is now timely in that it has been consistent with the ongoing federal devolution federal policy, but has been held up pending the settlement of the claims.

Rather than merely seeing claims in this way as a roadblock now removed, the GNWT is hoping to harness the momentum of the land claims process to pull the devolution cart. It argues:

> The result of the past approach (of separate processes for claims and for political and constitutional development) has been a largely ad hoc and poorly co-ordinated approach to political and constitutional development. While this has worked in a

fashion in the past, it will not any longer because land claims implementation and devolution have merged into a single process. Land claims have also added the requirement of a higher level of discipline, because claims agreements have set deadlines for the implementation of claims institutions, particularly public institutions which regulate the use of land and water...it does not make any sense to contemplate the implementation of public institutions created by land claims other than pursuant to territorial legislation. It would be inconsistent with federal and territorial policy and objectives. It would also be unworkable, certainly confusing and inefficient, if renewable and nonrenewable resource use continues to be regulated by a mixture of territorial and federal legislation.[21]

From this perspective, devolution and the settlement of claims are linked in that the latter provides an occasion for the former — for creation of a comprehensive territorial government regime for managing all the resources of the North, a development which would bring the span of powers of the territorial government very close to that of the provinces.

The issue of the relationship between claims-based resource management structures and those which devolution may provide arises in both Territories. An energy accord may itself not stir great interest in the Yukon because relatively few areas of the Yukon offer much promise of oil and gas deposits. As a result, relatively few areas of the territory are likely to be disturbed by energy exploration. However, to the extent that an energy accord will accelerate and provide precedents for the transfer of jurisdiction over mining, which does affect the Yukon very significantly, the linkage between the devolution of management and ultimately ownership of land and resources and aboriginal claims will be an important issue in both Territories. In the negotiations, the Yukon can be expected to advance the argument of the GNWT that resources can only be managed coherently if there is a single hand at the helm — the hand of the territorial government.

Aboriginal Self-Government

In the Yukon, devolution has not significantly influenced the Council for Yukon Indians' pursuit of aboriginal self-government. As has been noted, the Government of the Yukon has tried to avoid pushing the devolution process in a way which would complicate or pressure the negotiation of the claim. This has enabled the CYI to devote relatively little attention to devolution while developing the *Framework Agreement* for its claim, including the approach to self-government which it contains. This approach reflects the consensus that the Government of the Yukon has achieved its final form. It also reflects Yukon Indian political culture, which, as in the NWT, holds the local community to be the prime focus of political allegiance. As already noted, the lack of emphasis in the Yukon Indian *Framework Agreement* on a territory-wide Indian self-government makes a power struggle between it and the Yukon government quite unlikely, although conflict may arise over the transfer of powers to the community-based Indian nations. In theory, the issue of how governments — the aboriginal self-governments and the Yukon government — will share power over land use, when this power is devolved in the future, does relate self-government and devolution in the Yukon. However, this issue is largely resolved by the rather modest provisions of the *Framework Agreement*. For all of these reasons, while devolution is important to Yukon Indians, they have not felt that it has frustrated their pursuit of their claim; devolution has not motivated them to seek self-government.

The Northwest Territories presents a very contrasting picture. While many territorial residents would welcome the completion of the present evolution toward parliamentary government, this pattern is far from universally accepted. This is the case precisely because this model does not provide for the representation of aboriginal collectivities as collectivities.

Moreover, the aboriginal groups feel that past actions by the GNWT relating to devolution have undercut their interests and pre-empted opportunities for the development of aboriginal self-government. For example, the aboriginal groups supported the devolution of jurisdiction over health care out of a belief that the GNWT would decentralize the administration of this activity by empowering strong regional health boards. The aboriginal groups feel that their expectations were not realized and that the GNWT has denied them the power over their health care which they believed devolution would provide them.[22] The experience of the aboriginal groups regarding the signing of the enabling agreement for the Oil and Gas Accord in 1988 reinforced their belief that, when faced with a conflict between their interests and its own institutional growth, the GNWT would invariably opt for the latter.[23]

This feeling has caused them to fear that future devolution will continue to pre-empt aboriginal self-government. In some instances, as in the case of the Inuit position regarding health care and the Dene and Métis interest in forest management and fire suppression, aboriginal groups support devolution as a way of gaining much needed improvements in the quality of service. In other instances, such as the involvement of the Inuit in the Northern Accord process, they sense that they cannot stop devolution from occurring. Whatever the considerations which involve them in the devolution process, they are very concerned that they have as full an influence over its course as possible and that, in particular, future devolution does not limit the scope of aboriginal self-government which they may seek to put in place or the rights which they have negotiated as part of their claims settlements.

In this way, devolution has two impacts on aboriginal self-government in the NWT. First, the approach of the territorial government has added to the aboriginal groups' feeling that it is more interested in state-building than it is in respecting their interests. This suggests that the territorial government has little real interest in institutionalizing within its own structure the expression of the collective interests. This conclusion only adds to the argument for pursuing aboriginal self-government. Second, devolution can frustrate the development of aboriginal self-government if powers are devolved to the territorial government before the aboriginal governments have been established to receive them. The assumption is that once the territorial government assumes formerly federal powers, it will not be possible to cause it to share these powers.

If the territorial government and the aboriginal groups do not find more mutually satisfactory accommodations on devolution, the aboriginal groups can be expected to pursue strong forms of self-government. In the case of the Inuit, this will mean an intensified pursuit of division of the Territories. Should it become evident that this option is unattainable, the Inuit will probably fall back to a position of seeking the strongest possible forms of regional government. Several alternative futures could flow out of this situation. The first is that aboriginal self-governments in the West and strong regional governments in the East take shape and co-exist relatively successfully with the GNWT. Such a co-existence is unlikely, however, if the genesis of these governments involves tension between the territorial government and the aboriginal groups and if their jurisdictions overlap concerning such crucial issues as oil and gas management. A second, and more likely, scenario would involve the development of significant aboriginal and regional governments in the West and the East, respectively, and the development of conflict over policy and competition over resources between the territorial and the other governments. The hostility and waste of resources which would accompany this outcome would likely lead to calls for constitutional revision. In this way, if the GNWT does not change in the near future to represent aboriginal collectivities within its structures, it may find itself revisiting this issue 10 years from now. However, by then its structure may have become entrenched and the unique constitutional opportunity which the NWT presents may have been irretrievably lost.

This could also be the consequence of the third scenario, which is that strong aboriginal and regional governments do not come into existence. This scenario would lead the aboriginal groups back to the pursuit of restructuring the territorial government to embody aboriginal self-government, or at least directly represent their collective interests. Should they fail, the result will not be intergovernmental conflict as in the previous scenario. Rather, the government will continue to include aboriginal collective interests among a number of factors —

regional concerns, interest group desires, its own institutional needs; electoral prospects of its members — which shape its decisions. These decisions will likely serve aboriginal people better than have the similarly derived policies of the provincial governments because of the proportion of aboriginal people in the NWT is greater than in the provinces. However it will not give the weight to the collective interests of these aboriginal people which they need if their claims settlements, their land base and their culture and identity are to be secure.

The last two scenarios would produce the situation antici- pated at the start of this paper, a situation in which constitu- tional development is well advanced, but political development is blocked. The absence of a consensus on the appropriate basis of representation in the territorial government can only leave a part of the population alienated from the government, frustrated by its policies and difficult for the government to appeal to to support its initiatives. This situation, characteristic of many Third World nations, tends to reduce the responsiveness and the effectiveness of government. Particularly in a region experienc- ing the effects of rapid social change and economic challenges such as high unemployment and a dependence on natural resource production the pace of which is determined largely by factors which are global and hence out of its control, government needs to be as strong and well supported as it can possibly be. In other words, the issue of collective representation must be satisfactorily resolved if the GNWT is to be best able to provide its people with the effective government they need.

This is the context in the Northwest Territories in which devolution brings together the issues of the form of public government, land claims and aboriginal self-government. In- deed, devolution and claims represent two competing proc- esses. Each has the ability to shape governmental institutions, devolution by denying powers to aboriginal self-government and claims by denying them to public governments. These two processes also shape the motivations and tactical considera- tions of the government and the aboriginal leaders. Devolution without recognition of aboriginal collectivities reduces the pres- sure the government feels to involve aboriginal groups significantly in future devolutions or to make significant concessions to their concerns. On the other hand, it reinforces the determination of the aboriginal leadership to resist future devolution and to seek to go it alone through the development of aboriginal self-governments or division or, failing that, regional governments. The measure of the outcome of this struggle between devolution and claims will be the importance accorded to collective representation within the totality of government institutions in the Territory.

Devolution and the Attainment of Provincial Status

The Territories face significant opposition in their pursuit of provincial status.[24] However, to the extent that this concern focusses on the implications for fiscal equalization and the general amendment formula, other aspects of provincial status may be attainable by the Territories in the near future.[25] These aspects could include fuller participation at first ministers' conferences, the establishment of crowns in right of the Territories, and entrenchment of territorial institutions, alteration of which would require the consent of assembly of the Territory affected. However, status in the Canadian Constitution and in intergovernmental relations is only one of two basic sets of provincial attributes. The second is the range of powers which they exercise.

As with the linkages between devolution and other forms of constitutional development, the two Territories differ regarding the approach they have taken in relating devolution to their strategies for promoting the attainment of provincial status. The Yukon strategy has been to emphasize the status of provinces.[26] The GNWT has focussed its efforts on broadening the range of its powers.

By way of example, the Government of the the Yukon attacked the Meech Lake Accord most vigorously from 1987 to 1990. It condemned the provisions of the Accord which would have required unanimous federal and provincial approval for the creation of new provinces and which would have denied the government leaders of the Territories an entrenched role at future constitutional discussions. It even went so far as to launch an unsuccessful challenge to the constitutionality of the provisions of the Meech Lake Accord which affect the status of the territorial governments. For its part, the GNWT condemned the Accord and lobbied actively against it. However it avoided the stridency of the Yukon government. It recognized that the pursuit of provincial status would bring it immediately into conflict with the provinces on issues about which they felt strongly, such as the amending formula. It also recognized that it could not compete with the provincial governments on these issues, particularly in view of the insistence of all of the parties at the time that Meech Lake could not be renegotiated. In any case, provincial status would represent the fullest expression of constitutional development. While the Territories can continue, although at a significant cost, to develop institutionally in the absence of consensus on division, the form of public government and the role of aboriginal self-government, to grant provincial status would create a degree of constitutional development unacceptably ahead of the territorial level of political development. For this reason, and because it was blocked in seeking enhanced status, the GNWT emphasized gaining enhanced powers through devolution.

In this way, devolution has not been a significant part of the strategy by which the Yukon government has sought provincial status. In contrast, devolution has been the centrepiece of the GNWT's strategy. With the devolution of jurisdiction over health care completed, the GNWT now is responsible for all the major social development functions which the provincial governments carry out. Should it prove possible to negotiate a Northern Accord and thereafter the transfer of the jurisdiction over land and water which will enable it to legislate into existence the management regimes anticipated by the claims settlements, the territorial government will exercise a great deal of control over policy making in the realm of economic development. These functions involve large financial and personnel resources and the development of very substantial technical competence in the public service of the territorial government. Even if provincial status remains in the distant future, the GNWT will be able to deliver to the people of the Territory almost the full range of services that the provincial governments deliver. When provincial status does become attainable, this institutionalization of the territorial state which devolution has promoted will make it easier for the GNWT to credibly press its case to Ottawa and the provinces.

However, to the extent that this institutionalization does not rest on a societal consensus, then the other governments may resist provincial status for the NWT. At the head of the dissenters will be the federal government which will fear that the rights of aboriginal people, for whom it has a special constitutional responsibility, may be inadequately served by a government which is estranged from them. It will fear that some territorial government action may compel it to violate the norms of intergovernmental equality which have led it to deny itself the use of the disallowance power for the last almost half-century. Any resort to this power, however justified, would undoubtedly create a crisis in federal-provincial relations. While the likelihood of such a scenario is remote, Ottawa may feel that the prudent course in the absence of a degree of political development high enough to ensure the communication of aboriginal collective needs to the territorial government is to avoid taking the risk at all. In such a situation, provincial status would become impossible.

Conclusion

Devolution is linked to both political and constitutional development in Canada's northern Territories, and these two processes are themselves linked in ways significantly affected by devolution. While national factors such as equalization and the arithmetic of constitutional amendment will affect the growth of status of the Territories, regional factors will also prove influential. The more each of the Territories is able to demonstrate a societal consensus supporting or at least accepting the institutions it has developed, the more likely Ottawa and the provinces will be to accord it more status. Assuming that the aboriginal groups' collective consciousness and desire for collective representation do not dissipate in the face of assimilating forces, the obstacles they face in bringing their political agenda to bear on the debate about public government in the NWT represent a problem of political development which may impair its constitutional development.

The more power is devolved to the Territories, the more technically competent and similar to the existing provinces they will likely appear to be, developments which ought to weaken the rationale for discriminating constitutionally against them. If power is devolved and status accorded northern governments which are taking shape in ways which enjoy the support of the major social groups, then this process of empowerment can promote the development of the social consensus required for successful government. Here again, the ability of aboriginal groups to bring their potential political weight to bear on these issues and the responsiveness of government, particularly in the NWT, will be the deciding factors in striking the balance between collective and individual representation.

Until recently in the NWT, both of these factors contributed to a balance which tended to favour the latter over the former. This outcome encouraged aboriginal groups to seek separate vehicles — division, claims and self-government — rather than public means of representing their collective interests. The recent settlement of aboriginal claims has empowered the aboriginal peoples of the Territories, assuming the ratification of the Dene/Métis agreement, and has redressed the balance to a degree. It remains to be seen what status this development will encourage the territorial government to accord its aboriginal peoples. It could continue to respond to them as interest groups, albeit very powerful ones and risk the continuation of incoherence, of diverging values, loyalties and agendas. Alternatively, it could acknowledge that the devolution and claims processes have now converged; in recognizing its aboriginal peoples as "distinct societies" within it, it could lay the groundwork for resolving the difficult issues of political development and building the foundation of legitimacy on which further constitutional development should rest.

NOTES

1   Executive Council Office, Government of Yukon, *Yukon Indian Land Claim Framework Agreement*, (Whitehorse: Government of Yukon, 1989), Sub-Agreement 20.

2   Graham Eglington, "Matters of Confidence in the Legislative Assembly of the Northwest Terrritories" in Special Committee on Rules, Procedures and Privileges, Tenth Legislative Assembly of the Northwest Territories, *Third Report*, (Yellowknife: 1986).

3   See, for example, Canadian Arctic Resources Committee, *Aboriginal Self-Government and Constitutional Reform*, (Ottawa: CARC, 1988), p. 68.

4   Nunavut Constitutional Forum, *Building Nunavut*, (Yellowknife: Nunavut Constitutional Forum, 1985)

5   Geoffrey Weller, *"Devolution, Regionalism and Division of the Northwest Territories"*, this volume. See also John Merritt, *et. al.*, *Nunavut: Political Choices and Manifest Destiny* , (Ottawa: Canadian Arctic Resources Committee, 1989), Chapter 2.

6   Paul Quassa, President, Tungavik Federation of Nunavut, "Notes for an Address on the Signing of the Nunavut Agreement-In-Principle Between the Inuit of the Nunavut Settlement Area and Her Majesty in Right of Canada", Igloolik, April 30, 1990, p. 14.

7   Indian and Northern Affairs Canada, *Tungavik Federation of Nunavut Land Claim Agreement-In-Principle*, (Ottawa: 1990), Article 4.

8   Dene Nation and Métis Association of the Northwest Territories, *Devolution of Powers to the Government of the Northwest Territories: Provincehood and Aboriginal Self-Government*, Eleventh Legislative Assembly of the Northwest Territories, Tabled document No. 51-88 (2), tabled November 2, 1988, pp. 1 and 3.

9   Government of the Northwest Territories, "Opening Address of Commissioner John H. Parker to the Fourth Session of the Eleventh Assembly, February 8, 1989", p. 3.

10   Gurston Dacks, "The Quest for Northern Oil and Gas Accords", this volume.

11   Government of the Northwest Territories, *First Ministers' Conference on Aboriginal Rights and the Constitution*, (Yellowknife: GNWT, 1983) and *Directions for the 1990s*, (Yellowknife: GNWT, 1988), page 9.

12   This case is discussed in Robert Page, *Northern Development: The Canadian Dilemma*,(Toronto: McClelland and Stewart, 1986), pages 247-50.

13   Bob MacQuarrie, "Address to Standing Committee on Indian Affairs by the Western Constitutional Forum, March 21", 1984 reprinted in Western Constitutional Forum, *Partners for the future*,(Yellowknife: WCF, 1985,) p. 11.

14   Dene/Métis Negotiations Secretariat, Comprehensive Claims Branch (DIAND) and Aboriginal Rights and Constitutional Development (GNWT), *Comprehensive Land Claim Agreement between Canada and the Dene Nation and the Métis Association of the Northwest Territories*, (mimeo, April 9, 1990), Section 7 and Indian and Northern Affairs Canada, *Tungavik Federation of Nunavut Land Claim Agreement-In-Principle*, (mimeo, 1990), Article 4.

15   Yellowknife: Dene Nation and Métis Association of the NWT, 1981.

16   *The Globe and Mail* Wednesday, March 15, 1989, page B4.

17   Western Constitutional Forum and Nunavut Constitutional Forum, "Iqaluit Agreement", (Ottawa: Canadian Arctic Resources Committee, 1988), Part II.

18   Michael S. Whittington, "Political and Constitutional Development in the N.W.T. and Yukon: The Issues and Interests" in Michael S. Whittington, coordinator, *The North*, (Vol 72 of the research studies of the Royal Commission on the Economic Union and Development Prospects for Canada, Toronto: University of Toronto Press, 1985, page 81.

19   See for example Dene/Métis Negotiating Secretariat, op. cit., Section 30, and Department of Indian Affairs and Northern Development, *Western Arctic Claim: The Inuvialuit Final Agreement*,(Ottawa: DIAND, 1984), pages 15-16.

20   This question is examined in detail in Gurston Dacks, "The Quest for Northern Oil and Gas Accords" in this volume.

21   Letter from Bob Overvold, Principal Secretary, Office of the Government Leader, GNWT to Rick Van Loon, Senior ADM, Department of Indian and Northern Affairs, Government of Canada, April 12, 1990.

22   Dene Nation and Métis Association of the Northwest Territories *Devolution of Powers to the Government of the Northwest Territo-*

ries: Provincehood and Aboriginal Self-Government, 11th Legislative Assembly of the Northwest Territories, Tabled document No. 51-88 (2), tabled Nov 2, 1988, pages 1 and 3.

23   Ibid., page 5

24   See Gurston Dacks, "The Quest for Northern Oil and Gas Accords" in this volume.

25   See, for example, Gordon Robertson, *Northern Provinces: A Mistaken Goal,* (Montreal: Institute for Research on Public Policy, 1985)

26   Gurston Dacks, "The View from Meech Lake: The Constitutional Future of the Governments of the Yukon and Northwest Territories" in Rebecca Aird, ed., *Running the North: The Getting and Spending of Public Finances by Canada's Northern Governments,* (Ottawa: Canadian Arctic Resources Committee, 1988).

27   Executive Council Office, Government of Yukon, *Green Paper on Constitutional Development,* (Whitehorse: Government of Yukon, 1990), p. 10.

Index

Printed in Canada